D1429495

PLYMOUTH: A NEW HISTORY

Ice Age to the Elizabethans

PLYMOUTH
A NEW HISTORY
Ice Age to the Elizabethans

by

CRISPIN GILL

DAVID & CHARLES
Newton Abbot   London   North Pomfret (Vt)

ISBN 0 7153 4018 2

First published 1966
Second revised edition 1979
© Crispin Gill 1966 and 1979

Printed in Great Britain
by Redwood Burn Ltd., Trowbridge and Esher,
for David & Charles (Publishers) Limited
Brunel House Newton Abbot Devon

Published in the United States of America
by David & Charles Inc
North Pomfret Vermont 05053 USA

CONTENTS

5

LIST OF ILLUSTRATIONS

All the photographs are by Molly Gill except No 9, reproduced by permission of the *Western Evening Herald*, No 20, by permission of the *Western Morning News*, and No 24, by permission of Plymouth City Art Gallery. Maps: Nos 17 and 18 are by permission of the British Museum (Cott. Aug. Vol 1. 38), No 21 (Cecil Papers, Maps, Vol 1, No 35) by permission of the Marquess of Salisbury; and No 26 (M.P.F. 262) by permission of the Public Record Office.

MAPS AND PLANS

With the exception of Nos. 7 and 13, all the maps have been drawn by the author.

PREFACE

BEFORE 1941, the pattern of the streets of Plymouth told the history of the town; in them could be traced the pathways of prehistoric man, the farms and lanes of the first Saxons, the shape of the medieval town and the growth of the suburbs from Elizabethan times onwards. The wartime bombing and the subsequent rebuilding obliterated a great deal of this, and what is left of the pattern becomes more difficult to detect as, year after year, the new roads of the motor age cut into the city. So this history had to be written in my generation, the last one to grow up in the old city and to remember clearly its shape.

This book aims to explain why Plymouth is the kind of city we know today; why the streets take the shapes they do, when they were created, how the town grew; the economic and political forces that produced development at one moment of time and stagnation at another. It tries to do this, not just for the medieval settlement of Sutton, but for the whole area that makes up the modern city, the remote corners that were fields and farms until this century but which still have a history carved from the primaeval forests. One has to go back to the Domesday Book to discover why one side of Peverell Park Road is built up and the other side still open country.

It is no longer possible to do all this in one book, if it is to be acceptable to the ordinary reader, and so this volume ends with the reign of Elizabeth I. It makes a natural break, since it marks the birth of the modern naval port. One can even see naval importance beginning to elbow local commerce out of the way, a problem that is still with the city. And if, in the latter chapters, the reader finds himself on the shores of the Spanish Main as

11

much as in Plymouth Sound it is because there does not exist elsewhere as complete an account of the voyages out of Plymouth in these history-forming years, and because the local story is not otherwise really understandable.

PREFACE TO THE SECOND EDITION

Work on the history of Plymouth in the thirteen years since this book was published calls for some corrections. All stem from the labours of the archivist Jennifer Barber and her archaeologist husband James, now Director of Plymouth City Museum. In Vol 105 of the *Transactions of the Devonshire Association* (1973) Mrs Barber made it clear in her paper 'New Light on the Plymouth Friaries' that there never was a Blackfriars establishment in Plymouth (though the origins of that building are still unexplained), that the Woolster Street building which became the Mitre Inn could never have been the Franciscan friary but was a secular building (and the Hawkins family home after 1544) and that the Franciscan friary, or Greyfriars, was on the edge of the Hoe, bounded on the north by the top of New Street, on the east by Castle Dyke Lane and on the south by Citadel Green, in front of the United Services Inn.

In the same volume Mr Barber, in 'Yogge's House or Prysten House' makes it clear that there were three brothers Yogge, of Cornish origin, in Plymouth, that what we now call the Prysten House was built by Thomas as a dwelling house and that the house of the chantry priests of St Andrew's was smaller, further down Finewell Street and long since destroyed. John Yogge, when 'put out of the freedom' as a 'foreigner', retired to the family home at Duloe.

It has not been possible to correct all the passages which refer to these matters, but they should be read in the light of this new information. If I were writing the book again I would stress that my views on the Bilbury location of the first settlement were only a theory, and be less positive that the Southside Street area was altogether an Elizabethan suburb. I have no other reservations.

Crispin Gill, March 1979

CHAPTER ONE

PREHISTORY

THE first man we can trace in Plymouth was a hunter.[1] His world was getting colder and he was moving south in pursuit of his food, the elephant and the rhinoceros. He looked little better than a animal himself, his eyes peering out under heavy brows, his teeth protruding over a receding chin, and a great mass of hair that kept out the cold.

But three vital points made him more than an ape. By striking flakes from flints he was making knives, chisels, and axes. He used fire to keep himself warm. He could think; life after death was in his mind because he buried his dead with food and tools to help them in the next world, and he was capable of cunning in trapping the huge mammoths, or the savage lions.

Probably there were only about 250 of these hunters scattered over southern Britain, out on the fringe of the habitable world. They roamed the countryside in pursuit of their game and, with winter approaching and the cold of the first phase of the last glacial period of the ice-age creeping south, one family found shelter in a cave in the limestone hill of Cattedown.

After them there is a long silence. The Arctic ice-cap reached down to the north Devon coast. With so much water locked up in the ice the sea receded, as it had before in the glacial periods.[1] The water level was 200 feet below that of the present day; the North Sea and the Straits of Dover were dry land and the coast of Devon stretched out beyond Eddystone. The Plym joined the Tamar in front of the Hoe, and flowed as one river out to a bight in the coast, with the red rocks of Eddystone rising up on one side and the Hand Deeps making a hill on the other.

With the sea so low, the rivers cut deeper and deeper into the land, carving great valleys. The bed of the Plym was eighty feet lower than it is to today. With the unquarried white cliffs of Oreston and Cattedown just 300 yards apart, the river flowed through a minor Cheddar Gorge from Pomphlett to the Sound.

In these south-facing cliffs a new arrival found the cave[2] his predecessors had used, one glacial phase earlier. He turned out the hyenas which had made the two chambers into a den, and

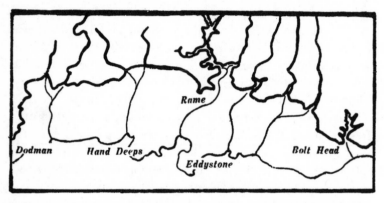

ICE-AGE COASTLINE. *The thick line represents the modern coast of south Devon and Cornwall and the rivers; the thin line the 60 fathom contour which must approximate to the coastline of the last ice-ages, and the probable courses of the rivers.*

used it himself as a base. The countryside around was open grassland, with a low scrub of birch and willow, and there he hunted the grizzly bear, wolves, reindeer, long-haired elephants and the woolly rhinoceros.

If his predecessor had been not quite like us, this new man was. His cousin in Kent's Cavern at Torquay had stone implements of some refinement, although none has yet been found in Plymouth, and at the centre of their culture, in the Central Massif of France, their relations painted lifelike pictures of animals on the walls of their caves. It was a kind of magic to help them catch the animals and, for the same magic, they disguised themselves as animals, which helped them in their stalking. These two groups of Plymothians rank with the first known men in England.

As the ice receded and the land became warmer, the scrub became trees, and the open plains gave way to forests of birch and pine. The great beasts which had afforded life to man moved away to the northern tundra, and middle Stone Age man had to adapt himself to a completely different environment. With half-inch long stone weapon-tips, inserted in rows on the end of wooden shafts, he hunted small game on open hilltops like Maker and Staddon, while his family gathered nuts, eggs and shellfish. These flint weapon-tips have been found on the high ground, and there is the evidence of collections of seashells at Mount Batten and Cattedown.

It was after these Mesolithic times that the Devon coast began to assume its present shape. The ice was back inside the Arctic Circle by 10,000 BC, and England was isolated from France by about 6,000 BC. A forest was drowned off Bovisand, and slowly the sea crept into the deep valleys on either side of Plymouth to make the vast estuaries we have today, the harbours that make the modern city. Originally, they cut even deeper into the land, with long creeks on either side of Plym and Tamar that the silt of centuries and the embankments of modern engineers have since turned into dry land. As the sea moved in, the climate changed to the wet Atlantic weather we now experience, and the forests from birch and willow to oak and alder.

Greater changes were coming from the Middle East. The river valley civilisations there were domesticating the ox and the boar; as well as gathering the fruits of the wood, they were planting seed and growing their own crops. Slowly this Neolithic revolution spread west, to bring farming to England by about 3,000 BC. One band of immigrants bringing these ideas moved across the Channel into Dorset and, later, Wiltshire became the centre of their culture. We know it as the Windmill Hill culture, after the site of their best-known monument. Hembury, in east Devon, and the site of a wooden house on Haldon, are the most western extensions of their habitations, but related groups of immigrants came across the sea into west Devon and Cornwall.

To farm, they had first to clear the forests. Their only available tools were stone axes, and quarries and axe factories were set up in the places—limited in numbers—where the best stone was to be found. Of all the axes scientifically examined, nine per cent are of Cornish greenstone, of which there are veins in Plymouth. Axe factories have been located at Penzance, Camborne and Callington, and Neolithic stone axes have been found in the city, at Thorn Park, on the Houndiscombe estate, and at Compton, all sharp, well-polished and showing no sign of use. Was there a local axe factory, or were they lost on the way from Cornish factories to customers on Salisbury Plain? As the ages unroll, we shall see that all these finds were close to ancient highways, and one such highway emerges in the next, the Bronze, age.

The hut circles on Dartmoor are the foundations of the homes of Bronze Age men, the pounds were their animal enclosures, and the stone rows and circles their places of ceremonial. Because stone axes could not do much forest clearance, or hand ploughs turn deep soil, the Neolithic men lived on the bare heights. Copper and bronze axes were not much more efficient, and the unwooded moorlands continued to serve the Bronze Age flocks and to provide small fields. But to get from the coast to the bare moor, these men had to make their way through the forests, avoiding the marshy rivers and valleys choked with scrub. A series of these ridge roads still reach in from the south Devon coast to Dartmoor, turning and twisting to avoid crossing streams, and are still followed by modern roads. One of them is the present Tavistock road out of Plymouth.

Its seaward end was a beach at the head of Sutton Pool and there, between two streams[3] to guard its flanks, the Bronze Age

men established a camp. Bilbury Street still preserves our oldest
place name; it means Billa's burgh, and a burgh was a defended
place. From Bilbury, the ridge road ran up North Street and
over the headland to the line of Mutley Plain and the present

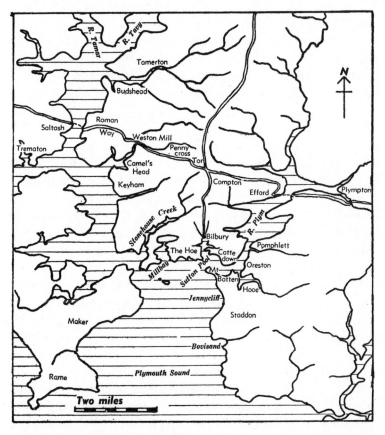

PREHISTORIC PLYMOUTH. *With the raising of the sea level after the last
Ice Age the tidal creeks and inlets cut far more deeply into the land
than now. The Bronze Age ridge road from the head of Sutton Pool to
Dartmoor is shown, following the watershed, and the east-west road of
uncertain age from Plympton to Saltash, crossing the Plym estuary by
a ford and the Tamar by ferry. Both routes can still be followed for
almost their entire length by present-day roads.*

Tavistock road, right out to Roborough Down, which takes its name (Rewberghe anciently, and still Rewbera in our Devon speech) from the fort, the burgh on the rough ground, which still caps the first rise on the down. There was another burgh near Millbay in Plymouth, called Romisbery, a place name so old that its location has been lost. But Bronze Age graves have been found close to both the Plymouth burghs.

The Bronze Age in the west runs from before 2,000 BC to about 450 BC, when it fades into the Iron Age, just as, in its beginning, it slowly emerged from the late Stone Age. Its people became the Dumnonni, the Celts.

MOUNT BATTEN

At Mount Batten, there was a settlement from Iron Age days to the end of Roman times.[4] The first clues came when a workman found five gold and eight silver coins in the angle of a rock there. The gold coins had been made by the Dubonni tribe of Somerset and Gloucestershire; one dated back to about 125 BC, the start of pre-Roman coinage, and the rest were of the first centuries BC or AD.

In the early 1860s, when Fort Stamford was being built above Mount Batten as part of the Palmerston defences of Plymouth, it was found that the guns would not bear down into Jennycliff Bay, and a gang of Irish navvies was set to take the top off the hill in front—which is why the slopes above the cliffs are so smooth and regular. It was then that an ancient burial-ground was found, with graves containing articles of bronze, earthenware, glass and iron, and parts of three bronze mirrors handsomely decorated on the back with the typical whirls and curls of the Celt. It was an Iron Age cemetery and the few pieces of Roman glass and pottery had no doubt been brought in by trade, just as the coins had come in from other parts of England. Soon afterwards, a Roman bronze statue was discovered in a garden at Hooe, a little figure of Mercury, that god of merchants and travellers much beloved (says Julius Caesar) of the Gauls.

There were many more such finds during the building of the Royal Air Force station at Mount Batten from 1917 to 1920, most of them from an ancient rubbish dump. Apart from a polished greenstone axe, everything dated from the late Bronze Age, about 1,000 BC onwards. There was the store of an itinerant bronzefounder, with some tools ready for sale—including a sickle, a chisel, two gouges, a knife and an axe—others broken and either in for repair or as scrap for melting down, and four cakes of founder's metal. This bronze had a tin content of ten to eleven per cent, and though it is tempting to think the tin came from Dartmoor—which would explain Mount Batten's importance— there is no evidence that any was found there before the twelfth century.

Other discoveries included Iron Age brooches of Iberian and French design, pins, and parts of bracelets which, with the mirrors, suggests enough wealth to support female vanity. Masses of broken pottery ranged in time from Iron Age (show- ing the influence of both Hallstadt and La Tene, the two main streams in Britain) to coarse Romano-British, mainly of the second, third and fourth Centuries AD. Of the gold, silver and bronze coins of the Iron Age, some were not identified, others came from tribes in Somerset and Dorset, Brittany and Gaul. Roman coins, with one or two small gaps, cover all the Roman emperors from Nero (who ruled AD 54-68) onwards.

So here was a trading settlement occupied apparently continu- ously from 1,000 BC to the end of Roman times, a period as long as from the end of the Roman era to the present day. It is a site with obvious advantages; with the Sound to shelter the narrow entrance to the river, a natural anchorage off a firm shelving beach on which boats could be run ashore, level ground behind the beach for a settlement, a narrow neck of land to the main- land and a steep hill at the tip of the isthmus, all admirable for defence. Less than a mile away, the almost land-locked Hooe

Lake provided perfect beaches for careening and repairing ships. It was an early British trading establishment which, with the arrival of the Romans, came increasingly under their influence. They found Britain a rich granary, though cattle and hides were probably Mount Batten's main export. Early in the third Century, when the Romans had exhausted their Spanish supplies of tin, they turned increasingly to Cornwall, and though the bulk of the Romano-British ware at Mount Batten dates from this time on, it is no proof that they were coming in for Dartmoor tin. Nor do we even know if Romans lived there, though they may well have set up a factor to manage their trade and he, in time, may have had his family and assistants with him.

GOG AND MAGOG

As the Roman ships came in to Batten from Bordeaux (goods went from there across France to Marseilles, and thence by sea to Rome), they would have seen two huge figures carved in the turf of the Hoe and outlined in the white limestone. Geoffrey of Monmouth in the early twelfth century explained them in his history of the Britons.

When Troy was sacked, he declared, a party led by Brutus sailed westward, landed in Plymouth, and took over the whole country. Brutus gave his name to Britain as one of his chiefs, Corineus, gave his to Cornwall. One day, when Brutus was holding a festival on the Hoe to celebrate their arrival, they were attacked by the original inhabitants, a race of giants. The Trojans, now Britons, drove them off and slaughtered all save one Goemagot. Corineus wrestled with him, eventually throwing him over the cliffs into the sea, and the battle was commemorated by the giant figures carved in the turf.

In our time, a distinguished archaeologist, T. C. Lethbridge, suggests in his book *Gogmagog* that we separate the facts from the legend. Brutus and his Trojans (he writes) came from the Mediterranean. The Dumnonni were related to the Veneti of

Britanny, and there were also Veneti at the head of the Adriatic, where the name survives in Venice. The Dumnonii were fighting people, and their Iron Age forts round Plymouth show that they had to defend themselves from their predecessors in the area. These are the facts on which the legend grew.

There are carved figures on other English hillsides, giants waving clubs, horses, sun-gods, sun-goddesses. Not many survive, but Mr Lethbridge suggests that these are the pagan gods of Iron Age times, of the two or three centuries before the Romans came. The giant with the club on the Hoe, like the Cerne giant near Dorchester and the Long Man of Wilmington in Sussex, was probably Helith, or Hercules, the sun god. The smaller figure, the other wrestler on the Hoe, may originally have been female, the older earth goddess. These figures had rôles to play in pagan worship, and the carved hillsides were their temples.

In Christian times their names and origin were forgotten, but they may have been vaguely remembered as pagan and evil, and so acquired new names from the Bible. In Ezekiel 38, there is the exhortation to fight the leaders of evil . . . 'Son of man, set thy face against Gog, the land of Magog'. So these figures became Gog and Magog.

If they were part of a pagan pantheon there must have been a considerable population to worship them there. Bilbury, for instance, must have continued in occupation for the name to survive. Then there was Romisbury and another settlement on Stonehouse Creek. In 1882, an ancient burial place was found at Newport Street, just below Stonehouse Bridge, and though everything has been destroyed, reports suggest that it may have been a Roman crematorium.

THE ROMANS

Why did the first Saxon settlers call this place Stonehouse? They must have found a house, or its ruins, remarkable enough to give its name to the area, and who could have built a stone house save a Roman colonist or a Romanised Briton of wealth? If one imagines the creek cleared from its sad industrial development, looking much as Mount Edgcumbe does just across the water, it is a perfect site for a villa of some size. Mount Edgcumbe is in the parish of Maker, and in Cornish 'Maker' means a ruin. What, again, was the ruin they found, unless it was a Roman villa? Only two villas have been located in Cornwall and one is just outside Camborne at a place called Magor, which comes from the same root and has the same meaning as Maker.

There are other Roman clues higher up Tamar. The Egyptian geographer Ptolemy in the second Century AD made the first map showing the West Country. Dumnonnia has four towns on this map, Isca (Exeter) and then Voliba, Uxella and Tamara in the eastern half of Cornwall. Tamara is close to the west bank of Tamar and is almost certainly Trematon, the mother settlemeant of Saltash. Probably there was a British village there, possibly a fort, too. Clearly the Romans knew it, and may have used it as an entrepot to clear the Tamar Valley produce, as Batten did the Plym. The little creek on which Trematon sits, opening out of the Lynher just before it joins Tamar, makes an admirable harbour for small craft, better than the bare waterfront of Saltash, which was the Tamar crossing-point.

On the other side of that crossing is King's Tamerton, with a Roman legend too persistent to be ignored. The street name 'Roman Way' perpetuates the nineteenth-century suggestion that there was once a Roman signal-station on the high hill overlooking the Tamar crossing. Mr E. N. Masson Phillips excavated the site in 1934 and will only term it 'an early fortification'. Roman Way's earlier name was 'Old Walls Lane', which clearly suggests an ancient memory, and soapwort has been found growing on a bank in the lane. The Romans used this herb for medicine, and it is normally found in this country only on the site of an old settlement.

Roman Way is situated on the second oldest route we can trace in Plymouth, an east-west road from the Saltash crossing to Plympton. It crossed the Ham brook at Weston Mill, then the head of the creek, the Tavistock road at Tor, and the Plym at Crabtree. This was the Ebb Ford to the Saxons, a name which, in the course of time, became Efford and moved up the hill, as place names will move. The construction of Saltram Park on the other side of the Plym in the eighteenth Century, obliterated part of the route, but beyond that it is still used into Plympton St Maurice. The ford was still marked on the 1809 Ordnance Survey map, and the road up the hill behind the 'Crabtree Inn' was known as Saltash Lane into recent times.

This east-west route may be very ancient indeed, and the Stone Age finds at Tor could mean that it was used by traders carrying axes from the Cornish factories to Dorset. If the Romans used it, they may well have set up a fort, or a signal-station, on the high hill at Roman Way looking down on the wide Tamar. In 1894, a crock of Roman coins was found in Compton Giffard, which is traversed by this route. It contained about a thousand coins, none later than AD 280, and the British Museum suggested that it could have been part of the pay chest of a Roman legion stationed in the area, or with temporary headquarters nearby. A similar collection of Roman coins has been found near Marazion, and two temporary Roman forts have also been identified in that area.

Roman roads west of Exeter are obscure. There was an ancient route along the north coast[5] crossing the Taw at Barnstaple, the Torridge at Torrington and the Tamar at Bridgerule. The main Roman road ran west through Crediton and north of Dartmoor, then down through the centre of Cornwall. A southern route has been traced over Haldon to Teign Bridge, near Newton Abbot, and this points to the Plymouth east-west route. A confusion is caused by Ridgeway at Plympton. The earliest written reference to it, in 1281, calls it 'Ryggeweystrete' and that street element always suggests a Roman link. It is certainly part of a ridge road leading from the site of Plympton St Mary Church to the Hemerdon area, but it is not on our east-west route. Probably, at some time, the Romans metalled and improved part of this old native trading route, and that is its only significance. Equally, our questionable south Devon route looks like an ancient trackway taken over at some time for Roman use, even if it was never a great military highway like the famous Roman roads.

THE DARK AGES

When the last Roman soldiers were called home in AD 410 what did they leave in Plymouth and its neighbourhood? A peninsula traversed by two main roads, a few isolated Celtic farms cut from the old forests, small seafaring communities at Mount Batten and Trematon, villas at Maker and Stonehouse, Celtic fishermen at Bilbury and Romisbery? All must have come under the influence of Rome and some would have been Christian and comparatively civilised.

But there were still 300 years of Dumnonni rule to come, and of those dark days our only knowledge comes from the missionaries who journeyed from Wales, Ireland, and France to keep the faith alive in Britain. Bishop Germanus of Auxerre in eastern France, for example, came to England in AD 429, and again in 447 to combat the Pelagian heresy. Tradition says that he spent some time in the Tamar valley and founded a Celtic monastery at St Germans. The church at Rame is dedicated to him and there is Germansweek not far from the Upper Tamar valley. When the Saxon King, Athelstan, made the newly-conquered Cornwall a separate diocese in AD 926 he founded a Saxon monastery at St Germans, and created its abbot Bishop of Cornwall. Was he promoting the old Celtic community, and had there survived a cult of St Germans strong enough to warrant making this place the seat of a new bishopric?

The name of St Budoc is remembered in St Budeaux. We can forget the legends, that his mother had a breast of gold, and that he crossed from Ireland in a stone coffin. He was, in fact, a great teacher, an abbot and Bishop of Dol in Brittany, and his arm is still preserved in the church of Plouin, his first parish. He founded a number of small monasteries in the islands off Paimpol, and there are churches dedicated to him at Penryn and in South Wales, all close to the Celtic trade routes of the western seaboard.

Legend says that he sailed into the Tamar in AD 480, landed in Tamerton Creek, and set up a little church which was later dedicated to him.[6] That first church was at Budshead, beside the water. Leland, writing about 1540, described 'a creke going up to Mr Budokes side wher is his manor place and St Budok Chirch'. It was moved to its present hilltop site in 1566. But whether Budoc himself came or not, there must have been sea links between Brittany and Tamarside, and people living there who, hearing sailors' stories of the great bishop across the sea, named their church after him and survived to keep his memory alive.

Cornwall is rich in associations with these saints through legend and place name, though they were not in our modern sense of being men and women through whom God worked great miracles. Rather were they faithful members of the church—those whom the Prayerbook calls 'the communion of saints'. Further up the Tamar is St Dominic, founded according to legend by the Irish woman missionary who is said to have landed at Tamerton with all her company in the closing years of the sixth Century. Tamerton Foliot Church was dedicated to her son, St Indract, until its re-dedication to St Mary in 1318.

In places, the Irish missionaries set up stones inscribed in both Latin and Ogham, a primitive form of writing. Such stones have been found at Buckland Monachorum (now in the vicarage garden at Tavistock), Fardel, near Cornwood (now in the British Museum), and Yealmpton (still in the churchyard, but without Ogham marks). So they were close around Plymouth.

There were other, less friendly, invaders from the east and north, the Angles and Saxons who gradually overran all England and, in time, brought pressure on the west. Some of the

Dumnonni fought them, and out of such struggles led by Roman-ised, Christian chiefs against the pagan forces of darkness came the legend of King Arthur. But for the most part the Dumnonni moved out of Devon, westwards into Cornwall, or back across the Channel into western France. So many went that Amorica changed its name; it became Brittany, little Britain. But enough remained to give their tribal name to the county (ask any true man of Devon today the name of his county and, if he is off his guard, he will say 'Demn'). Their place names can still be found in Plymouth, and it is not surprising that they are mainly on the Cornish side of the peninsula, near their fellow Celts across the Tamar.

Pennycomequick means 'at the head of the creek' in the Celtic tongue, and it was at the head of Stonehouse Creek until the tidal waters were damned back. Camel's Head takes its name from Kemel, probably a British name, and Keame, the oldest form of Keyham, has a similar ring. Whether as Saxon slaves or isolated smallholders, Celts must have survived here to remember the names, as they must at St Budoc and even further east in Ply-mouth, at Romisbery and Bilbury.

One puzzle remains, Pennycross. The name is Celtic, and it has that inexplicable little church dedicated to St Pancras. He was a boy martyred in AD 304 at one of Rome's gates which was subsequently named after him. There are five St Pancras dedications in Devon. The Exeter church is close to the east-west axis of the Roman town, and Pancrasweek, in north Devon, is beside Bridgerule where, if a Roman road existed, it crossed into Cornwall. St Pancras at Rousdon is where a coastal Roman road came into Devon from Dorset, and Plymouth St Pancras is close to that east-west route we suspect to have been used by the Romans. So all the Devon dedications have Roman links, almost gateway suggestions, save St Pancras at Widecombe-in-the-Moor. To prove a survival of Romano-British Christianity here is impossible. To wonder about it is permissible; no more, because the great days of the Pancras cult came after the Romans had already left Britain. But when St Augustine brought Christianity a second time to eastern England (it never died in the west), he dedicated his first church at Canterbury to St Pancras. The cult spread rapidly, and it might be safer to think of Pennycross[7] as an early Saxon foundation in Plymouth.

CHAPTER TWO

SAXONS AND NORMANS

FROM Wessex the Saxons moved slowly westwards, peacefully where they could but fighting when they had to. They had to fight five battles between the years 614 and 682 before Dumnonni were finally subdued in Devon, and the still militant rump left more or less at peace in Cornwall. The Tamar, and the Otter in north Cornwall, became the frontier of Wessex.

In AD 705, a new diocese of Sherborne was set up for the religious control of the new territory and in that year King Geraint of Cornwall, no doubt as a peace offering, gave the bishop five hides of land at Maker. This explains why Maker remained a part of Devon until 1844, and may well date the beginning of the Cremyll Ferry, for Sherborne was also given land at Exmouth and established a ferry across the estuary to Starcross. It also gives us a date for the Saxons' arrival in Plymouth Sound.

Their armies had come by land, but the settlers came in by sea, which is indicative of the state of the land communications. This freshly-conquered territory was King's land, and he gave estates to any of his men who would go and settle there, and so consolidate his hold. These settlers were Christian; they built their own churches beside their houses, and when, about AD 800, the parish system was set up, these churches became parish churches, and the estate of the owner of the church was the parish. As churches are dedicated in perpetuity, parish churches have normally remained on their original site through innumerable rebuildings. There is no such reason for keeping a dwelling-

28

house on the same site and, over the centuries, many squires have moved their manor houses. But it is a safe assumption that the parish church marks the site of the original settlement.

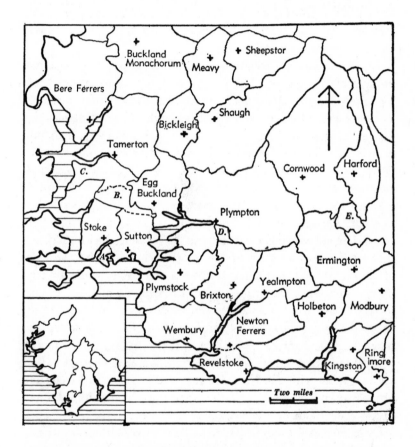

SAXON SETTLEMENT. *The parishes of south Devon. Note how the churches, marked by crosses, in the coastal parishes are close to the sea or the heads of creeks, and inland the churches tend to be near the southern or western borders of the parish. Stonehouse (marked by the letter* A), *Weston Peverel* (B), *and St Budeaux* (C) *were originally part of the parish of St Andrew's, Sutton. Plympton Erle* (D) *and Ivybridge* (E) *are clearly small urban parishes cut from the original pattern at a later date. The inset map shows the hundreds of south Devon, reaching from the coast up to the Forest of Dartmoor.*

The map of south Devon clearly shows the parish churches close to the sea, with the parish stretching away inland. This was the work of the first Saxon settlers. New arrivals set down their house (and their church) just over the edge of the first estate and cleared their estate further inland. So the parish map of south Devon shows the pattern of settlement, with nearly every church on the southern edge of the parish.

In Plymouth, the reclamation of many arms of the sea has obliterated this pattern, but St Andrew's is close to Sutton Pool, Stoke is still beside Stonehouse Creek, Tamerton within a stone's throw of the tide, and even Egg Buckland had salt water at the bottom of the hill until medieval times. All round the Plymouth arms of the sea the pattern is the same, Bere Ferrers beside the Tavy, St Stephens Saltash on the hill above Trematon, Yealmpton and Brixton close to arms of the Yealm, and Plympton reached by the sea until a few centuries back. In all these cases one can imagine the safe landlocked anchorages and the rich alluvial meadows, not even in need of clearing, welcoming the new settlers. Less easy to explain are the windy clifftop churches of Rame, Maker, Wembury and Revelstoke. Were these already church sites when the Saxons came (for, even with churches, one looks for Saxons in the valleys and Celts on the hilltops), were they built by men who had the second pick of land, or were they much later settlements? Wembury is dedicated to St Werburgh, a royal lady of Mercia; Maker to St Julian, a Roman saint but very popular with the early Normans. Plymouth has a clifftop church in St Katherine-upon-the-Hoe,[1] but it comes into written history later than St Andrew's and was most probably a chapel built in medieval times to counteract the lingering pagan appeal of Gogmagog.

Devon was made a county before AD 800, and divided into hundreds, our original form of local government. The south Devon hundreds reflect the sea settlement pattern even more than the parishes, for they are all long, narrow strips of land reaching from the sea to Dartmoor. Plymouth was at the southern tip of the hundred of Wachetona (the modern spelling is Walkhampton, but the rustic pronunciation has not changed). It was an important hundred for it guarded the mouth of two rivers and the frontier with Cornwall as far up the Tamar as the tide flowed.

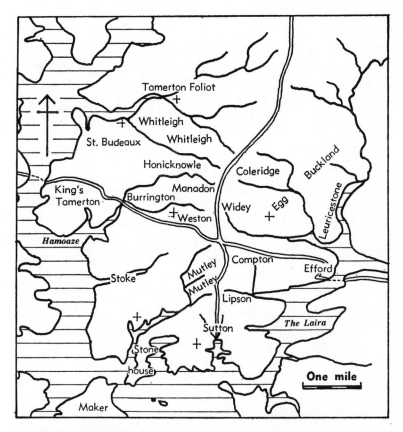

DOMESDAY MANORS. *The names given are in modern spellings with the exception of Leuricestone, which is now Leigham. The two roads shown and the rivers were natural boundaries and by placing the names on the map where they are found today the shape of the manors becomes clear. Many of these boundaries survived into modern times; the stream between the two Mutleys and Stoke for example, was the boundary between the boroughs of Devonport (Stoke) and Plymouth until the amalgamation of 1914.*

The Crown kept the hundred firmly in its own hands right up to Norman times.

It is odd to think of Walkhampton, away in the northern corner of the hundred, as being its centre (later it became the hundred of Roborough, and Horrabridge the seat of the hundred court). Professor W. G. Hoskins, the leading historian of Devon, thinks that Walkhampton was a royal hunting-lodge from which the Saxon kings could enjoy their sport on Dartmoor. There is an odd reference in Domesday Book to Sutton, King's Tamerton and Walkhampton manors being required to contribute 'one day's supply' and Maker £6 in cash. These were the royal manors in the hundred, and when the King arrived at Walk-hampton each had to send one day's supply of food for the Court, except Maker which, perhaps because of the difficulties of the water crossing, had to give money instead.

Just as it is clear that this frontier hundred remained in direct royal control because of its strategic position, so it is obvious that the King kept these other royal manors for strategic reasons. Sutton commanded the head of the Sound and the entrance to the Plym, while King's Tamerton covered the vital Saltash crossing of Tamar. When possession of Maker passed from the Bishop of Sherborne to the Saxon kings is unknown, but its value in guarding the mouth of the Tamar and as an advanced position in Cornwall is apparent. With Maker, it would be reasonable to take over Stonehouse as well and so completely control the mouth of the Tamar. Our first clues to ownership come in Domesday Book when, though Stonehouse was certainly not royal, it was the only small manor on the Plymouth waterfront, and an exception to the pattern. Standing on a long narrow peninsula thrusting out into the river, with what early documents call 'a great ditch' cut across its thin link with the mainland, it is a natural partner to Maker on the other side of the river. Both areas have been linked throughout history, and land ownership is a conservative, slow-changing process.

Sutton was the south town or 'ton'—the word is Saxon for

The mouth of the Plym. Stone Age men lived in caves in the cliffs behind the oil·tanks (left) and a Romano-British trading post occupied Mount Batten (right). At the head of Sutton Pool (below) an Iron Age fort was established. The warehouses are on flat ground recovered from the sea; the fort at the foot of the hill behind, between two streams.

North Street is on the line of an Iron Age ridge road which ran from the fort at the head of Sutton Pool along the watershed to Roborough Down and Dartmoor. It crossed an east-west trackway from Plympton to Saltash, of uncertain antiquity, at Tor, where there is still set in a garden wall in Tavistock Road the head of a medieval granite cross (below) flanked by boundary stones of Compton Gifford and Weston Peverell.

farm—at the very southern extremity of Walkhampton hundred, the southern end of the ridge road. When, in medieval times, the town proper grew up the original Sutton, the first farm, became the Old Town, and Old Town Street led up to it. That is the major clue to its position. It is not difficult to envisage the original settlers sailing into Sutton Pool, landing at Bilbury, the innermost point, and deciding to set their farm on the north bank of the little stream a few hundred yards up its course. They would be sheltered from the westerly winds, have gentle south-facing slopes for their fields, and the stream to water themselves and their cattle. A detached house in its own garden (it was called Norley latterly, to confuse the issue) stood on the site until, in our times, the telephone exchange was built there. The church was set up a few hundred yards south along the ridge and, with church and farm established, the old ridge road altered course to meet them, leaving the North Street line and moving to the present line of Tavistock Road and Mutley Plain to Old Town Street.

The other royal manor, King's Tamerton, embraced not only the hilltop housing estate that bears the name today but all that area of the township now known as Lower St Budeaux, and all the Bull Point waterfront round to Saltash Passage. In Domesday, it was of the same size and value as Sutton and has an equally obvious name, the King's ton on the Tamar. Probably, the main farm was Barne Barton, and a branch of Weston Mill Creek would have taken the tide almost up to it.

Three other fat manors, all larger and wealthier than these two royal estates, were obvious sea settlements of the first generation. Largest of all was the other Tamerton, with its church at the head of the creek and probably the manor house beside it, where Cann House now is. The stream running into the creek was the manor's southern boundary, northwards it reached far up Tamarside and along the Tavy, nearly to the present edge of Dartmoor. By Domesday, sixteen farms and six smallholdings had been carved out of the woods, and there were seven slaves at the manor farm who also had to operate the saltworks on the marshes. It was their task to guide the sea into shallow pans, wait for the sun to evaporate the water and then to gather the remaining salt.

Second largest of the manors was Stoke (a Saxon word for dairy farm). Its church, again on the southern boundary, is beside Stonehouse Creek, with the manor running north along Tamarside to Weston Mill Creek where the Ham brook reached the

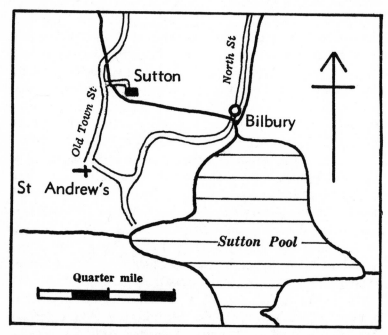

SAXON SUTTON. *Both the positions of Bilbury, the original Celtic settlement, the Sutton, the first Saxon farm, are conjectural, based in geographical evidence. Bilbury was at the end of the ridge road, and the two streams made it defensible. The Saxons first need for their farm was water and a sheltered position; given an empty countryside the position marked is the logical answer and Old Town Street, as the town grew up between the church and the harbour, was the street leading to the old town, or old farm, of Sutton. If Celts survived at Bilbury they would have made their own path to the church, with a side path down to the beach where boats were kept.*

estuary. At the confluence large mud flats formed, early maps mark them as the Ham ooze (or Ham mud), and so there emerged the modern name of the Tamar estuary, the Hamoaze. Stoke church no doubt marks the original settlement point but at some time the manor house moved to the north bank of the Keyham Creek and took the Celtic name of Keyham. It was a long creek, reaching right up to Swilly (a hollow place), and at its narrowest point there was a ford which gave its name to our modern Ford.

The third big estate was Egg Buckland, and though it is difficult now to imagine how it could have been reached from the sea, the tide then flowed up a side branch of the Plym over the present wet fields of Marsh Mills to the flat alluvial meadows less than a quarter of a mile from the church. Egg Buckland could even boast the only other saltworks in the area.

Two other settlements from the sea, though quite small, were Lipson, at the head of another creek of the Plym, and Leigham, on the main stream of the Plym, at nearly the highest point reached by the tide at Plym Bridge. Leigham's Domesday name was Leuricestone, which starts an interesting hare. The river Tamar's name, like those of so many English rivers, is old, older even than the Celtic language. The river Plym is believed to have got its name by a back inversion from Plympton, the first place in the valley to achieve any importance. Yet it is on a side stream, and the main river must have had an older name. Its estuary is still called the Laira, and a point of land in the estuary, between the Lipson and Tothill creeks, is called 'the Leurie Point' on a seventeenth century map. Beside Leigham are still farms called Mainstone and Rock; was this stone or rock also called Leurie's Stone, the stone beside the Leurie?. And was Leurie, or Laira, the original name of the river Plym? After all the lower estuary, the Cattewater, took its name from a land feature as did Cattedown. Probably there was a rock which looked like a cat; it may have been the feature across from Fisher's Nose which later maps called the Bear's Head Rock.

Squeezed between the fat manors of the sea settlements were a dozen little manors. Efford, at the Ebb Ford on the old east-west road, touched the Plym and there was a fishery there. St Budeaux on the Tamar was round St Budoc's church. Between them were Compton, two little Mutleys, Widey, Manadon, Weston, Burrington, Honicknowle, and two Whitleighs. Even by Domesday, the manors were not necessarily continuous. They started as clearings in the forest which were gradually expanded, the land between the clearings being left waste. During the reigns of the first three Norman kings all this waste was made the royal forest of Devon, in which the people had certain rights of grazing, though the severest laws forbade them to touch any game. Grazing cattle would stop trees regenerating, and gradually the old forest would become as much open moorland as woodland. Not until 1242 was Devon granted a charter of dis-afforestation, when the Crown retained only the modern forest of Dartmoor, in which every man of Devon (save the inhabitants of Totnes and Barnstaple) still has the same grazing rights as his forefathers enjoyed in the ancient forest of Devon.

Were these little manors a no-man's-land of the early Saxon settlement, left to be developed by the latecomers or by the people elbowed out of the first settlements? It is the highest land in the city, much broken up by steep-sided valleys. There is evidence in Wessex, supported by other parts of the country, that the Saxon settlements lay along the river valleys, while the Celtic remains are on the plateaus above. It may be that the original Celts found the woodlands beside Plym and Tamar too tough to clear, and so confined their riverside settlements to the new alluvial flats. It is equally likely that they found the ridge road from Bilbury and the cross road from Plympton to Saltash led them to the higher ground round Tor and Pennycross where the woods were less dense, the undergrowth less luxuriant, and the patches of open ground larger. Certainly it is curious how frequently suggestions of early settlements in this particular area keep cropping up.

All these little manors may well have been Celtic farms origin-ally. Professor Hoskins envisages a period when Saxons and Celts lived as neighbours, each following their own laws and customs. 'This,' he writes, is surely what William of Malmesbury means when he says that the Britons and English inhabited Exeter (and presumably the rest of Devon) *aequo jure*, until Athelstan made an end of their "equality" and caused Wessex law to reign supreme.' Of these small manors, only St Budeaux and Weston had their own chapels but they, along with all the other hill manors, were in the pastoral care of St Andrew's of Sutton, ex-cept Efford and Widey which were in Egg Buckland parish. Leigham was also in Egg Buckland, and Stonehouse in St Andrew's.

They may, on the other hand, have been merely late clearings from the forest, and Domesday actually provides a picture of just such a new manor emerging. In 1066 Coleridge, which stretched eastwards from Tavistock Road (where Seaton Barracks has turned Coleridge Lane into its main road) between two deep valleys which meet at the top of the Forder valley, was still waste. The name means the ridge of the coal- or charcoal-burners. By 1086, when Domesday was compiled, it was a manor with a demesne farm, two small holdings, and a beast for the plough, presumably an ox. It was worth fifteen pence, and there were still thirty acres of woodland.

Apart from the barracks and some housing close to Tavistock Road, Coleridge has not changed. It is still the network of fields cleared by that pioneer of 900 years ago from the coppice oak of the charcoal-burners, with the surface stones pushed aside to make the hedges. In the middle of the fields stand four walls and a barn, all that is left of the manor house, its approach roads having long since become grassed over and choked. It is a typical Devonshire long house that would at one time have housed the owner at one end and his cattle at the other, a type becoming rare in Devon, let alone inside the city boundaries. The spring that watered the farm is now making a swamp of the yard, and down

where the two streams meet are two farms, Bircham and Lower
Bircham, no doubt the smallholdings of 1086. Their names first
appear in documents of 1270, and indicate the birch woods from
which they were carved. All but one of the Plymouth manors
had this very Celtic pattern of separate isolated farms and smallholdings, even Tamerton and Egg Buckland which developed
central villages as well.

Only Compton seems to be different, to follow the normal
Saxon pattern. Domesday records six farmers and four smallholders, and the tithe map of 1840, drawn before the urban
growth of Plymouth had made any impact, shows no scatter-
ing of farms, but one central hamlet. The land was divided
among ten tenements, the fields of each being intermixed. On the
plateau south-west of the village, reaching out to Tavistock Road,
the tithe map shows six fields. Two are unnamed, but the others
are Compton Great Field, Compton Field, Mannameads and
West Mannameads. Mead means 'meadow', and the prefix
(according to *Devon Place Names*) means 'common, general, and
may refer to some feature belonging to the whole village or community.' Surely these six fields together make up the great field,
or common meadow, of Compton, like Braunton Great Field in
north Devon and the great field of the Midland nucleated villages, owned collectively and cultivated in strips? It matches the
pattern of the scattered field holdings, just as the ten farmers and
smallholders of 1086 match the ten tenants of 1840.

The whole map, and its field names, evoke a picture of a
countryside hardly changed from Saxon times. From Tavistock
Road the village is reached by way of Lower Compton Road,
and the road on to Egg Buckland is cut deep into the hillside by
centuries of the passage of human feet and packhorses, and by
rain. At the top, where it meets the Plympton-Saltash road, there
is an inn (which was Hooper's Beer House in 1840, and is the
'Rising Sun' today). The village sits with its back to the hillside
and in its centre Calloway's Tenement, once a farm house, once
perhaps the manorhouse, is now the 'Compton Inn'. In front, a

valley slopes down (Compton is the ton in the coombe) to Lipson. Beside the stream is Washing Brook Field, where clothes were washed as they are still beside the streams of Brittany. At the bottom, the stream filled a millpond which served to turn Lipson Mill and grind the corn.

THE VIKINGS

This pastoral world which the Saxons carved out enjoyed long years of peace. Tamar was an effective guard against the Cornish, and such armies as the Saxon kings had to move against them used the easier crossings above the tidal reaches. Cornwall was firmly in the Saxon fold by the tenth century, and Tamar just a county boundary. But now a new enemy was in the Channel, the Vikings, whose worst raid was made in AD 997.

'This year,' says the Anglo-Saxon Chronicle, 'went the Army about Devonshire into Severnmouth and equally plundered the people of Cornwall, North Wales (that is Wales, as distinct from West Wales, or Cornwall) and Devon. Then went they yp at Watchet, and there much evil wrought in burning and man-slaughter. Afterwards they coasted back about Penwith-stert (the point of Penwith, or Land's End) on the south side, and turning into the mouth of the Tamar, went up until they came to Liddy-ford, burning and slaying everything that they met. Moreover, Ordulf's minster at Tavistock they burned to the ground, and brought to their ships incalculable plunder.'

Tavistock Abbey was then barely twenty years old, and Lyd-ford was one of four towns, the first in Devon, built by Alfred for just this kind of defensive rôle against the Danes. But it is impossible to believe that the Vikings sailed up to Tavistock unaware of the little farms and villages hiding in all the creeks of the Sound. Indeed, this raid explains not only why Sutton was hidden away behind the Hoe, invisible from the sea, but why places even further from the sea, such as Stonehouse and Stoke, Keyham and King's Tamerton, Trematon, St Budeaux and

Tamerton, were all tucked away inside creeks invisible from the main river. The Danes had been raiding these coasts since 851, and would certainly have known where to find the villages. One can only hope that our forefathers had some warning and were able to take to the woods with their wives and children before the longboats came pushing into the creeks. They must have remained hidden for many anxious days before the marauding Danes came back down the Tamar, and set off up the coast again.

Wooden houses burn well but can be rebuilt. How much was burnt, how many slaughtered, we shall never know, but enough survivors came creeping back from the woods to rebuild the flourishing communities that the Normans took over in 1067.

NORMAN LORDS

After the Hastings campaign, King William returned to Normandy in May 1067. Trouble in the west, where the dead King Harold's mother had large estates, brought him hurrying back, and in December he besieged Exeter, captured it, and built the castle of Rougemont to keep the peace. He was not back at Winchester until the Easter of 1068 and had probably spent the winter making sure that the west was going to stay at peace. To this end he ordered castles to be built at Totnes, Plympton, Trematon, Restormel and Launceston, and if they mark the order of his route he must at least have passed through Plymouth. The castle at Totnes was given to the Breton, Judhel, but the other Devon castles went to William's second cousin, Baldwin Redvers, who was made Earl of Devon. The Cornish castles went to William's half-brother, the Count of Mortain. The Conqueror was taking no chances with the west; it was King Harold's mother who had stirred up Exeter and when Harold's two sons did land in south Devon in 1089, they were beaten back as the result of William's precautions.

Plymouth now had two powerful neighbours, Plympton castle

on one side and Trematon on the other. These Norman castles could be thrown up quickly, and comprised little more than a mound of earth with a wooden tower on top, and a pallisade which enclosed both the mound and a large courtyard. When time permitted, a stone keep could replace the tower, and a stone wall the pallisade. Plympton and Trematon are both still in a good state of preservation, with the earth mound, the stone keeps and curtain walls protecting in one case the Plym valley and in the other the Tamar.

But though William gave these strongpoints to relations who had fought beside him at Hastings, he had no intention of allowing them to become too strong. Most of the land in Plymouth he gave to Judhel of Totnes, and the Count of Mortain had to be content with only two Plymouth manors, Lipson and Honicknowle. Earl Baldwin had none, though his family later acquired a small parcel still remembered in the name of a row of houses in Alma Road, Earl's Acre. Mortain installed Reginald de Valletort at Trematon, and he was also tenant of Lipson and Honicknowle.

Judhel kept his richest Plymouth manor, Egg Buckland, in his own hands at first, but it was later let to Stephen, his tenant in Compton. Within a century, Stephen's descendant was known as Guy de Bockland, and his grand-daughter, Isabella, brought the estate to her husband, Osbert Giffard. The Giffards continued until 1342, and their name is perpetuated in Compton Gifford, whereas Buckland, oddly enough, retains the name of its last Saxon owner, Hecche, in Egg Buckland. (Buckland or 'Bocland', means land granted by charter, or book, by a Saxon king).

Judhel's other Plymouth manors, Leigham, Coleridge, East Whitleigh, Manadon, Weston, Burrington and the two Mutleys, were held by Odo. The Buzon family, who may be Odo's descendants, continue until the early thirteenth century, when the estate split up. By 1241 Hugh Peverell had Weston, and his name survives in Weston Peverell.

The other Plymouth manors were held directly from the King.

Alfred the Breton (so-called to distinguish him from another adventurer rewarded with English lands, Alfred the Spaniard; which shows what a mixed crew these Normans were), was rewarded with Tamerton and St Budeaux, with Blaxton (north of Tamerton) and Peter Tavy away on Dartmoor. Robert Foliot owned these estates in 1188 and on his death in 1199 they were divided among his grandchildren. Foliots[2] continued in Tamerton until 1253 (hence Tamerton Foliot), when Reginald Foliot exchanged the estate with Ralf de Gorges for Skipton, in Yorkshire. In that 1199 division Budshead and Ernesettle went to 'Alan Buddekeside and partners'. It marked, perhaps, the emergence of tenant farmers into the yeoman class and, in due course, into landed gentry. The ruins of their manor house can still be found at Budshead. Robert the Bastard received Efford and Stonehouse, and continued there until 1368 when Gonilda, daughter of the last male Bastard, and her husband, William Snapedon, made over the estates to Stephen Durnford.

Stoke, Widey and West Whitleigh went to Robert d'Albemarle. There is a story that he was named after his shield, which bore the device of a white blackbird, an albino 'merle'; but it is more likely that he was from Aumale in eastern Normandy. His family remained in Stoke until about 1300, with his name anglicised into Stoke Damerell. His tenant in Widey and Whitleigh was Osulf, who may have been the Osulf who owned Compton before the Normans took over. Otherwise, all the Saxon names disappear: Alwin of Tamerton, who also owned Stonehouse, Higher Mutley, Efford, St Budeaux and Burrington; Godwin of Lower Mutley, Lipson and East Whitleigh; Wado of West Whitleigh, Honicknowle and Widey; Brismer of Stoke, Ulnod of Weston, Edmer of Coleridge, Saulf of Leigham, Colbert of Manadon, even Hecche of Buckland. Some may have become tenant farmers like Osulf, but they fall out of sight as landless, dispossessed men.

Yet the manors went on much as they had before the Normans arrived, farming communities gradually reducing the waste adding to their fields, increasing their flocks, growing their corn and grinding the flour in the lord's mill. An 1155 deed of Geoffrey de Weston mentions the land of Ham, on the west side of the road from the mill. The road is still called Ham Lane, and it still crosses the river at Weston Mill. When Stephen Durnford bought Gonilda Snapedon's land in 1368 the deed conveyed 'all her estate in Stonehouse next the township of Sutton within the great ditch together with the grist mills of Sourpool, Stenmafri and Tolfri.'

The main change in this farming community was the position of the individual. Serfs had been slaves. Even smallholders and farmers were not free to leave the manor and were obliged to give the lord so many days work a week. The lord would move from manor to manor, going to the food rather than having it brought to him and his family. So, for much of the time, the manor was in the hands of a reeve or steward. In turn, the lords possessed their land in return for giving military service, so many days or so many soldiers, to the King when he called. Neither were popular forms of service; gradually the gentlemen gave money so that the King could hire paid soldiers, and the smallholders and farmers gave money to be excused day labour. So farm wages came into being, together with labourers and tenant farmers. The manorial system, and feudal England, died slowly, but the Black Death of 1345, which made labour scarce and wages high, wrote an end to the chapter.

A detailed picture of this farming world in 1086 emerges from Domesday Book. Of the present area of Plymouth, nearly two-thirds was then under management. The rest was waste, or mud-flats in the creeks and estuaries. By far the greater part of the farmland was arable, with only a small proportion of meadow and pasture. There were something like 135 families living on the 8,000 odd acres of farmland, scattered through 21 manors, 107 farms, and 40 smallholdings. Spread through these manors were some 350 acres of small woods, and three very big woods, each over a mile long.

Most of this William the Conquerer used as rewards for his soldiers, but he kept for himself the old royal manors of Maker, King's Tamerton, and Sutton. Only in Sutton does the farming pattern begin to change into something quite different.

CHAPTER THREE

THE TOWN IS BORN

WHEN William the Conquerer died his sons fought among themselves for twenty years as to who should possess Normandy. The issue was finally resolved when King Henry I of England beseiged and captured Tinchebray in 1106. Among the Cornish knights with Henry was Renaldus de Valletort. The defender of Tinchebray was the Earl of Mortain, who was imprisoned for life and forfeited all his estates.

Now Valletort was Mortain's man, and held Trematon, Lipson and Honicknowle from him. Between the battle of Tinchebray and Henry's death in 1135 the King gave to Valletort the three royal manors in Plymouth, Maker, King's Tamerton and Sutton. The gift must have been made soon after the battle and looks remarkably like a reward for supporting the King, even though Mortain, the feudal overlord of Valletort, had turned the other way.

These Valletorts, who became key figures in the early story of Plymouth, had a flair for supporting the right side. Ten years after Tinchebray, King Henry gave the Mortain title and lands to his nephew, Stephen, and when, after Henry's death in 1135, the long Barons' War between Stephen and Matilda raged for the throne of England, the Valletorts were on Stephen's side. A Valletort witnessed a grant by Reginald, Earl of Cornwall and Brittany, to St Michael's Mount in 1140, in gratitude for the safety of King Stephen.

Renaud de Vautort was at Hastings.[1] There is a Hugo and a Reginald Valletort in Domesday Book, but as Reginald is spelt in varying ways, and may or may not be Rainaldus,

45

and as similar confusion haunts the family down through the generations, it is as well simply to deal with the family as a whole. They were the main agents of the Count of Mortain in Devon and Cornwall, holding the honour of Trematon, twenty-three manors in south-east Cornwall, and land right across south Devon from Modbury to the Clyst valley. The Valletorts came from Torteval,[2] close to Mortain itself, a strongpoint about fifteen miles from the Bay of Mont St Michel, and well sited to watch the Norman frontiers with both Brittany and Maine. They can have owned little land there, for when the choice had to be made between England and Normandy, even though the Earl of Mortain most valued his Norman possessions, the Valletorts fought for England. They appear to have been adventurers who made their fortune with the English conquest. In England, they multiplied, acquiring estates in Cornwall, Devon and Somerset, marrying into the best families, giving land to the abbeys at Torre and Buckfast, witnessing the foundation deeds of both Plympton and Buckland abbeys, founding Modbury Priory themselves.

SUTTON MANOR HOUSE

When they acquired the manor of Sutton soon after 1105 they seem to have built a new house there in which they lived from time to time. Some years they had tenants there, and from their leases and from the eventual sale documents the site of their manor house can be precisely located. It was on the west part of Church Hill, that is the hill dominated by St Andrew's. It stood between the highways from Sutton to Sourpool, and from Sutton to Stonehouse. Sourpool was a vast saltwater lake with a narrow link to the sea in Millbay, and stretched from Stone-house to the foot of modern Royal Parade. The foundations of the Pearl Building on Royal Parade cut through a beach that was once the shore of Sourpool, and a downpour of rain at high tide still puts Derry's Roundabout under water. For those who knew pre-war Plymouth, these roads are simple to follow. The road from Sutton came down Bedford Street and then forked. The left-hand route down George Street and along Millbay Road led to the grist mills worked by the tide rushing in and out through the narrow neck of water between Sourpool and Millbay—hence the name Millbay. The Sourpool[3] was not 'sour' water, and most probably took its name from sorrel, the red-

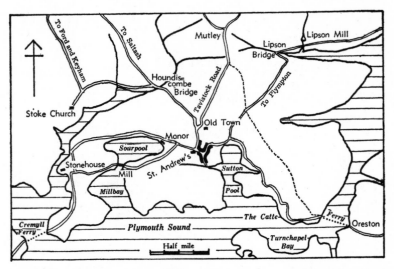

NORMAN PLYMOUTH. *As the village of Sutton grew so the road pattern developed. The Valletorts built their new manor house beside Sourpool between the roads to Stonehouse and to the pool.*

seeded summer plant that was called 'sure' in old English and still grows thickly round the salt estuaries of south Devon and Cornwall. The right-hand fork went down Frankfort Street and King Street and Clarence Place, to Stonehouse High Street.

Both routes skirted the edge of Sourpool, and reference in a 1370 document to 'Vautordis parke atte Pole' now becomes clear; it is the park of the Vautorts at the pool. Vautort is a phonetic rendering of Valletort. A secondary title of the modern Earls of Mount Edgcumbe is Viscount Valletort, a courtesy title held by

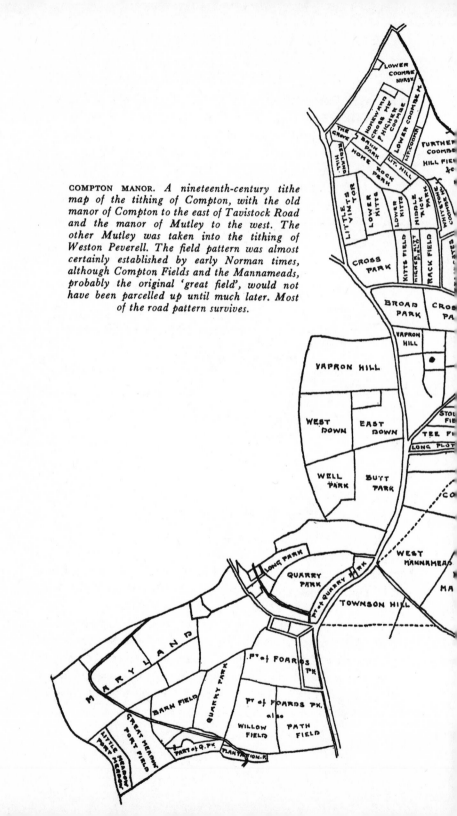

COMPTON MANOR. *A nineteenth-century tithe map of the tithing of Compton, with the old manor of Compton to the east of Tavistock Road and the manor of Mutley to the west. The other Mutley was taken into the tithing of Weston Peverell. The field pattern was almost certainly established by early Norman times, although Compton Fields and the Mannameads, probably the original 'great field', would not have been parcelled up until much later. Most of the road pattern survives.*

LOWER COOMBE NURSE

HOMEWARD CROSS PK

HIGHER COOMBE

LOWER COOMBE PK

LIT.COOMBE

The Grove

BARN PARK

HOME PARK

REDLAND HILL

ROCK PARK

LIT.HILL

FURTHER COOMBE

HILL FIELD

LITTLE VINTOR

LOWER KITTS

LOWER KITTS

MIDDLE RICK PARK

WHITSTONE COOMBE

KITTS FIELD

HIGHER KITTS

HIGHER KITT RICKER FIELD

RACK FIELD

CROSS PARK

BROAD PARK

CROSS PARK

VAPRON HILL

VAPRON HILL

WEST DOWN

EAST DOWN

STOU FIE

TEE FI

LONG PLOT

WELL PARK

BUTT PARK

CO

WEST MANNAMEAD

MA

LONG PARK

QUARRY PARK

Pt of QUARRY PK

TOWNSON HILL

MARYLAND

BARN FIELD

QUARRY PARK

Pt of FOARDS Pk

Pt of FOARDS PK. also

WILLOW FIELD

PATH FIELD

LITTLE MEADOW PORT MEADOW

GREAT MEADOW PORT FIELD

PART of Q.PK

PLANTATION.R

the eldest son of the earl, and the family still pronounce it 'Vautort'.

The site is very similar to those of other Valletort houses in the area. The first one, Trematon, is close to the water of Forder Creek but away from the town at Saltash. Moditonham is on a deep creek on the Cornish bank of Tamar, not far from Botus Fleming, but still isolated. Inceworth was close to the water but away from Millbrook. Empacombe still has its own little harbour, but keeps aloof from Cremyll. Houses still standing on these sites can be studied in their unchanged rural setting, and the site beside Sourpool had the same characteristics. Clearly this is Sutton Valletort.

As lords of Trematon, the Valletorts owned all the waters of Plym and Tamar, and all the fish therein. Even after centuries of over-fishing there are still a dozen different varieties of edible fish to be caught in Plymouth Sound, and in those early days they must have been even more plentiful. One cannot imagine that dwellers on this shore, even though farmers by trade, would have ignored this source of food. After all, they could not even feed their cattle throughout the winter. A few were kept for breeding, the rest were slaughtered and the meat salted down. Fresh fish must have provided a welcome change of diet. Even their church was dedicated to St Andrew, the patron saint of fishermen.

Mr Robert Pearse, the historian of the Cornish harbours, suggests[4] that when the Valletorts moved into Sutton they also moved the manorial seine net there from Trematon. The Hamoaze may have been a rich fishing-ground but Plymouth Sound was richer and bigger, and Sutton closer. The net could have been brought into Millbay, where it would be under the eye of the new manorhouse, but the pattern of the other Valletort houses shows that the villages were kept at arm's length. The Stonehouse shore of Sourpool was also owned by another family, and Sutton Pool was a more sheltered base.

There may already have been fishing-boats there, perhaps even some sale of fish, but the support of Valletort, and the use of the manorial seine net, would make a vast difference. A seine net is hung from a line of floats and laid in a circle, either between two boats for herrings, mackerel, and pilchards, or run out from a beach for other fish, and the circle closed so that all the fish inside are trapped. Such methods are still used in the Tamar and in Cornwall. As more fish would have been caught than could have been eaten fresh, even if there had been a sale to people further inland, the surplus would have had to be salted down.

Salt was producd locally at Tamerton, Egg Buckland, and Bere Ferrers, but the method of obtaining it by evaporating sea water requires a stronger sun than ours to produce any quantity.

Such salt pans are still worked on the south coast of Brittany, and in medieval days, La Rochelle was a good source of supply, while further south Gascony offered a ready market for salted fish. So here was the foundation for a sound two-way trade, out with fish and home with salt. It was a pattern already established in the south Cornish ports, and soon developed in Sutton. One can imagine a fishing village growing, then becoming something more as bigger boats and larger crews were wanted for the overseas trade. An early Valletort document names the first Plymothians: Roger de Fletehenda and Reginald de Veifer (with surnames taken from the place where they lived), Gilbert Cytharista (a harper), William Pistore (a baker), John Boscher (a woodcutter); the names show the occupations of a community which was beginning to specialise.

There were other small towns already in the neighbourhood. Saltash had a market at the time of Domesday, and Richard Valletort gave the town its charter in 1190. At Tavistock, there was the great Benedictine Abbey, founded in 974, well-endowed by the Saxon royal family and already the richest abbey in Devon. A small town developed outside its gates and the abbot gave the townspeople a market in 1105, adding a three-day August fair in 1116.

PLYMPTON

Plympton had two centres of interest, priory and castle. The priory was a Saxon foundation, dating back to Alfred's reign, but Henry I closed it down in 1121—because 'the monks would not give up their concubines'—and refounded it for the Augustinians. Ranaldus de Valletorta witnessed the deed of foundation with the Queen, the archbishops, and the great nobles and prelates of the day. There are undated gifts by the Valletorts to Plympton Priory which probably date from this time; the right of fishing in Sourpool (in front of the new Valletort house), and Drake's Island with its rabbits. Drake's Island was then St Nicholas's Island, named after the little chapel which stood there. There were other such chapels around Plymouth in medieval times, probably those of religious hermits, and one still stands on Rame Head. The mention of rabbits in the Valletort gift is believed to be the earlier reference to them in England, though the early Normans are known to have set up warrens in places where they were not likely to damage their crops. There was one in the tangled Efford hills above Marsh Mills.

Plympton Castle was one of the seats of the Redvers, Earls of Devon, who also held Okehampton and Exeter castles, and 159 Devon manors. In the Barons' Wars, they backed Matilda, and King Stephen himself beseiged Baldwin Redvers in Exeter. The King sent down a party of a hundred men to deal with Plympton Castle, which surrendered without a fight. The castle was slighted, made ineffective for any further rebellion and, after three months, Baldwin had to surrender at Exeter and retired into exile. But as Earl of Devon, Lord of the Isle of Wight and a descendant of an illigitimate son of William the Conqueror's grandfather, Baldwin was still a powerful figure and he was back in Devon within three years, as prosperous as ever. Plympton Castle was still one of his seats and it was in the shadow of the castle, not at the priory gates, that the new town of Plympton Erle—the earl's town—grew up.

The priory stood on a damp, exposed site where the Ridgeway reached the tidewater, but at that point the creeks split, one arm going up over the Colebrook area and the other reaching up to make a small harbour right under the walls of Plympton Castle. Further down the Plym, even in Saxon times, people could wade across the ebb ford there at low tide, and though this meant that Plympton harbour was only accessible at high water, it was here

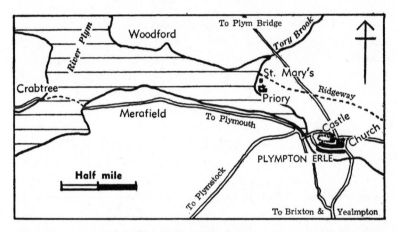

THE PORT OF PLYMPTON. *The Earl of Devon's town grew up round his castle and the road which led from the northern side of the castle to the little harbour is still called the Barbican, which means the water gate. The road shown to Plym Bridge is now marked by a pathfield, part of Station Road, and a hedge line, but beyond the urban development is still a good road.*

that the medieval trade of the district began. There was the produce of a rich farming district to take out, the needs of a rich priory and a wealthy man's castle to bring in. The first cargo of which there is any record is a cargo of slates from Plympton to Southampton in 1178. The town must have grown rapidly, for the fifth earl gave it a market in 1194 and, after various other grants, Plympton Erle was made a borough in 1242.

If the castle had the town, the priory had the church. St Mary's, built beside the priory, was the mother church of the entire parish, a very large one. A new parish for Plympton Erle was carved out of the old rural parish, and its original dedication to St Thomas à Becket (murdered in 1170) gives a clue to its date. The priors established their right to appoint the priest at Plympton Erle in 1288, but it was their only authority in the town.

TIN MINING

The real impetus to the growth of these new little Devon towns, Plympton and Tavistock, came from the discovery of tin on west Dartmoor. The earliest reference is in 1156, and almost at once Dartmoor became the largest source of the metal in Europe. There was virtually a tin rush. No mining was required, just a spade and a bucket, the patience to find alluvial deposits in the streams, and the courage to endure the Dartmoor weather while washing the river sands for tin. Later, the miners dug back the banks of the streams in search of buried alluvial deposits, and worked upstream towards their original sources. Essentially it was an industry of small men, and as all the miners were under the King's protection it attracted not only small farmers and merchants from the neighbouring villages but runaway serfs and others dissatisfied with their medieval lot. It must have been a rougher and tougher business than anything Klondike or California saw in the last century. The marks of the old miners can still be seen in the south-west Dartmoor valleys, where the bottoms have been cut back to a U-shape, and where uneven heaps of stone lie just as they were thrown aside. The marks are clearly seen in the Plym just above Cadover Bridge, and, indeed, Brisworthy, just north of Cadover, and Sheepstor, are the first names mentioned in tin records, as early as 1168.

From 1160 to 1190 the output of Devon tin was at its highest. It was refined into blocks, each of 160 lb, much too heavy to go far by packhorse, and shipped away, mainly to London. Three stannary (the word means tin) towns, Tavistock, Ashburton and Chagford, were named where the tin had to be taken for marketing under royal supervision. Each block was weighed, and a corner (coign) cut off so that its purity could be tested (coignage), before receiving the royal stamp. The miners had their own courts, and even their own prison at Lydford, where a castle was built in 1195 for that purpose. In 1198, Richard Coeur de Lion appointed a Lord Warden of the Stannaries to control the trade, with officers at each stannary town, a weigher for the Plym and Meavy valleys, and officers at the ports to see that no uncoigned tin was smuggled out.

Which were the tin ports? Tavistock almost certainly used the quays beside the Tamar at Morwellham, where the abbots of Tavistock had a hunting lodge (the building is still there, high above the river). It seems a long way upstream but it was still handling the output of mines in the last century. Whether it could handle all the west Dartmoor tin is another matter. King Richard, for instance had 254 thousand weight of tin shipped to him at La Rochelle in 1195. Was some taken downriver to Saltash and trans-shipped? Did Sutton have any of the trade? There is a record in 1313 of 129 ingots of tins being confiscated at Sutton, after having been found hidden under other cargo in the *Grace Due* of Fowey.

If tin did come down to Sutton, then the pack horses would have jogged from Tavistock through Whitchurch, over the Walkham at Horrabridge (the boundary bridge; three parishes met there) and up to join the old ridge road to Sutton. There is evidence that a branch road to Plympton became important soon after the tin trade started. A disused section can still be traced north of Roborough aerodrome, after which it follows the modern Plym Bridge Lane to Plympton. The river is crossed just above the tide mark, originally by a ford but in 1238 there is mention of Plym Bridge, quite the earliest bridge in the Plymouth area. It was also an alternative route from Plymouth to Plympton when the Ebb Ford was impassable at high tide, and the route through Compton and Egg Buckland, crossing the Buckland Creek and the Forder Valley just above the old tide-mark, is still in use.

But the fact that a bridge replaced the ford at Plym Bridge soon after the start of the tin trade is significant.

Plym Bridge was also distinguished because a chapel dedicated to St Mary the Virgin[5] stood upon it. A Papal letter of 1450 directed the Prior of Plympton to depute fit priests to hear confessions there and to absolve 'the great multitude of faithful from divers parts of the world' who resorted to the chapel 'on account of the many miracles which God has wrought therein.'

When Plympton became a stannary town in 1328 its initial petition asked that the coignage should be moved there from Tavistock since it was a maritime town where the tin could be straightway put aboard ship, whereas Tavistock was so far inland that transport costs were very high. Their petition was successful (after all, the jury who made the decision was largely drawn from men living near Plympton). Tavistock was furious and protested so strongly that, in the end, it kept its stannary and Plympton was added as a fourth Devon stannary town.

PLYM MOUTH

But Plympton in 1328 was very worried about its maritime trade, which it was losing to Plymouth, and the reason lay in this very tin business. Tin streaming sends a lot of waste matter down the rivers to add to the silt Nature has been sending down for centuries. Protests about silt in the Plym caused by the tinners form an endless record, continuing right into Elizabethan times. The Plym, the Meavy, and the Tory Brook which comes down through Plympton, were all tin-streaming valleys on Dartmoor, and were all being exploited by the middle of the twelfth century. So, from 1150 onwards, the Laira estuary and the creek up to Plympton must have been getting more and more shallow, while the fords at Ebb Ford and across the Plympton creek, from Woodford to Merafield (where the little road crosses the railway shunting-yard today) became bars to the passage of ships. The times when ships could get up to Plympton must have become more and more limited either side of high water and, increasingly they would have to anchor at Plym mouth and wait for high tide before going up with their cargos. Reloaded, they would have come down from Plympton on the tide and then awaited at Plym mouth for fair winds or weather to take them on their voyage. The pattern is the same today, with our bigger ships waiting at anchor in the Sound until the top of the tide will taken them to the quaysides of Cattedown or Millbay or the Dockyard.

Those waiting ships could anchor safely in Turnchapel Bay whatever the weather, though they might have been a little uncomfortable with wind against tide. But on the other side of Plym mouth there was the full shelter of Sutton Pool. There, too, was the little fishing village of Sutton, with its own ships trading to western France, with carpenters, sailmakers and riggers if wanted, victuals or water available, and ale of an evening. Seamen have not changed over the centuries.

The longer tin mining went on, and the longer the waits at Plym mouth, the greater became the inducement to use Sutton at Plym mouth as a terminal port instead of Plympton. It is hard to put dates to the process, but the first record of the name Plymouth, and the first cargoes, appear in the Pipe Rolls for 1211. There was a shipload of bacon for Portsmouth, and wine for Nottingham.

So Plymouth came into being as a port at a time when events in Europe were bringing the western Channel ports into prominence. After the trouble experienced by the First Crusade, it was decided that the second should go by sea. A fleet of 164 ships was assembled and sailed from Dartmouth. When they reached northern Portugal weary and battered, they were asked, 'Why go all the way to the Holy Land to fight the infidel? We have him here. Help us clear our land of Moors.' So the chivalrous knights agreed, Lisbon was freed, and there was born a trade in wine and fruit between Dartmouth and Portugal that continued for centuries.

In 1154, Henry of Anjou became King Henry II of England. With his own and his wife's estates, all the western Atlantic seaboard was under one rule, from Ireland through England and Brittany down to the Pyrenees. Trade was unfettered; there was La Rochelle for buying salt, Bayonne for selling salt fish, and Bordeaux for buying wine. Salt fish is a thirsty business. The vineyards around Bordeaux are still the best in the world; and when Englishmen took to claret as their national wine, Plymouth built its commercial fortune on it.

Another King, John, saw Brittany become independent again and, in 1204, Normandy broke away from the English Crown. There were still vast lands in western France acknowledging English rule, but to reach them involved the long haul round Ushant and across the Bay of Biscay. And that was a voyage calling for West Country ships built for the Atlantic, and West Country seamen brought up in that trade, rather than the shallow-draught ships of the Cinque Ports, which had been the link through Normandy. Now, Dartmouth, Plymouth and Fowey had a new place on the map.

In 1244, Seville was freed from the Moors and rapidly became the entrepot where all the riches of the Mediterranean were brought into the Atlantic for purchase and reshipment by the merchants of the Channel and northern Europe. It was a simple and logical extension of the Biscay voyages. No wonder Sutton was growing in importance.

MARKET GRANT

But to take advantage of their new opportunities the people of the little town had to be able to buy and sell, to conduct business. They had to be a market town, and the market itself would be a useful source of revenue to whoever owned it.[6] The Valletorts were the lords of Saltash, where the market dated back to before the Conquest. At Tavistock, the Abbot had set one up in 1105, and the Earls of Devon had been given a market at

Plympton Erle in 1194. Sutton received its market in 1254, and the rights went to the Prior of Plympton. Until them, all the Priors had possessed in Plymouth was the right of fishing in Sourpool.

King Henry III was in winter quarters with his army in France when, on 27 January, 1254, he signed the grant giving Sutton its market and so making it a town. He had been King of England for nearly forty years but had little love for the English. The barons plagued him as they had his father, John, and he far preferred the French relatives of his wife. Indeed, his ambition was to win back all the French lands of his great namesake and grandfather, Henry Plantagenet. That was why he was wintering in the dusty little fortress town of Bazas, on the edge of the vineyards of Sauterne, awaiting better weather to drive out again across the sandy wastes of the Landes and clear Aquitaine of the French. Now the affairs of England were before him as he sat in council with the Bishops of Bath and Hereford, the Earl of Hereford and Essex, Earl of Warwick, and other gentlemen. Who presented the petition about Plymouth is unknown, but it was presumably the Priory. Perhaps Prior Baldwin himself had made the voyage from Plympton to Bordeaux the previous autumn, and then ridden the forty miles out to Bazas when the Royal army had finally settled down.

One can imagine the King considering the claim, and pondering its implications. The Earl of Devon, he would recall, was lord of the hundred. True, Baldwin de Redvers was only about ten years old and a ward of the Queen's uncle, but his mother's family were arrant rebels. The lord of the manor was Ralph Valletort. His wife, Joan, had been mistress of the King's brother, Richard (whom he had made Earl of Cornwall and so lord of the Honour of Trematon many years earlier). The affair had gone on for ten years and there was a son. Richard's wife was the Queen's sister, and even if he did not care what his brother did, had there been complaints from his sister-in-law to his queen? Plympton Priory was rich, it managed its large estates well, and the Pope and the Church had always been good friends to the King—which was more than could be said for most English landowners.

So the charter was sealed, granting to the Prior and Convent of Plympton and their successors a weekly market[7] on Thursdays at Sutton in the county of Devon, and a yearly fair there on the eve, the day, and the morrow of St John the Baptist. All the lords around the table signed, as they signed State papers day after day.

Plympton Priory, an Augustine foundation, had been set up by Bishop Warelwast of Exeter, nephew and chaplain of the Conqueror, as part of a plan to bring the Saxon church, whose priests were appointed by lay landlords, under central discipline. The Augustines were a preaching order of canons who ministered to the people in the parishes round their priory, and whose churches came under priory control. The active interest of Warelwast brought many local parish churches into Plympton's hands but, increasingly, the canons either lived in their parishes as normal priests or resided in the priory and appointed vicars to the parishes, just like any lay holder of an advowson. In the twenty-six parishes[8] to which Plympton Priory had the right to appoint priests at the Dissolution, only two of the eighteen canons of Plympton were acting as vicars, Henry Luxton at Shaugh and Bernard Cole at Wembury. A thirteenth century minstrel-turned-monk wrote of the Augustines: 'Among them one is well-shod, well-clothed and well-fed. They go out when they like, mix with the world, and talk at table.' They were not tonsured but wore a black biretta, long black cassock and hood. By 1288, Plympton Priory was the second richest religious house in Devon; by the Dissolution, it had even outstripped Tavistock in wealth.[9]

The Prior of Plympton had upheld his right of presentment to St Andrew's against the Valletorts as early as 1159. Perhaps in those early days a canon of Plympton did officiate in the parish of Plymouth but, by 1333, the Priory was complaining to the bishop that the vicar of St Andrew's had so increased his income (evidence of the rapid growth of the town) that the amount payable to them should be increased and the vicar's share reduced accordingly. At that time the vicar of St Andrew's returned to Plympton as 'a professed religious' or monk, and another canon was nominated to St Andrew's as incumbent. Two years later St Andrew's was being held in plurality by Ralf de Ryngstede of Lincoln who was also a canon and prebend of Exeter Cathedral, as well as holding offices in Bangor and Wiltshire. He declared that if he was allowed only two offices he would keep the Exeter and Plymouth posts. The Bishop of Exeter nominated the vicar in 1334 and in 1472 licensed the perpetual vicar of St Andrew's, John Stubbes, with authority also to officiate at St Lawrence Stonehouse. It would appear that Plympton's only interest was in drawing its annual pension from the church, just as the new market town was a strictly commercial venture.

The Earl of Devon saw that he had missed an opportunity by letting the priory get a market grant for Sutton in 1254, so in 1257 he obtained one as well. But it was only a paper entry, for the Earl was then actively engaged in the war with Simon de Montfort against the King, and died in 1262, poisoned, it is said, at the table of the King's uncle, Peter of Savoy, who had been his guardian. He was the last Redvers, Earl of Devon, and when his mother, Amicia, founded Buckland Abbey in 1273 it was in honour of his memory and his father's. Amicia gave to the new abbey the Redvers rights to the Hundred of Roborough, but there is no mention of any market held by her family.

Ralph Valletort, the cuckold, did not argue. He gave the prior a site at Sourpool for a mill, the right of way along the old fishing-path to reach the mill, and the manorial right to grind the corn of everyone in the manor. He died soon after, and his son, Reginald, died young and without heirs. His uncle, Roger, succeeded to the Valletort estates and began to dispose of them. Richard, Earl of Cornwall, who had been defeated with the King by the barons at the battle of Lewes, was strengthening his position in the west. To Launceston he had added Lostwithiel and

Restormel Castle, and in 1270 he bought Trematon Castle, and all the feudal rights which went with the Honour of Trematon. Successive Earls and Dukes of Cornwall have held Trematon and all the rights it gave them over Sutton and the waters of the Sound. Roger Valletort died insane in 1275 and his two nieces began a long series of law suits claiming that the sale of Trematon and the rest should be set aside on the grounds that their uncle had been mad when he sold their patrimony. But it availed them nothing.

One other sale made by the mad uncle is interesting. The vital deeds are undated but, in the first, Roger de Valletort grants to Ralph, son of Richard, all Cremyll and Maker; later deeds add the Cremyll ferry rights and the fishery of Tamar. It is suggested that the Richard named is Richard, Earl of Cornwall, that his son Ralph was the result of Richard's union with Joan Valletort, and that his son's family took the name of 'de Stonehouse' after the village of west Stonehouse, which then stood at Cremyll.

The Valletorts survived, but in Plymouth they were reduced to their manor of Sutton. There long lingered in Plymouth a memory that the family had lost its overlordship to the Crown through some villainy. The story was embroidered over the years, and in about 1540 Leland wrote 'I hard say, that the landes of Valletorte were for a morther doone by one of them confiscate, and sins the great part of them have remaynid yn is the kinges handes.' No murder in fact, it would seem; just an unfaithful wife and a mad uncle.

Perhaps we can forgive Joan Valletort, for Richard was the King's brother and the most ambitious man in Europe; he was even elected Emperor of the Holy Roman Empire. Of the Stonehouse family, believed to be the offspring of her union with Richard, the heiress in 1369, Cecilia, married Stephen Durnford, a land speculator from Tavistock, who had already bought Stonehouse. The next year they bought the Valletort manor house in Sutton, and in 1386 Rame was added to the estate. A century later there were no male Durnfords left; the daughter, Joan, married Piers Edgcumbe, whose father made his fortune in the service of Henry VII and built Cotehele. Until recent years the Earls of Mount Edgcumbe owned nearly all these estates, heirs of the long Valletort story that goes back to the Conqueror.

The Valletorts may well have provided the initial stimulus which started the growth of the small fishing community between St Andrew's Church and Sutton Pool. But by 1254 they bowed out, content to remain rural landlords at Sutton Valletort. The new town became Sutton Prior, one of many such monastic boroughs created by Henry III, every one of whose histories is a long story of struggle by the townspeople against their clerkish overlords.

CHAPTER FOUR

THE ROYAL PORT

A MARKET cross was the centre of Sutton Prior, and stood in a triangle[1] at the junction of three streets: Whimple Street, leading to the parish church; High Street, to the waterside, and Buckwell Street to Breton Side and the road to Exeter. Around the cross every Thursday the market stalls were set up, and the Prior's steward moved through the shoppers, collecting toll from the stall-keepers, checking their weights and measures and settling any disputes between stall-holder and customer. Serious argument would be referred to a court which he would hold the following Monday morning, sitting with the leading men of the town.

But change was to follow change. In 1272 Richard, Earl of Cornwall, died. His son Edmund (by Richard's second wife, the lovely Sanchia of Provence, King Henry's sister-in-law) lacked his father's European ambitions but was concerned to pull his earldom of Cornwall into a profit-making entity. His palace was at Lostwithiel, and his secondary centres at Launceston and Trematon. By 1274 the townsmen of Plympton, their market damaged to some extent by the new rival at Sutton, complained to King Edward I that the bailiff of Trematon was using the port of Plymouth without payment or acknowledgement, had taken over the ferry from Sutton Pool to Hooe (a good route through Plymstock to Plympton) was taking sand from the estuary for agricultural purposes, and has gone into the fish business in Sutton. Edmund of Cornwall was still King Edward's cousin, and, what is more, as lord of Trematon, he had undoubted rights over the waters of Plym and Sutton Pool.

64

The 'ebb ford' over the Plym at Crabtree crossed from the slipway (right) to what is now the hedge of the reclaimed land, and along the hedge line to firm ground; it served the ancient trackway and was the main road before Long Bridge was built about 1620. Below, Devil's Point from Mount Edgcumbe; until quite modern times the ferry across the Tamar mouth came from a cove where the Victualling Yard buildings end to this beach between Cremyll and Barn Pool.

The Saxons settled at the head of the many tidal inlets like Tamerton Creek, where St Budoc is believed to have landed on the left bank in the Fifth Century.

An arm of the sea once reached up from Marsh Mills to the valley below Egg Buckland Church.

By 1280, the abbot of the new monastery at Buckland had been installed and, by gift from Amicia of Devon, he was now also lord of the hundred of Roborough. As such, his court at Horrabridge was the legal authority right down into Sutton. Clearly there was a tangle of claims, and two inquiries into them were held in Exeter in 1281. At the first, John Valletort claimed that he was lord of the manor of Sutton. The Prior of Plympton declared that he owned the 'ville' of Sutton, with assize of bread and ale (the administration of mercantile law, as distinct from the civil and criminal law cases heard in the hundred courts).

The second inquiry of 1281 reached positive decisions that were of major importance to Sutton's future. To understand the decisions, one must realise that the town—that is, the built-up area—was on the north bank of an arm of Sutton Pool which reached up across the present day Parade. Summarised, the judge's findings were that :

> Sutton was on the coast of the port of Plymouth, but no part of it was on the King's soil.
> Part of Sutton north of the coast was on the soil of the Prior of Plympton, where he had assize of bread and ale, and certain rents.
> Part of Sutton south of the coast was on the soil of John Valletort, where he had certain rents, but the Abbot of Buckland had assize of bread and ale.
> The port of Plymouth belonged to the King, and paid £4 a year to the Exchequer.
> It would prejudice neither the King nor anyone else if Sutton were made a free borough and its inhabitants free burgesses.

The two vital points emerging from all this, apart from this last apparent claim for freedom by the inhabitants, was that the Prior's authority and ownership was limited to the urban area, that the Valletorts were still lords of the rest of Sutton, and that the harbour belonged to the King. It would seem that this claim rested on the fact that Sutton had once been a royal manor, and that this royal authority over the water was exercised as a tenant by Edmund of Cornwall, through Trematon.

War was to make this royal claim of new importance, for when, in 1294, the French king tried to seize the English possessions in western France, Edward I, a soldier all his life, retaliated. That year, a fleet sailing from Portsmouth to Gascony was scattered off the Cornish coast and reassembled in Plymouth. The following year, a fleet again assembled at Plymouth and this time the King's brother, the Earl of Lancaster, sailed with it. Corn for the army was brought to Plymouth from all the western counties. This expedition, which was repeated in 1296 and again in 1297, was the start of Plymouth's long connection with the Crown as a naval base. As such, Plymouth rapidly outstripped its neighbouring rivals to become the pre-eminent port of the western Channel.

Dartmouth and Fowey have anchorages as sheltered as the Cattewater and Sutton Pool, and perhaps roomier. But both are approached through narrow entrances between high cliffs where the wind can play tricks, whereas the approach to Plymouth is across the wide Sound which gives shelter in all but a southerly blow. Again the land approaches to Dartmouth and Fowey are steep and difficult; even the railway never got to Dartmouth, and only reached Fowey with difficulty. By the time Edward I wanted a western base Plymouth had a reasonable road to Exeter, with all the rivers bridged, and so to London.

Plymouth could water the ships and the soldiers, either from the little streams flowing into Sutton Pool or from the town wells, remembered today in street names: the west well, the buck well (where clothes were bucked or washed), the fyne well, Lady well (where a hermit had a little chapel, probably dedicated to Our Lady). Buckland Abbey was a Cistercian house and the Cistercians were the great agriculturalists of the day; with an estate of 20,000 acres stretching between Plym and Tavy they were a ready-made victualling organisation. The massive tithe barn at Buckland still bears testimony to the size of their undertaking, and it is not surprising that when the Hundred Years War started Buckland was at once given permission to fortify itself; whereas the defence of Tavistock, Plympton and Buckfast abbeys was not considered necessary until forty years later. Yet Plympton was a rich establishment, fit to offer hospitality to royal personages and great nobles, a place where the war chest (for it had to travel with real gold, in those pre-banking days) could be guarded, away from the press of soldiers and sailors.

King Edward was himself in Plymouth for over a month in the spring of 1297. He arrived at Plympton between 6 April and 10 April, and signed a document at Sutton as late as 8 May. So long a stay shows the importance he attached to the expedition he was fitting out for Gascony, for he had just finished a campaign in Scotland, had trouble on his hands from Wales, and was planning a summer expedition through Flanders as well as this western campaign. He resolved to stay at 'Plemmuth' until he had seen his fleet sail. Every corner of the west was searched for ships to serve as transports, and to carry food. Again, corn came in from all the western counties, and a year's output of tin was appropriated to finance the expedition.

The impetus to the growth of Plymouth in those years must have been immense. When Edward called his first Parliament in 1295, it was attended by burgesses from the older towns of Tavistock and Plympton. For the second Parliament of 1298 these two were joined for the first time by burgesses from Plymouth, William of Stoke and Nicholas the 'Rydlere'.

THE WINE SHIPS

War, tin, fish, hides, lead, wool and cloth; these were the export trades of Plymouth. On the import side there was war again (expeditions moved both ways), wine (a little from Spain and Portugal as well as Bordeaux), iron (from Bilbao in northern Spain), fruit, woad (for dyeing cloth), onions, wheat and garlic. No customs returns are available for Plymouth but these goods appear in the records of other south Devon ports, whose trade can have been little different.

The lead was a side product of the mines of Bere Ferrers and Bere Alston, where silver had been discovered about 1290. Mines were royal property, and silver a welcome gift to a monarch with a war on his hands. Some 270 lb of silver were shipped from Maristow to London in 1294 and, between 1292 and 1297, the Devon mines yielded £4,046 in silver and £360 in lead. By 1297, the King had 284 miners from Derbyshire and 35 from Wales at work at Bere. Two years later he leased the mines to Americo Frescobaldi, one of the great Florentine bankers, the Lombards, who had replaced the Jews in England as merchant bankers to the Crown. Lombard agents were to be found all over England, and their badge of three golden balls is still the sign of the pawn-broker. They handled Cistercian wool and, quite likely, the annual crop from Buckland Abbey. Americo Frescobaldi was very close to the King, and had the wine customs of Bordeaux, making a strong financial link between west Devon and Bordeaux.

From an almost indecipherable roll in the Public Record Office emerges the names of the first Plymouth ships[2] carrying wine from Bordeaux. The record is for 1303 :

28 September *La . . . de Plenmue*	47 tuns
30 September Navis *Santi Salvatoris de Plemua*	49 tuns 1 pipe
1 October Navis *Sancta Michaelis de Plemua*	79 tuns

A tun of wine was equivalent to four barrels or hogsheads of sixty-three gallons each. Two barrels made a pipe—half a tun. The size of a ship was calculated on the basis of how many tuns of wine she could carry, and complicated measurements were made to arrive at this figure without actually loading. So the tunnage, or tonnage, of a ship originated.

There is a gap in these Bordeaux customs records until 1308. Then in the roll beginning 11 May, and listing forty-four ships, there occurs :

19 June Navis *Santi Andrei de Plomuth* portagium 124 tuns. Rector Ricardus Baykins.

This is the first recorded name of a Plymouth sea captain, Richard Baykins, and a French clerk, using the Norman French of the day, is making as big a hash of English names as his descendents do today. Was the rector (master) really Captain Bacon, or is it an H? It would be nice to call him Haykins, or Hawkins. Fittingly the ship (navis) was the *St Andrew*, no doubt named after Plymouth's parish church (thirty years earlier, in the taxation of Pope Nicholas I, it was named S. Andree).

That autumn, with the wine harvest in, there were seven Plymouth ships braving the equinoctial gales round Ushant and, as like as not, fighting off French, Breton and Norman pirates. All told, they carried nearly 200,000 gallons of wine. There are more records for 1310, and from them all eleven Plymouth ships emerge, eight of over 100 tons. There were other West Country ships in the trade, six from Fowey and one from Polruan, four from Looe and one from the Fal. The Cornish ships were not as big as the Plymouth ones, though there were even bigger craft sailing from Bordeaux for up-Channel ports.

Some financial returns show the rate of Plymouth's growth. The Crown, to save itself the cost of collecting dues, rented out or 'farmed' their assets to private individuals. In 1296 the farm fee for Sutton Pool was 49s 6d a year. By 1334 it was £17 10s, a sevenfold increase in forty years. Sutton was worth more than all the Cornish ports put together. Exeter and Dartmouth kept higher trade figures than Plymouth all through the fourteenth century. Exeter was the centre of Devon's new cloth industry and Totnes (for which Dartmouth was the outport) the second centre. Plymouth had only the coarser cloth of Tavistock, and some of the Ashburton output.

FRIARIES

Round the turn of the century the friars, too, were moving in; no doubt there was need of their ministration in the rapidly growing seaport whose population was liable to multiply many times over when the royal expeditions brought in soldiers and sailors by the thousand. Seaports with men of half-a-dozen different nationalities fresh in from sea, garrison towns with soldiers for whom tomorrow meant war and imminent death, and yesterday a battle they were lucky to have survived; these are never gentle places. On top of that, it was a raw new town, growing fast, with new populations moving in mainly from the neighbouring rural areas, but bringing in, too, all kinds of unsettled people.

No wonder all three orders of friars[3] moved in as well. There is no written evidence of the Black Friars, either of their foundation or their dissolution, but legend is firmly attached to the one friary building which has survived, in Southside Street. It would have been on Valletort land, on the 'south side' of Sutton, the first building there. The friars originally owned nothing, but, as time went on, they had to have places in which to live and churches in which to serve the people and, since they still refused to own any property, these buildings were often vested in the town or the bishop. This may explain why the Black Friary of the Dominicans became town property after the dissolution.

The Grey Friars (Franciscans, and followers of St Francis of Assissi) had probably built a leper house, on the 'headland' above the town by 1300, and this Maudlyn, with its thatched roof on the healthy hilltop, was Plymouth's first hospital. 'Goddeshouse' it is called in the raw words of the Dissolution accounts of 1538, 'for the relief of impotent and lazare people'. There were fourteen inmates then, though sometimes there had been twenty or more. Beside their 'mansyon house', they had funds from certain lands given them by the charitable, worth in all £4 7s a year. In 1566, Plymouth Corporation was buying reeds for its roof, and the building seems finally to have disappeared under the Civil War defences of 1643.

The Grey Friars probably settled from the start on the royal waste where they eventually built their friary, just across the Parade inlet from the Blackfriars between the town and the harbour. The White Friars, who were Carmelites, built on Valle-tort land east of the town as early as 1314. Notice that none of these friaries was in Sutton on priory land; the established church had no love for them and there were constant battles between the Plymouth friaries, the vicars of Plymouth and the Bishops of Exeter. Whether the friars were usurping the work of the vicar, or doing the work he was neglecting, is not clear, but certainly their friaries were as close to the town and the people they

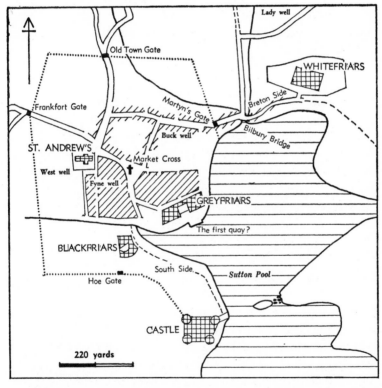

PLYMOUTH 1400. *The built-up area is uncertain but the friaries were sited round the edge of the town. The gates have been marked on their sites, and as roads forked just outside these gates they had probably not changed position. The dotted line can be no more than a suggestion of the site of the walls, although there is evidence for the line between Martyn's Gate and Old Town Gate.*

came to serve as they could get; the ring of buildings gives a fair idea of the size of Sutton. They may early have bred in Plymouth a critical view of the established church; they certainly created a taste for sermons and they were able to offer sanctuary, with freedom from arrest, for forty days. They were outspoken to the end, even if their friaries did eventually become as sumptious as any buildings in the town. John of Gaunt lodged with the White Friars in 1386; it is recorded as the 'Palace of John of Gaunt, at the Carmelite Friary'. These friaries were close to the harbour, more convenient than Plympton Priory, and one wonders how often they housed the royal persons whom the French wars brought to Plymouth?

SELF-GOVERNMENT

These wars saw a lull in the early days of the fourteenth century, while Edward II wrestled with problems closer home, and with the Scots. In 1302, 1308 and again in 1310, Sutton was ordered to hold ships in readiness to sail north against 'The Bruce'. But little happened and, meanwhile, the men of Plymouth were taking a close look at their own affairs.

The town's growth was being cramped by the priors, but, in 1310, a 'final concord and agreement' (which suggests a long argument) was reached in the presence and at the mediation of the Bishop of Exeter and others, between the Prior and the burgesses of the commonalty of the town of Sutton. Here is evidence that the burgesses, the chief men, were working together and forming the first local government. They had no corporate being in law, and Richard the Tanner had to affix his seal on their behalf. He is called the Prepositus, which means reeve or bailiff, but he cannot have been the prior's bailiff or he would never have signed for the townsmen. Clearly then, he was the townsmen's leader, holder of the office that in time merged into the mayoralty. A writ of 1254 to the bailiff of the port of Plymmue may refer to the King's officer, but by 1289 there was a writ to the Bailiffs and Commonalty of Plymouth, the first signs of any corporate life.

The agreement related to Sutton's market where, around the central stone cross, stalls had been set up for the sale of fish, flesh, and other victuals. These stalls belonged to the Prior, and though townsmen had no right to set up any others without his permission, they had been doing so. Now it was agreed that there should be eighteen stalls round the cross, for which the burgesses should pay a penny a year, this rent to be paid to the Prepositus for the time being. It was further agreed that they should not put up any more stalls, there or elsewhere in the town, without the licence of the Prior. This looks as if the Prepositus was expected to change frequently, or perhaps even to be elected annually. Certainly it indicated a body of townspeople strong enough to fight for their rights.

In 1310, Earl Edmund of Cornwall died heirless and his estates passed to the Crown, together with all the Trematon rights in Plymouth. Three years later the Crown was taking the Prior to court to prove his rights, and it was decided that he held the view of frankpledge (the right to try criminal cases less than felonies), of ducking-stool and pillory (for punishing minor offenders), the assize of bread and ale, the fishing of all the Cattewater, and the right to grant the lease of houses.

In 1317, the burgesses of Plymouth were themselves at court petitioning to be granted, for an annual rent, certain waste places belonging to the Crown.[4] The Prior and two Valletorts, John of Moditon and John of Clyst (in east Devon) opposed this, claiming that the King had no land in town, that the Prior was lord of two parts and the Valletorts of the third part. This must surely have meant that the town was growing out beyond the original land of the Prior, into Valletort land.

Plymouth's witnesses at the hearing in Exeter are interesting. Among them were John Gifforde (the Giffords were still the owners of Compton), William Kemell (from Camel's Head) and Walter Colrigg (from Coleridge). Either these nearby gentry were

taking a hand in the town's trade, or else these were younger
sons moving into the town to make their fortunes.

The Sheriff of Devon found that, before the foundation of the
ville of Sutton, the Kings of England had a piece of waste land
near the port of Plymouth, five perches long and one perch
broad, and a six-acre piece of land recovered from the sea where
a certain house of the town was built. At this place according to
the Sheriff, the King's ancestors, by their bailiffs, had held their
courts, and fishing-boats of the town and other places were
accustomed to resort there to dry their sails and nets, and to put
their fish up for sale. They had paid the King a rent of twelve
pence, and a penny on each basket of fish, and the proceeds had
amounted to £4 a year.

The oldest streets of Plymouth were built on the slopes running down from the church and the market cross. Between the
foot of the hill and the water's edge today there is an area of
more than six acres, on which no housing development took place
until Tudor times. Part of it is still called Sutton Wharf, and this
must be the six acres formed 'by the withdrawal of the sea', whose
royal ownership resulted from it having been part of the sea bed,
and so part of the honour of Trematon. It was the base of the
fishing fleet, and the site of the wholesale fish market, as distinct
from the retail fish market licensed by the Prior at the market
cross. There is a similar story of royal ownership, through the
duchy of Cornwall, of the foreshore at Dartmouth.

Why was the court concerned with that other piece of land,
five perches by one? It was not very large, just $27\frac{1}{2}$ yds by $5\frac{1}{2}$
yds, but it must have been important. The perch was commonly
used as a measurement of stonework, and this may be the clue.
Was it, perhaps, the first quay in the harbour? It would be long
enough to berth a ship of the times, make loading and unloading
easier than from a ship run on to the beach and unloaded into
carts, or anchored off and unloaded into boats. The first sketch
map ever made of Plymouth, when Henry VII was surveying
the defences, shows ships moored along Sutton Wharf and round

the corner of Guy's Quay, into the Parade inlet. There is still a piece of quay wall there which fits the measurements, and it may have been that very first quay in Sutton Harbour.

What becomes very clear from all this is that the influence of the Prior of Plympton was confined to the town, and his powers to appointing the vicar, holding the minor law-court, and collecting rents and market dues. Otherwise, he was limited to the position of any other landlord and, moreover, had to contend with a strong body of townspeople already developing their own form of self-government.

In shape, Plymouth was similar to many little towns which grew up in the days of Edward I, with parallel streets at right angles to one another, the church and the market place standing apart, the market place the rallying place from which streets ran out to the perimeters of the town. But in the case of Plymouth, Edward I was there to see it taking shape and, through the port so firmly established as belonging to the Crown, he built up its prosperity.

An army assembled again in 1324, when Edward II, having made a truce with the Scots, could turn to the perpetual nibblings of the French kings at Gascony. A fleet was assembled in Plymouth, 200 foot soldiers were sent from south Wales, and 800 archers came from south and south-east England. But royal troubles at home kept the fleet from sailing, and it must have meant a rowdy summer for a town of under 900 people to have a thousand idle soldiers and the crews of an idle fleet kicking their heels in the port. The ships were private vessels pressed into the King's service, and while they waited they earned no money. Small wonder that many slipped off to their normal business; trade never yet stopped for war.

THE HUNDRED YEARS WAR

With Edward III on the throne, a soldier like his grandfather, he resumed the French wars in real earnest in 1336. This was the start of the Hundred Years War and Plymouth was many times to pay the price of being a royal port; regularly were the townsmen to see the red glow of their burning houses and each time it was part of the major design of the war.

In 1337, the French King assembled a fleet at Marseilles for a Crusade; instead, he brought it north to the Channel to help his Scottish allies. Edward invaded the Low Countries.[5] The French fleet attacked Hastings, Dover and Folkestone. Southampton was burnt. Eighteen French galleys and pinnaces were sent down Channel and descended upon Plymouth.

'They brent certain great ships and a great part of the town', says Stowe. The French were driven back by the Devon militia under the eighty-year-old earl, and it is claimed that 500 were drowned. This seems a large number, but those Mediterranean galleys ranged up to 1,200 tons and carried 180 rowers each, strong paid men, not slaves. The cost to the defenders was eighty-nine men killed. It must have been a considerable battle but whether it took place in Sutton Pool or the Cattewater is impossible to say; we are not even sure whether there was just one raid, or a second in 1339, for the chroniclers all give different dates.

The battle of Sluys in 1340 brought a respite after this first raid and for the next twenty years the English were to be masters of the Channel. England had learnt the importance of sea power. In 1344, the bailiff of Plymouth, in common with those of Bristol, Hull, the Cinque Ports, Exeter, and Dartmouth, had been ordered to send two men with a knowledge of shipping to London, to advise the King. Portsmouth sent only one. In 1345, for the Duke of Lancaster's expedition, Plymouth sent fifteen ships[6] compared with Dartmouth's nine, and the Plymouth crews totalled 300 men. For the siege of Calais in 1347, for which the Channel ports were scoured for ships and men, Fowey found 47 ships and 770 men, Dartmouth 31 ships and 757 men, and Plymouth 26 ships and 603 men. Seven of the Plymouth ships had more than fifty men in the crew and the biggest had eighty; the size of Plymouth ships was growing considerably.

The year after Calais, 1348, a fleet of forty western ships assembled in Plymouth to take the King's daughter, Joan, to Bordeaux. It was hoped to marry her off to the King of Castile and so attract him away from his friendship with France. The large fleet was probably meant to impress him. It was also a necessary defence. After fifty years of war and legitimate commerce-raiding, there was a vast amount of piracy going on. In 1342, Plymouth men captured a Breton ship carrying salt for England, brought it into their home port, and sold the cargo. Even a ship carrying royal envoys from Spain was boarded in the port and the cargo stolen. The *Trinity* of Fowey, carrying wheat and victuals for Bordeaux, was plundered off the Lizard by Plymouth men and, four years later, a ship loaded with wine and salt from La Rochelle for Bristol was attacked by a Plymouth ship in a Cornish harbour and its cargo stolen. This piracy was by no means confined to Plymouth men, but had become so widespread that a law was passed in 1353 to deal with it, after which conditions began to improve.

In the year that Princess Joan sailed from Plymouth, her brother was also in the port. The Black Prince, although just twenty, had won his spurs at Crecy two years before, and been made Duke of Cornwall. As such, the honour of Trematon and the royal claims in Plymouth were his, and the duchy of Cornwall was established as the property of the Sovereign's eldest son, as it has remained ever since. In 1348, the Prince was returning from Gascony, where there was temporary peace. He dined at Plympton with the Prior, before journeying on. He was to come again.

Two years later Plymouth was raided by the French, but the town was so well defended that the invaders were only able to destroy 'some farms and fair places around', possibly the hamlet of West Stonehouse at Cremyll. Plymouth had learnt the lesson of that first raid.

In 1355, the Black Prince was appointed Lieutenant of Gascony and mounted an expedition designed to put an end to the constant nibbling by the French King. All through that summer the Prince's forces were assembling at Southampton and Plymouth. The first orders went out on 24 April and the ships began to gather in May. The Sheriffs of Devon and Cornwall were ordered to send hurdles and gangways to Plymouth by 14 June, the hurdles to corral the horses ashore, and the gangways to get the baggage trains aboard the ships.

Trade was at a standstill. No ship was permitted to go to sea unless well-armed. Ships in harbour had to anchor close inshore. Local men had to be armed in case of attack. Fire-beacons were set up to warn of the approach of any invader. Fighting men came in from all over England, archers from Wales in green and white uniforms, archers from Cheshire who were given twenty-one days pay before they started the 275 miles march to Plymouth. The Prince's retinue comprised 433 men-at-arms and 700 archers. All told, his force totalled about 3,000, including 1,000 men-at-arms, 1,000 horse archers, 300-400 foot archers, and 170 Welshmen. They came from all corners of the kingdom, among them a fair sprinkling of goal-birds hoping to win their pardon. Theft, rape, abduction and prison-breaking were among their crimes; there were even 120 murderers.

What a summer Plymouth must have seen, even if only half the army was there. How did a population of under 2,000 cope with all those stores, horses, and men? Devon, Cornwall and Somerset were scoured for wheat, wine and firewood. Did the men who could not be billeted in the town camp out on the neighbouring hill-sides, setting the slopes above the town a-flicker with their camp-fires at night? Could any hen or sheep within miles have survived their cooking-fires? Were there no fights of a night-time outside the alehouses, between locals armed against invasion and the soldiery, or between the Englishmen, the Welshmen and even the Germans who made up the army?

The ships were supposed to be assembled by 11 June, but more were still being sought in July. The Prince was due in Plymouth on 1 July, but did not arrive until 26 July. Problems of supply, and of assembling the army, caused yet more delays. Strong winds held back the up-Channel ships, and it was not until 9 September the fleet finally sailed, and Plymouth could breathe again.

During those forty-five days of his stay the Prince lodged at Plympton Priory, attended by four veterans of Crecy, the Earls of Suffolk, Warwick, Oxford, and Salisbury. With him, too, were other distinguished soldiers and Crecy knights such as Audley, Stafford and Chandos; and his chamberlain, Sir Nigel Loring. It must have been an expensive visit for the Prior, and some local merchants, like one who was instructed to buy gold for the Prince, would have done well. But many who sold stores to the army had to wait a long time for payment.

The Prince and his officers would have done much of the planning for the campaign at Plympton and he must frequently have ridden into Plymouth to inspect ships, men, stores, meet local merchants, and to confer with the bailiff and chief citizens about the problems of so large an influx into their town. Not since the days of his grandfather, Edward I, could Plymouth have seen so much excitement.

Even greater must have been the excitement two years later when the Black Prince sailed into the Sound again. He went as the hero of Crecy; he came back with Poitiers added to his laurels, and for this first and last time a King of France was brought captive to England. The English army had marched to the Mediterranean coast and back to Bordeaux, then north to the Loire. Then the French King cut them off, and the English choice was literally victory or death. The French were sure of themselves, the English hardened veterans. They stood firm and one after another, the French divisions broke upon their ranks. King John of France led the last desperate charge, only to fall prisoner with his younger son, Philip. The Constable of France and sixteen nobles lay dead upon the field, 2,000 Frenchmen around them. The rest were scattered.

All that winter the Black Prince rested at Bordeaux, and

Plymouth sent out to him hay, oats, corn, and even gold. In March 1357 a truce was signed; in April, the Prince sailed for home. His royal prisoner was in another ship, and both reached Plymouth about 1 May. Three weeks later they were in London, amid tremendous rejoicings and excitement, such as there must have been in Plymouth for the few days the Prince rested there while his ships were unloaded and men and horses recovered from the voyage.

In the resulting treaty, King Edward III renounced his claim to the French throne but was established in Gascony. The French King was ransomed for three million gold crowns. Most of the English leaders did well in ransom money, but there were other rewards. Sir Nigel Loring was given the manor of Trematon, and the Black Prince gave his porter, William Lenche, who lost an eye at Poitiers, the rights of Saltash ferry. The Prince was in Plymouth again in 1362 and again in 1364, when he made the award to Lenche, and there is a legend that he was rowed across to Saltash by the women of that town, whose fame as boatwomen has come down through the ages. A room in the gatehouse at Trematon is shown as the chamber in which he slept.

During all these Plymouth visits in the course of his travels to and from Bordeaux, the Prince busied himself with the affairs of the duchy. In 1358, he ordered a warship to be built in Plymouth, the first written evidence of local ship-building, though it must have already been a well-established trade. Old enough, too, to have labour troubles, for the men struck for more wages. The Sheriff of Cornwall was ordered to send in men to finish the job and the contractor, William le Vennour, was told to pay them reasonable wages.

At one time, a complaint was brought to the Black Prince by the master of a Hamburg ship. The Saltash ferry-boat was under repair and the Cremyll ferry was being used in its place. The German captain was incensed when his boat, in turn, was taken to serve as the Cremyll ferry, and he was not even given a share of the fares. In the same document the Prince is recorded as making a grant to some 'poor brothers', friars perhaps, at Plymouth.

The town was now growing steadily, and Professor Hoskins[7] calculates that, by 1344, when Bristol was the biggest provincial town, Exeter ranked twenty-third and Plymouth twenty-fifth. By 1377, Plymouth moved up to the twenty-second place, one above Exeter, and had a population estimated at 1,700. Today, Chagford with 1,500 people, Moretonhampstead with 1,600 and South Brent with 2,000, are of the sort of compactness of fourteenth century Plymouth, and offer a comparison in size.

TRADE

Trade flourished in spite of the brief halts called by war. Wine from Bordeaux and La Rochelle was transhipped at Plymouth for Calais and North Sea ports. In 1362, the town was licensed to trade with Portugal, and, two years later, it received further licences to export 2,000 coloured cloths and 2,000 packs of cloth from Devon and Cornwall to Gascony and Spain. One merchant alone exported ten packs of cloth, twenty coloured woollen cloths, and ten tons of hake. This fish, caught by fast trawler round the Eddystone, was always a Plymouth speciality. There was another licence in 1364 for 30,000 hake from Plymouth and Mousehole for Gascony. Tavistock and Ashburton were the nearest wool towns, and no doubt Plymouth was shipping their tin as well. Worth calculates from a customs scale of Richard II that the goods passing in and out of Plymouth included wine, honey and mead, coloured, russet and close cloths, canvas, hides, hake, herrings, pilchards and other fish, salt, coal, iron, cheese, soap, hemp, cords, wax, cornboards, pitch, tar, and slate. Wheat and malt were brought from Weymouth in 1375.

In 1373 there were four large merchant ships at Plymouth valued at 70,000 livres, an immense sum. This may have been the first appearance of the Genoese carracks, big ships which carried not only the rich cargoes of the Mediterranean but the

spices of the East as well. Certainly there was a carrack in Plymouth in 1376 and another in 1387. As a rule, they sailed from
Italy right through to the German ports. Sometimes they waited
for fair winds in the virtually deserted mouth of the Fal (hence
the Carrick Roads as the name for the Falmouth anchorage),
preferring to avoid busier ports where they offered too much
temptation. One at Dartmouth in 1373 was described as being
'under arrest', and in 1403 the burgomaster of Bruges complained to the Bishop of Lincoln, who was passing through, that
goods belonging to his town had been seized on board a Genoese
carrack at Plymouth. One sheltering in Plymouth in 1433 was
plundered 'by certain evil-doers'. At sea, they were more than a
match for our smaller craft; 'orrible grete and stout' runs an
English description of these new ships in the Channel. But we
could learn from these fast, two-masted ships; the steeply-raked
bowsprit of our cogs became a foremast and, by the mid-fifteenth
century, we had three-masted ships, with a fore-and-aft rig on the
mizzen that enabled them to sail closer to the wind.[9]

When the carracks first appeared in Plymouth they joined
shipping from half Europe. Baltic ships brought in linseed oil,
rosin, tar and masts for ship-building, and took away wine from
the south. After 1386, the wine ships ran in convoys to beat the
Breton pirates, and Plymouth was the starting and finishing point
for the convoys. Hides were going from Plymouth to Holland,
and salt came back from Zeeland. Ships were plying to Spain
and Portugal; the *Trinity* of Plymouth, for instance, regularly
traded as far south as Lisbon.

The trans-shipment of cargoes was so important that special
facilities were given in 1393 for merchants, local seamen, and
foreigners to land goods at Convers (or Conyers) on St Nicholas's
Island without payment of customs duty, provided that the goods
were not put up for sale. The reason given was that, in past times,
the town's greatest aid and chief advantage came from merchants
who entered the port for 'safety, refreshment and victuals', and
that they were now ceasing to call because customs officers were

demanding duty. The beach on the north side of the island is well-sheltered and isolated enough to stop pilfering; it must have been useful too for storm-damaged vessels who could lighten ship and make temporary repairs on the beach.

PILGRIMS

There was a two-way trade in pilgrims. Inward-bound, they were going to the shrine of St Thomas à Becket at Canterbury. The shipman from the west whom Chaucer met at Southwark with the Canterbury Pilgrims might have been William Hawley of Dartmouth, with a personally conducted tour of foreigners he had brought over in one of his ships and for whom he provided horses and guidance. The church at Kingswear is dedicated to St Thomas à Becket, as originally was the church of Plympton Erle.

Outward bound were English pilgrims going to Santiago (the Spanish form of Saint James) de Compostello; where the bones of the Apostle were miraculously discovered in the ninth century and inspired the war against the Moors. Edward I had made this a fashionable pilgrimage for the English. In 1361 a party of twenty-four men and women, with their horses, left Plymouth for Bordeaux and the long journey overland. In 1384, Plymouth was named as a place where passports to leave England could be obtained, and in 1389 it was decreed that no one, save merchants and known soldiers, should leave the country other than by Dover or Plymouth. These were the only legal routes for pilgrims and, as they had to be rich to make such a journey, it was a lucrative business. A man from Landulph had ships engaged in it and, in 1395 alone, there was one party of eighty pilgrims and two of sixty, one party sailing in the *Margaret* of Plymouth.

All this went on against the routine background of war, and it took the fitting-out of the Poitiers campaign in 1355 to put a stop to the pilgrim trade. There were also regular calls from the Crown for ships and services, and a request from the King

in 1369 for mercantile officers was addressed for the first time to
the 'mayor 'and bailiffs of Plymouth. A document of the previous
year carries Plymouth's first seal, with the device of a single
masted cog on the sea, rounded to fit the circular shape, and
the legend round the border *Si Commvnitatis ville de Svttvn
svper Plymovth*. In 1370 there appears the name of the first
mayor so addressed, Maurice Berd, and in the same year the
Black Prince's youngest brother, John of Gaunt, led a fleet from
Plymouth to Bordeaux.

It was from Bordeaux that the Prince had, since 1362, ruled
Gascony, virtually as a sovereign with a lavish court, but suffering
constant French raids on his frontiers. In 1371, he came home
through Plymouth with his wife, the 'Fair Maid of Kent' and
his son, Richard. He was a dying man. He rested a few days in
Exeter, on his way to London, and Plymouth saw him no more.

PROTECTING THE TOWN

Times were changing. The command of the sea, which England
had won by smashing the French fleet at Sluys in 1340 and kept
by defeating the Castillian navy in the Channel in 1350, was lost
when the English fleet was beaten by the King of Castile in 1372.
Calais, and a narrow coastal strip from Bordeaux to Bayonne,
were all that remained of English possessions in France. Once
again, the English coast was open to the raiders.

In 1374, the aged King Edward gave orders for the defence
of Plymouth. Letters patent were sent to William Cole, Stephen
Durneford, John Sampson, Roger Boswines, Robert Possebury,
Geoffrey Couch, John Weston, William Trevys, William Gille,
Maurice Berde, William Bourewe junior, and Humphrey Passour, burgesses of the borough of Sutton. They were to survey all
the weaknesses of the town's defences and put them right; they
were to see that there were arms for all the men of the town, and
do all they thought expedient for the safety of the town. 'Moreover the mayor and bailiffs and all and singular the inhabitants

of the town were to be obedient and aiding in the performance and execution of these premises.' The abbeys at Tavistock, Buckfast and Plympton were ordered to raise men to guard their estates.

Hardly was Edward dead in 1377 than the French fleet was off the English coast. Dover, Rye, Hastings, Portsmouth, and Plymouth were all attacked with fire and pillage. The new king, Richard II, who had visited Plymouth with his father, the Black Prince, in 1371, realised that while defences could be ordered, they had also to be paid for. So, in 1378, and because Plymouth was in great danger and neither enclosed nor fortified, he made a grant for its defence of six years customs duty to the 'mayor, bailiffs, honest men and commonalty.' He also granted a hundred marks a year for twenty years, to be spent on walling under the direction of the Prior.

He also launched a roundabout offensive against France, and in 1381, and again in 1385, expeditions fitted out in Plymouth for Portugal. These set that country free, enlisted new support for England against the Kings of Castile and resulted in the foundation of England's oldest alliance when John of Gaunt's daughter married the King of Portugal. But basically, these expeditions to Lisbon were designed to keep Castillian galleys out of the Channel. They were also the background to a bitter dispute among the men of Plymouth as to who ruled the town.

King Edward's defence order had been addressed to the men of the port, and the mayor and bailiffs were to be obedient to them in matters of defence. These port men can, in some cases, be indentified from ship records, but there is another clue to their authority in the port. Three of them, Thomas Cole, Geoffrey Couche and Humphrey Passour, together with Thomas Fishacre (is this a significant name?) were licensed by Richard II in 1384 to alienate six acres of land held of the King in chief to the Grey Friars. These six acres of royal land can only have been the six acres of the earlier 'royal waste' dispute, and on it the

Grey Friars built a new convent, just behind that piece of quay five perches long.

King Richard's order had gone to the mayor. Since the 1311 market agreement, the Prior's steward had ridden into Plymouth on the first Monday after the feast of St Michael, 29 September, to swear-in twelve of the Prior's tenants, who had then elected a reeve or Prepositus. He was presented to the Prior's steward and, if acceptable, took the oath. Thereafter, he was head of the court which sat in Plymouth every Monday, exercising for the Prior the assize of bread and ale, authority over weights and measures, millers, bakers, butchers, sellers of wine and those who brought bread in from outside the town; and with jurisdiction over transgressors. He collected all debts due to the Prior, rents, dues to the Sourpool manorial mill, and market stall rents, and he rendered an account of all this to the Prior's agent at the end of the year. He was the chief magistrate of the town, and was known as the mayor from 1369 onwards. But, though elected by his fellow townsmen, he was still acting on the Prior's authority, exercising the Prior's rights, and subject to the approval of the Prior.

In September 1384, John Sampson was so elected. He had been to Westminster in 1369 with Thomas Fishacre, as one of the King's shipping advisers, and was one of the port men to whom the defence order of 1374 had been addressed. Clearly he was in the shipping business, (there had been a Sampson who was master of a wine ship in the 1310 fleet), and the 1369 service shows that he was not a young man. He was in for a stormy year.

A number of the burgesses of Plymouth elected a rival, Humphrey Passour, who not only set himself up as mayor without the approval of the Prior but, from January onwards, prevented John Sampson from sitting at the Monday court by force of arms. The authority he and his friends quoted was that 1374 writ which ordered the burgesses to see to the defences, and the mayor and burgesses and all and singular to be obedient to them.

Passour's name had been the last on the list in that 1374 writ, and it was his first appearance in the town records. It appears to have been a case of youth versus age, of young Passour anxious to shake off the Prior's domination and old Sampson (who was also in that 1374 list) content to accept it. These were times of rebellion; the Lollards were preaching equality, and the voice of John Ball had not gone unheeded in the west. When the peasants of Kent marched to Blackheath in 1381 the first John of Gaunt expedition to Portugal had been fitting-out at Plymouth. When news came that Wat Tyler had been stabbed to death in front of the boy king, Richard II, the noblemen and gentlemen at Plymouth[10] had hurriedly embarked in their ships, and anchored well off the land, in spite of stormy weather, for fear of West Country uprisings. There must have been local rumblings then; now there was a real challenge to authority.

The Prior protested to the King, who ordered an inquiry. The King's officers, Walter Cornu and Richard Gripston, swore in their jury at Egg Buckland one Wednesday early in June 1385. If one takes the Plym Bridge route, then Egg Buckland is half way between Plympton Priory and Sutton Prior, and so might be considered as neutral ground. The jury consisted of twelve local men, independent, in theory, of both parties but close enough to the scene of conflict to be able to bring their local knowledge to bear. But their names suggest that they were all country gentlemen who could be expected to find for the landowner. This they did but, on the evidence, they could hardly have done otherwise. They found the Prior proved in all his claims to authority in Plymouth, and that there had never been a mayor there before the previous January, only the Prepositus of the Prior.

Passour tried again to uphold his claim, in the courts the following year, quoting all the documents of Edward III and Richard II addressed to the mayor of Sutton Plymouth, and claiming that such forms of address were appointing the people of Plymouth to have their own mayor. But the address on a letter

meant nothing against the sealed charters of the Prior. Passour's
blow for independence failed, but it was not forgotten.

There was still the money granted in 1378 for defence.
Richard's reign ended in turmoil and the grant may soon have
dried up, though there is evidence that the mouth of the harbour, at least, had been made impregnable by 1403. It is most
likely that during those twenty-five years a chain was stretched
across the harbour mouth at the narrows where the entrance piers
now are, that a windlass to raise and lower it was set up on the
Sutton side, and two towers built at the cliff to prevent an enemy
attacking the windlass or cutting the chain.

In a warehouse wall at the bottom of New Street there is still
to be seen an ancient stone into which has been cut the words
'HE SAMPSON'. It is not on its original site and, as a rule, only
stones of importance were preserved. There was a Henry Sampson in the town in 1395, and may it have been that the two
towers, the start of Plymouth's medieval castle quadrate, were
built at this time? Was Henry a son of John Sampson and the
man entrusted with the building, and was his name placed over
the main entrance? One can only surmise. There may have been
a start on a town wall, possibly no more than a ditch with the
earth thrown out to form a bank on the inner side, and surmounted by a wooden pallisade.

PLYMOUTH BURNT

With weak government in England, the French were at our gates
and there were two or possibly three major attacks on Plymouth
at the turn of the century. The 1399 raid is described as an attempt to fire the town, and was repulsed with the loss of 500 men.
How these optimistic round figures of enemy losses echo down
the centuries.

There are two versions of the 1400 raid. One is that James
de Bourbon, Count de la Marche, coming into Plymouth on his
way to help Owen Glendower in Wales, set fire to the town but

lost twelve of his largest ships in a gale. The other is that Bourbon was coming back from Wales and chased seven trading ships into the Sound, where their crews abandoned them and escaped into Plymouth. It is said that the people in the countryside around crowded into Plymouth in wild alarm but were forced out again when the town shopkeepers doubled the price of provisions for outsiders.

The raid of 1403 is clearer in the records. A strong force, 30 ships and 1,200 men-at-arms led by Le Sieur du Chastel, came into the Sound on Wednesday 10 August from St Malo. They sailed into the Cattewater and landed their soldiers within a mile of the town. This suggests that the entrance to Sutton Harbour was strongly defended, but that the guns covering the chain could not be trained to cover the Cattewater. Probably, the soldiers landed on the Cattedown ferry beach opposite Oreston and marched along the road to Plymouth, looking down on the little town and laughing at the guns that could not reach them.

They entered at the 'bak haf' of the town, under the White Friars convent (now Friary Station) and ravaged, burnt and plundered throughout the night. An attempt to storm Old Town was beaten off, and many of the Bretons were killed or captured there. One can imagine the hand-to-hand fighting in the narrow streets leading up the hill; for towns are still hard nuts to crack even in modern warfare. The invaders spent the night in the lower half of the town and withdrew at ten o'clock on the Thursday morning, taking their dead and wounded with them.

The old town that clearly was never taken must be the original town round the market cross, not the old farm. Until 1789 Martyn's gate[11] stood on this side of the town at the foot of the hill, the entrance from Exeter (it is still Exeter Street), and there is evidence of a wall running at right angles to the main road. If this wall had been started by 1403, even if only a bank and pallisade, it may explain why the old town held out. In the raid, 600 houses are reported to have been destroyed, but so many would have housed the whole town. Fire will travel fast along narrow streets of wooden dwellings, and it may be that the Bretons found fire was invading where they could not, and so left it to finish their work. It must have been a grim Thursday morning for Plymouth.

The part the Bretons did occupy, outside Martyn's Gate, has been called Breton Side ever since (though a modern council has moved the name uphill into old Plymouth to a 'bus-station, and so confused the issue). It is believed to be a memory of this Breton raid, though the earliest spelling was Britayne Side, and it is also the site of Bilbury, that Celtic fort whose name survives today. John Harris in his 1810 history of the town suggests the name implies that there had been a colony of descendants of the ancient Britons living outside the town proper. Similarly, Professor Hoskins thinks that the Bartholomew Street corner of Exeter, once also called Britayne, was the British quarter where they survived until they were expelled by Athelstan in the tenth century.

King Henry IV (he was Henry Bolingbroke, John of Gaunt's son, and had ousted Richard II in 1399) at once ordered a reprisal. It was mounted from Dartmouth the same autumn (which shows that Plymouth had not recovered sufficiently to play its usual rôle) and did much damage around Quimper. Next year, the Normans attacked Portland and the Bretons Dartmouth, but both were defeated; du Chastel, who had led the Plymouth attack died in Dartmouth itself. A Te Deum was ordered in Westminster Abbey to celebrate this success and twenty famous Breton knights were English prisoners. Clearly, these were not just cross-Channel rivalries, but part of the national war.

In 1404, King Henry ordered a wall of stone to be built round Plymouth; the wording of the order suggests that there were already perimeter defences but, clearly, these had not been enough. To sharpen the need, there was another minor raid in 1406 by ships from Castile.

In the Channel there was complete anarchy. In the 1370s the Dartmouth ships under John Hawley, and the Plymouth ships under Roger Boswines, formed a western squadron that virtu-

ally ran the war in their own waters. John Hawley certainly had
the King's licence which permitted him and his captains 'at their
own charges, under the King's protection to attack and destroy
his enemies.' This letter of marque was common up to Napoleonic
times; the holder was a privateer to his own side and a pirate to
the other, for in the heat of a sea battle it is hardly possible to
examine the other man's papers before firing the first cannon.
Ships mixed legitimate trade with privateering and, at times,
straight piracy; King's officers could turn pirates and vice-versa.
Harry Pay, the great Poole pirate at the turn of the century,
finished up as the water bailiff at Calais. John Hawley, leading
a fleet of Bristol, Dartmouth, and Plymouth ships in 1403, took
seven vessels carrying goods of Genoa, Navarre, and Castille, and
refused to make any restitution.

Richard Spicer of Plymouth had been on the King's service in
Portugal, but he twice captured galleys belonging to the Florentine Society of the Albertine. He was probably the principal
pirate out of Plymouth at this time. When the *Trinity* of Plymouth was captured by the French off the Isle of Wight in 1403,
it was Spicer who rescued her. In that year John Kyghley was
named as a banned sea-robber. In 1404 he sailed into Weymouth
and cut out the *Marie* of Bordeaux as she lay at anchor, and he
was in command of one of Spicer's ships. Spicer was not alone.
In 1403 Henry Don of Plymouth was summoned to appear before the Privy Council on a charge of piracy.

THE CASTLE BUILT

Ordinary trade was going forward. Plymouth had ten ships in the
1409 wine convoy. The seamen were willing to fight their ships
through their legitimate business but they wanted to be sure that
they would not come home to find their houses burnt down and
their wives ravaged in a ruined town, But first, they had to get
unity in the town; the division between the seafarers in the King's
port and the traders in the Prior's town had to end, and each

must learn to live with the other. In particular, the nonsense of the two mayors of 1384 had to be done with.

So in 1411 a petition went to Parliament. The inhabitants of Sutton Prior and Sutton Vautort, commonly known as Plymouth, asked that in future they might elect a mayor each year and that they might be a body corporate, capable of purchasing lands without licence from the Crown. The town, it was explained, was close to a large port which was liable to attack in time of war. Being unwalled, the town was exposed to great danger. To build the wall, they wanted to be able to levy tolls on cargoes discharged in the port.

Here were two problems. Until they became a body corporate, they could not own property, nor buy land. No one would want a town wall built across his land unless someone would pay him for the land. Thus the land and the wall had to be paid for, and it seemed reasonable that ships seeking the protection and the facilities of the port should contribute.

But the port customs were royal prerogatives, and the right to collect them was farmed out at a fat fee. The King was a chronic invalid, sick and suspicious. 'Let the petitioners compound with the lords having franchises,' came back the answer, 'before the next Parliament, and report having made an agreement.' The pigeon-holes of government are ageless. There was no agreement by the next Parliament, nor by the next quarter-century. It would seem that the townsmen got on with the wall as best they could; they had acted in the past as if they were an incorporated borough, and they could do so again.

They may well have found more unofficial support from Henry V, who came to the throne in 1413. His Lord Chancellor, Bishop Stafford of Exeter, granted indulgences in 1416 which helped them to repair the causey[12] at the entrance to Sutton Harbour, and to build two towers of the castle.[13] They put Bishop Stafford's arms on one tower and it was long known as the Bishop's Tower. Probably, it completed the castle quadrate. In 1449 Bishop Lacy granted another indulgence for the new castle and ditch but this looks more like a maintenance appeal for something already built.

So in all likelihood the castle and the wall—of stone in the most vulnerable points, wood elsewhere, and with mound and ditch—were completed in Henry V's time. The castle and wall were all on Valletort land, which explains the later story that they built it all. Certainly it could not have been built without their consent, and the limestone quarries which furnished the stone were on their land, too.

Henry V also helped in other ways. He built up the naval forces and passed another anti-piracy law in 1414. It is significant that, after the record of Henry Quental of Plymouth capturing three Breton ships in 1412, there is no further piracy suggestion against Plymouth until 1419, when certain Bristol merchants brought into Plymouth carracks and other ships loaded with merchandise from Genoa. Thomas ap Reece, the leader of the Bristol men, asked that certain of these goods should be sold to him, for which he most certainly would pay—which rather looks as if the Welshman was talking his way out of detected crime. But piracy was not entirely stopped, and in 1422 three Bristol ships, with one from Plymouth, plundered a carrack in Milford Haven.

That year, Henry V died and weak government was back. The King's ships were sold up, and privateers licenced in their place to give naval defence. The argument that the anti-piracy laws hurt legitimate trade became so persuasive that they were suspended in 1435. The rogues were in full gallop again. The notorious William Kydd of Exmouth cut a Breton ship out of St Pol de Leon harbour in 1436 and brought it into Plymouth. That year, John Zeelander of Fowey captured the *Mighell* of Dartmouth in the very entrance to Plymouth Harbour. Zeelander was one of the Flemings who had settled at Fowey and made that port's name a by-word. The 'Fowey gallants' were cock of the Channel, and had even fought a pitched battle with the men of the Cinque Ports. There were Cornishmen in the business at Fowey along with the polygot settlers; John Mixtow once brought in a carrack he had captured off Cape St Vincent, even though English merchants were actually aboard at the time.

Out of this desperate world, while the dissensions of York and Lancaster were raging around the monkish King, and Joan of Arc was driving the English out of France, Plymouth finally won its independence and its self-government. The struggle for freedom, which started with Humphrey Passour in 1384, saw final success in the charter of 1439.

CHAPTER FIVE

THE YOUNG BOROUGH

LYMOUTH obtained its charter largely through the exertions of William Venour. A Walter de Venour received royal orders to detain ships in 1358, and had been mayor of Sutton Prior in 1377. It was an old family, and of some substance. William Venour had married Thomasine, sister of Richard Trenode, Sheriff of Bristol in 1422, mayor in 1432, and three times Member of Parliament for the town. Venour sought his brother-in-law's aid in securing the Plymouth charter and the two men acted as the town's agents. Neither were young men; indeed, Venour died in the middle of the charter negotiations and one of Plymouth's first acts as a borough was to set up a chantry priest in St Andrew's Church to say daily prayers for the souls of the Trenode and Venour families 'in consideration of the labour and charges sustained' by them in securing the charter.

Bristol had been subject both to the counties of Somerset and Gloucester, as Plymouth had been subject to the courts of the Prior of Plympton and the hundred courts of the Abbot of Buckland. So the charter that Bristol had obtained in 1373 was used as a pattern for Plymouth's request in 1439. In accordance with the 1411 command, the petition was addressed to Parliament—a sign that, with the weak boy King Henry VI, on the throne, Parliament was fast growing in strength.

Plymouth, said the petition, was made up of the town of Sutton Prior, the tithing of Sutton Raf, and the hamlet of Sutton Valletort. It was an important port and had often been burnt 'by reason of a defect in the enclosure or walling of the same', the

inhabitants despoiled of their goods and 'many carried away to
foreign parts by the said enemies, and cruelly imprisoned until
they have made fines and ransoms'. And, the petition added,
'all these things might happen again'.

'The 'proper remedy' which Plymouth asked for the relief,
fortification, and bettering of the town, was five-fold; that they
should be a free borough, with one mayor, a perpetual commonalty and a common seal; that they should be capable of owning
land, and capable of suing and being sued in the courts. These
five points were held to be the essential points of incorporation.

The petition set out the boundaries and asked for the fee farm
of the borough at forty shillings a year (other boroughs had to
pay up to £50). It asked for authority to fortify the town, that
William Kethrich, one of the more honest and discreet men living
in the town (an ambiguous compliment) should be their first
mayor, and that certain rules should govern the annual election
of a mayor thereafter on the feast of St Lambert (17 September).
There are full details of how Plympton and Buckland were to be
compensated (Plympton with a fee farm rent of £41 a year), and
the town was to buy the advowson of Bampton from the Prior of
Bath and give it to Buckland.

The assent to this petition declared that it should not affect the
manor of Trematon, the borough of Saltash, the water of Tamar,
or the Crown land. The next step should have been to obtain
the letters patent, but they were never entered on the Patent
Roll; either the Chancery clerks were lax, Plymouth did not pay
the necessary fees, or the death of Venour may have introduced
complications. But there must have been letters patent, for they
were copied into the town's 'Black Book' in 1534.

The 1439 charter was amateurishly drafted and, though it
might have sufficed for towns with long-established government,
it was not enough for Plymouth. A new professional charter of
1440 added the right of Plymouth to have its own quarter ses-
sions, which kept county magistrates, and the hundred powers

The Normans defended the Tamar Valley with a strong castle at Trematon *(above)* near Saltash and the Plym Valley with another castle at Plympton *(below)*. Plympton was 'slighted' in the wars between Stephen and Matilda.

All that remains of the Castle Quadrate built about the time of Henry V to guard the entrance to Sutton Harbour and Plymouth's new maritime importance. By Elizabeth's time it was necessary to defend the whole waterfront and Drake's Island (below), then St Nicholas's Island, became a major strongpoint.

of Buckland, out of the town. The mayor also became a justice and the town was given a recorder and a coroner. There was authority for a merchant guild, for weekly markets on Mondays and Thursdays, and for two four-day fairs, in September and January.

William Kethrich remained mayor until September 1442, when Walter Clovelly was elected, and was probably in office until the whole transition was complete. But 'between 12 November 1439 and 25 July 1440 Plymouth obtained the powers and privileges which, with some very minor changes, were to last it until 1835, and which still to some extent affect its constitution. In the course of nine months an unprivileged and divided market town had become a borough with powerful rights and privileges.' It was the first town in Devon to be incorporated. Totnes followed in 1505, and Exeter in 1537. Plymouth also was the first town in England to be incorporated by Act of Parliament.

How close to the heart of Plymouth was the need for defence set out in the petition for incorporation, and how proud the people were of their new castle, is shown in the mayor's first seal. In place of the old ship design there now appeared the cross of St Andrew and, between the arms, four castles, representing the castle quadrate. It is still the centre of Plymouth's coat of arms. Around the seal was the legend *S'officiz maioratus burgi ville dni regis de Plymouth*. 'The King's burgess town'; here was the final shaking off of the Prior's town label and the victory of the King's port.

The boundaries set out in the charter used the Stonehouse and Lipson creeks on the landward side, so that the new borough had only a narrow land link[1] with the rest of Devon. It took in just two Domesday manors, Sutton and Lipson, both Valletort holdings. The petition said that Plymouth was made up of the town of Sutton Prior (which was just the built-up area by the harbour), the hamlet of Sutton Valletort (the rural area centred in the manor house by Sourpool, and the few cottages which had probably grown up beside it), and the tithing of Sutton Raf. The

word 'tithing' survived (in the tithing of Compton Gifford, for
example) into the last century to mean a self-governing part of
a parish, and probably has the same meaning here. Raf, or
Ralph, was a common Valletort Christian name and Sutton Raf
looks like the old Lipson manor, which was originally between
the Lipson and the Tothill creeks, extended southwards to take
in Cattedown when that part was cut off from Sutton Valletort
by the growth of Sutton Prior.

There turns up in the seventeenth century a new manor,
'Uletts fee, als Lulytts Sparke als Luletts fee.' From the evidence
of property deeds it was clearly between Sutton Valletort and
Sutton Raf, stretching from the northern edge of Sutton Prior

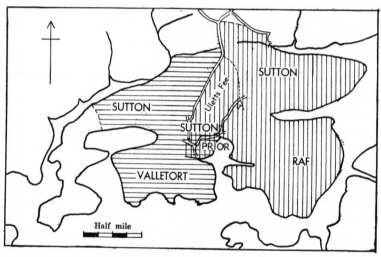

THE BOROUGH OF PLYMOUTH. *The tideline made up most of the boundary
of 1439, with the 'great ditch' at Eldad marking the division from Stonehouse. From the head of Stonehouse Creek, or Houndiscombe Bridge, the
southern branch of the Houndiscombe Brook (now under Central Park
Avenue, Dale Road, and Ermington Terrace), was the line up to Mutley
Plain, on the old ridge road. Eastwards the southern edge of Compton
Manor was followed to Elm Road and thence to Lipson Bridge, approxi-
mately the site now of St Augustine's Church. The shaded areas indicate
the probable geographical locations of Sutton Prior, Sutton Valletort and
Sutton Raf which were joined to make the new borough.*

up to the headlands, the slope still remembered by old people as Vinegar Hill. The Sparke family in the seventeenth century had acquired the Whitefriars, and Vinegar Hill is believed to recall the vineyards of the friars (it would be quite possible to grow vines on this south-facing slope). Quite possibly, this is the estate of the White Friary, a further wedge between Sutton Valletort and Sutton Raf, but this is a doubtful conjecture, for old deeds show the priors granting land at the 'Headland'.

From early references to street names and from old maps, the shape of the town can be established.[2] The southern edge was Notte Street, or Nut Street, in all likelihood looking across a little stream running down to Sutton Harbour, with hazel bushes on the far bank. On this bank, the south side, a path ran past the gates of the Blackfriars, with a tower and a cross on one gable, to the four-towered castle dominating the harbour entrance. The western edge was Catherine Street, St Andrew's Churchyard, and Old Town Street, with the backs of the houses looking across open ground to the town wall. Only the St. Andrew's end of Old Town Street was built up, and a line from the present top of New George Street east to Exeter Street would mark the northern edge of the houses. Between them and the wall on that side were still the fields of Old Town, and it was significant that the first street built here in the Elizabethan expansion was called Week Street, for the name comes from 'wic', meaning dairy farm. The wall turned south to Sutton Harbour on the line of the modern Bilbury Street, with Bilbury Bridge outside, then the strange suburb outside the wall of Britayne Side, and then the White Friary. An imposing building this, with a spire to its church, its own gateway, and a wall round the conventual buildings. Between the town and the waterside was the Grey Friary, with its domestic buildings looking across a cloister garth to the church and a crenellated wall enclosing the whole.

The town had four gates which, in time, became impressive stone structures, reflecting local pride as much as defence, for they always seem to have been more substantial than the walls that linked them. The Barbican, or watergate, was really part of the castle. Hoe Gate, in the south wall, led to the Hoe. Frankfort Gate was in the west wall; outside, the roads forked to Stonehouse and to the manor mills on Sourpool. Old Town Gate in the north wall was the dividing point of the roads to Tavistock and Saltash; Tavistock road up the old ridge way and the Saltash road across the head of Stonehouse Creek at Pennycomequick, Keyham Creek, and then Camel's Head Creek at Weston Mill Bridge. In the east wall there was Martyn's Gate, with the Exeter road climb-

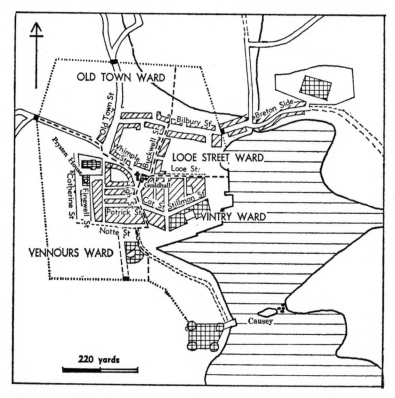

PLYMOUTH 1500. *By this date thirteen street names are given in various documents. By mapping them, and the known buildings, as has been done above, the shape of the town becomes clear. One or two unnamed streets have been drawn in although they are no more than 'probables'.*

ing up Lipson Hill, winding down the steep slope beyond to the head of Lipson Creek, and then following its northern shore to the Ebb Ford and so to Plympton. Looking across the long-disused Ebb Ford until 1974 was a public house, the 'Crabtree Inn'. It probably marked the oldest inn site in Plymouth, where people must have waited for the tide to fall enough to let them cross, and where shelter and refreshment were no doubt provided. One can remember the channels in these muddy rivers being marked by branches of trees stuck upright and irreverently called 'winkle-trees'; were there even earlier such branches to mark the line of the ford and were these the 'crab-trees'? From Martyn's Gate, another road ran out over Cattedown to the Oreston ferry, and an inn there is still called the 'Passage House Inn'. It must share the antiquity of Crabtree and of the inns at Saltash Passage.

Between the town centre and the waterfront one area was not developed until late. The main streets there now are Looe Street and Vauxhall Street. Looe means pigs (as at Looseleigh, which means the pig-clearing in the forest), and Vauxhall is a polite spelling of Foxhole; direct references to the rural state of early Plymouth.

LOCAL GOVERNMENT

Plymouth was basically a commercial centre, and the merchants very much its rulers. They were given a guild in the charter of 1440, and very soon the usual form of government of a guild, the twelve and the twenty-four, was the form of the town council. The twelve were aldermen—itself, originally, a guild term—and the twenty-four were councillors. The Plymouth merchant guild was that of 'Our Lady and St George', and in the early days everyone who ran a business or traded in the town was a member. A guild meeting was a meeting of all the townsmen. The guild enforced trading regulations, saw fair business done, made sure that there was no unfair competition. The town council were the senior members of the guild, acting as the executive committee of the guild and of the town.

As the town grew, as some men became richer and others poorer, as the number of apprentices becoming masters grew fewer and the number becoming employees grew more, so the merchants' guild became more exclusively the club of the big men. So, in turn, trade guilds developed, for men of certain crafts. In Plymouth, a tailors' guild was set up in 1496, the only one of which there is record, though no doubt there were others.

Only freemen could hold office in the borough and, to tighten the circle, the council decreed in 1471 that every freeman had to be a brother of the merchant's guild. Half-brothers paid sixpence a year to the guild, full brothers a shilling, councillors an extra eightpence and aldermen another shilling. Discipline was strong. In 1516, it was resolved that anyone disobeying the mayor should be punished by him, and freemen would be imprisoned in the guildhall. Anyone betraying council secrets could be put out of the council and dis-enfranchised for ever, and so could anyone who sought outside help from any lord to oppose the mayor. In 1520, it was laid down that no freeman should leave the town without special licence during the twenty-eight days prior to mayor-choosing, unless he could be back in time, and that every freeman should be at the guildhall for mayor-choosing.

How tight this governing clique grew over the years is shown by a council resolution of 1683, when the mayor and seven of the town's twelve magistrates (magistrate and alderman appear to be synonymous by this time) decreed that for the next five years they would select the townsmen to serve on the council and councillors would have no say in the matter. The trouble was that when the councillors had been invited to elect into their ranks people nominated by the mayor and magistrates, they had persisted in electing people of meaner condition, to the neglect of people of quality and known loyalty. There is a memorandum under this entry declaring that this was contrary to the practice of the town, where it was customary for the whole twelve and twenty-four to elect burgesses to fill any vacancy. Patently, the town council was a self-renewing body.

The council met in the guildhall. Originally, this was the meeting place of the whole guild, and as the council comprised the elders of the guild they met there, too. Not until 1873 did the council attain a chamber separate from the guildhall, and, to the present day, Plymouth has retained the feeling that the guildhall is the meeting place for all the people of the town, and the council chamber a place apart.

There is no written evidence of the location of the first guildhall, but when a new one was built in the market triangle in 1606 the old one had first to be demolished, so fairly clearly it was on the same site, and it is the most logical position. It must have been built beside the market cross soon after the charter of 1439 for, in the town accounts of 1480, there is a note of eightpence having been paid to Watkyn, the mason, for work at the guildhall (the first written reference). It must have been repair work; there was more done in 1494, and in 1501 it is referred to as 'the old geld hall'. Next year, it was 'made fine' with plaster of Paris, a glass window was mended in 1503, and a clock[3] installed in 1526.

The ward boundaries of the town met in the market place, running north, south, east and west along street lines as far as they would serve. Old Town was to the north-west, Venours to the south-west (named in honour of the man who won the charter and who had a house in this area), Vintry to the south-east (note that the port area is given a name meaning 'the gathering place of wine merchants'), and Looe Street to the north-east. The first three wards are named by 1480; Looe Street, the last area to be built up, does not appear until 1500.

The mayor was chosen on the first Monday after St Lambert's Day, as in Priory times, but did not take the oath and office until Michaelmas Day. One custom prevailed right up until the Reform Acts changed the council composition; on Michaelmas Day the council would assemble at ten in the morning and wait until eleven before the mayor took the oath. It was a legacy of the old days, when the burgesses had to wait for the Prior's officer to arrive before their choice could take office. After the oath, the mayor and corporation went in procession through the town; they had two standards (coloured or 'stayned' in Totnes) and a great banner by 1486. By 1572, the aldermen had to have red robes, and in 1580 (Drake's mayoralty) the councillors had them as well.

Between St Lambert's Day and Michaelmas Day the town boundaries were beaten, a significant choice of date whereby the new mayor was reminded by his predecessor of the town's extent. It was a day's holiday, and in 1496 there were two gallons of wine 'for ye mayer and his bretheren when they sawe ye franchyse abut.' In 1516 there were pears, apples and nuts for the children on this holiday, and ale for their elders. Granite boundary stones began to be set up in 1518, 'ffredome stones', the old records call them.

This Freedom Day gradually developed into one of the chief holidays of the year, with a battle between the Old Town Boys and the Breton Boys to finish it off. Old Town by now is the town within the walls, while the Breton Boys came from the suburb east of Martyn's Gate. It seems an odd way to remember the Breton raid of 1403, and could have been a remnant of the old animosity between the town and the 'Britayns' outside their gate. History became more confused when the Freedom Day fights became too much for the town and were moved up the hill to the open spaces of what became known as Freedom Fields, because it was also the site of the vital Civil War battle. The Freedom Day fights eventually became drunken brawls, the Breton Boys' name degenerated into Burton Boys (still remembered in a public-house name), and the whole affair was finally suppressed after a number of bones were broken in 1792.

CORPUS CHRISTI

The other great holiday of medieval times was Corpus Christi, the Catholic festival in honour of the Sacred Host, in early June. On this day, a church-ale was held in aid of St Andrew's Church funds, and everyone in the town would gather up their friends and acquaintances, men and women, and go to St Andrew's churchyard. It was an all-day party, for they could take with them whatever food they liked for dinner and supper, except bread and ale. These they had to buy, and this made the money for the church. To ensure a good profit, no tavern in the town was permitted to sell wine or ale on that day.

The great event of the day was the procession. The rules of the Tailors Guild ordained that they should 'make a pageant yearly into Corpus Christi', just as it was earlier ordained that each ward should 'make an ale' on that day. There were rules too, about the men who 'carried the ship'. One imagines that the mayor went in procession with his gilded maces and his officers and his banners, that each ward and each trade guild followed with a tableau, and that the ship was a massive model of canvas and wood carried shoulder-high by the Corpus Christi guild—a symbol of the town's main interest and the source of its prosperity. The parading of a model ship on May Day continued until quite late in Cawsand and Stonehouse; in some Breton churches such ship models are still stored in the church from one feast day to the next, together with giant figures of St George and the Dragon, the Virgin, and so on, mounted on carrying poles. No doubt the Plymouth Guild of Our Lady and St George had its gaudily-coloured models, too.

What the old records variously call the 'Corpus Christi Ilde' and the *Fraternitat corpis xpi* must have been a religious brotherhood formed to run this great church day, and not a trade or craft guild. People left money and property to it as they did to other religious bodies, and the guild was a tenant of the town in 1490. By 1645, the town had acquired certain property and fields which were called 'Corpus Christi', and there was a Corpus Christi House in Bedford Street as late as 1874.

There were other feasts, too, unconnected with the church. May Day and Midsummer's Night were celebrated with Morris dancing, and visits by teams from Bodmin, Stonehouse, St Budeaux and Tavistock are recorded. One year, there was a hobby horse; on another, a maypole was painted. There were waits on Midsummer's Night (singing men were not limited to Christmas carols), and wine for the mayor and his brethren that night at 'High Cross'. This must have been a cross upon the Hoe, near the little chapel of St Katherine, and the figures of Gog and Magog, which were fresh cut each year. It was an odd survival of pre-Christian dances beside pagan images, and perhaps there may still have been undertones of witchcraft, of pagan abandon which chapel and cross had been set up to combat.

Christmas was the winter feast; in 1566 there were ten shillings for the schoolmaster and children from Totnes 'whiche played in Christmas', and there had been minstrels in 1495. Six players gave an interlude in the mayor's house on the Saturday before Twelfth Night in 1539, and the mayor and his brethren watched a juggler on St John's Day. Strolling players and minstrels began to appear, often under royal or noble patronage, the 'King's Joculars', for example, in 1523. In 1529, the servant of the Duke of Suffolk appeared with a dancing bear and a dancing wife, perhaps a more refined entertainment than straight bearbaiting. A 1516 entry reads 'Reward to luskum for his dogge at the Bere baytynge, iiijd.' Bull-baiting was an every-day entertainment; it was thought to make the meat more tender and butchers were fined for not having their animals 'bayted'. There was a bullring on the Hoe and another just below the guildhall in High Street. That was right in the heart of the town, and if a bull broke away he might well finish up in a china shop.

CRIME AND PUNISHMENT

There were strict rules of business for butchers, bakers, brewers and the shopkeepers. No strangers were to be in the town for more than two days unless their business was known. No man was to walk up and down on working days to ale and wine unless he was a man of substance, or a merchant waiting on a gentleman. No innkeeper was to give shelter to any suspicious person, or let any man and woman lodge together unless he knew they were man and wife. Nor was he to keep in his house any harlot or strumpet.

People were no better than they are now. In 1502, a coroner's inquest found that John Croste, a groom of Lipson, had stabbed and killed Robert Matthews in his house at Stonehouse, and that the dead man's wife, Elizabeth, had been an accomplice. Murders and death in brawls were not unknown; men were not to carry arms without the mayor's consent and everyone was to be indoors by eight o'clock, when the town gates were closed. Not that this stopped crime, for there are records of theft, false pretences, breach of covenant, even stealing a man's wife as well as his goods, and breach of promise.

John Meyow of Plympton was arrested to 'answer' Joan Collins, the daughter of a Bickleigh man. She was an honest maid, said her counsel, replete with many honest and womanly qualities, but that had not stopped John Meyow on 4 August in the Vintry ward. 'Blinded by inordinate concupience he did with force of arms with knives and daggers, and false promises of marriage, provoke her to consent to his filthy lust of the flesh and so with her did execute the act of carnal copulation, abusing her body so that he hath begotten her with child.' He had then declined to marry her, and Miss Collins was suing for a hundred pounds, which was more than the whole town's expenditure in some of these years.

Punishments were hard. In 1486, there was a pennyworth of

straw for prisoners in the clink, which was probably in the base-
ment of the guildhall. Iron bars closed its window. A gallows
was set up in 1498 to hang a thief, and the town accounts, as
they so often do, set out all the grisly details: fourpence for timber, a shilling for building, tenpence for a ladder, fivepence for
a halter and a rope to bind the arms, a penny each for six men
to be guards at the hanging, and fourpence for their ale. Another
man was set in fetters and a blacksmith was paid to smite on
the gyves. There were stocks,[4] and a pillory set up beside the
market was regularly used. Down by the harbour there was a
ducking or scold's stool; this was a seat on the end of a long pole
which pivoted so that an offending woman could be tied on
and dipped into the sea. All these ranked as public amusements
in those rough and hardy times, when death was commonplace,
plague was ever present and war never far away.

Even the twelve and the twenty-four had to be ready to stand
to arms. The mayor was also commander-in-chief and, when
danger threatened, he took charge of the north-east tower of the
castle quadrate, the key-point overlooking the harbour. The rest
of the council were divided among the four towers, the three
aldermen and six councillors of each ward to their own tower.
These wards were strictly for administrative and not electoral
purposes. Town finances were collected on a ward basis, each
ward had its own rules for keeping the streets clean, and in each
ward the aldermen appointed constables who kept the peace.
No doubt they also organised archery practice at the butts on
the Hoe.

TRADE DEPRESSION

Though they were warring days when Plymouth won its charter,
trade was still going on. In 1437, two years before the town's
incorporation, there are records of cargoes reaching Plymouth
from Guienne, Landerneau, Brest, Guerrade, Oporto, Lisbon,
Norway, Denmark, Genoa, Dusant (or Fusant), Spruce, London,
Dartmouth, Guernsey, Exmouth, Fowey, and Exeter. Fish was

being sent to Bristol and there was a trade with southern Ireland. It was the old pattern, but it was changing. In 1420, men from the east coast ports and Bristol began to fish off Iceland, and the wealth of cod they found there cut deeply into the dried and salted fish trade of the west Channel. The wine trade with France, too, took a mortal blow when the English were finally driven out of Bordeaux in 1451. It had survived the tramp of armies through the vineyards, the depredations of pirates, the discipline of convoys and the doubling of prices. And, because the Bordelais, living sixty miles up the Garonne, were never seamen, the English had taken over their export business, set themselves up as factors in the port, married and settled down—no doubt with Plymouth men amongst them. But after 1451 no Englishman was permitted to live in Bordeaux, and the wine trade fell into the hands of the Hanseatic League, and the Flemings, those merchants of the Baltic, of Bruges and Ghent, who had no love for the west Channel men. The wine trade gone, the Plymouth business in pilgrims went as well, and even the salt trade fell into the hands of the 'Eastlanders.'

The first twenty-five years of the new borough must have been difficult times. With failing trade and weak government, it is no wonder either that piracy was abroad again. In 1449, Robert Wennington was ordered to 'cleanse the sea of pirates' and assembled a West Country fleet at Dartmouth. He met a convoy of about a hundred Hanseatic and Flemish ships carrying salt off Portland, and set about it to such effect that all the ships surrendered. All the government could do was to pay compensation, and then only the Flemings got any of it. That same year Fowey men (still the arch pirates) came out of the Cattewater and took a Barcelona galley anchored in the Sound off to their home port, together with a cargo worth £12,000. Not only were half the gentry and lawyers of Cornwall named in successive court actions as owners of pirate ships and as receivers, but James Durnford and Thomas Tregarthen, distinguished Plymouth men, were also accused. Some of the booty was even found in Tregarthen's house, but he claimed that it had been put there while he was away in London.

THE WARS OF THE ROSES

With the final eviction of the English from France, the Wars of the Roses, long smouldering, turned into open civil war. Devon had been generally Lancastrian in sympathy, with the Earl of Devon and his Courtenay relations the chief supporters, but the Bonvilles,[5] a powerful family in east Devon, were Yorkist and the two families conducted virtually a private war in the 1440s and 1450s. This anarchy on land, and the weak rule of the Lancastrian King at sea, which left the Channel a playground for pirates, began to produce a strong Yorkist faction among the merchants and in the seaports. In Plymouth, Vincent Patilysden, mayor of 1453, 1454 and 1456, wore the red rose of Lancaster in his hat when he went to church and the aldermen and burgesses followed his example 'but which, as they saw the York faction arising (writes an old diarist) they afterwards did prudently decline.'

In the vital year, 1461, when the young Duke of York, although beaten at the second battle of St Albans, seized London, was proclaimed King Edward IV and then crushed the Lancastrians on Towton Moor, the French King sent a force into Plymouth to try and help the Lancastrian cause. There is reason to believe that the local Lancastrians knew what was afoot, for when William Champernowne of Modbury, a Yorkist (and a relation by marriage of the Bonvilles), sent his men towards Plymouth to repel the French, he was intercepted by Courtenay men (the Earls of Devon still held Plympton) at Yealmpton and kept out of the town.

Plymouth must have suffered from that French 'visit' for a merchant, William Savage, went to law with a complaint that, when the Frenchmen were at Plymouth 'and spoiled the town', he had been robbed of his goods, save some jewels which he sent away by a servant, and they were taken by a servant of Thomas Carewe. After York's triumph, Baldwin Fulford tried to raise Devon to rebellion in support of Lancaster but he was quickly taken and beheaded.

That autumn John Page succeeded William Yogge as mayor of Plymouth; he wanted the vicar to offer prayers for the success of Lancaster but the vicar prudently declined. Then the new King's brother, the Duke of Clarence, came to Plymouth and the mayor quickly changed his tune : 'this very mayor[6] in the same year (to quote the diarist again) feasteth the Duke of Clarence . . . right royally, here in Plymouth, and drinketh long life and a prosperous reign to King Edward IV.' It looks like a disciplinary visit, and a new regime which was taking no chances. John Rowland was mayor for the next three years 'a man of great interest and sway, and closely attached to the house of York. He was chosen mayor more from fear and awe, than reverence and love. . . .' He was also a member of Parliament in a Yorkist-packed Commons.

But Plymouth was clearly impoverished by the falling off of its old trades and the anarchy that reigned by land and sea. When Edward IV renewed the town's charter the annual rent to the Prior of Plympton was reduced from £41 to £29 6s 8d, because of the town's poverty.

William Yogge was mayor again in 1470, when the Lancastrians once more used Plymouth in an effort to regain power. Warwick the Kingmaker, who had put Edward IV on the throne, had now turned against him and seduced his brother, Clarence, from his loyalty. The two landed at Plymouth with the Earls of Pembroke and Oxford, and were dined by William Yogge in the guildhall, where Henry VI was proclaimed king again. They marched away and were briefly successful, until Warwick was defeated and killed in the battle of Barnet; Clarence, who had twice dined in Plymouth Guildhall, returned to his brother's side, only to become suspect again eight years later and be drowned in a butt of malmsey.

William Yogge, who had been four times mayor, disappears from the records in 1470 and in the following year the town council resolves that no 'foreyn' man shall be a freeman—which means a 'foreigner's' exclusion from all office.[7] The next entry in the town's records is 'John Yogge, John Shipper, and other foreyns putte owte of theyre ffredom.' It may all be coincidence but it does rather look as if the Yorkist element in Plymouth was in control again, that old Yogge—who had been in office during each of the Lancastrian landings at Plymouth—was now dead, and they were determined to have no more trouble with a Lancastrian family. So a foreign origin (European trade had brought Dutchmen and Bretons to settle in Plymouth for a century past) was being used as an excuse to put Yogge's son out of reach of any possible future authority.

Edward IV proved a strong king who restored the mercantile life of the country and brought discipline back into the Channel. He captured the pirate leaders of Fowey by a trick, hanged them, and got the men of Dartmouth to take away their ships and their harbour defence chain. Piracy still lingered on but the changed conditions can be seen in a 1474 report. Raulyn Pape, of Dieppe, was anchored in Falmouth when Henry Hornebroke, of Plymouth, cut out his ship. Pape says that he and his crew were 'bete and wounded' by the attackers, and then cast adrift in an open boat without a compass. Rescued by a French vessel, Pape had no hesitation in going to Plymouth where he bearded the mayor, Nicholas Heyncott, 'and in the presence of many and divers notable persons then all being in the chirche of Plymouth shewed unto him his hurtes and damages and required him to put under arrest the goodes of the said persons. . . .'

This is the last fifteenth century reference to a pirate from Plymouth. Thereafter strong central government not only made punishment more certain but, by restoring trade, made an honest life more profitable. But with Edward's death uncertainty and unrest returned. His brother, Richard Crouchback, made himself King, declared his brother's sons illegitimate and imprisoned them in the Tower where they were later put to death. The true line of Lancaster had disappeared but a new claimant arose in Henry Tudor, Earl of Richmond. From Brittany, he organised a rising in the west to synchronise with the Duke of Buckingham's revolt in Wales.

For the third time Plymouth was chosen for a Lancastrian landing; evidence of Plymouth's sympathies and of the fact that the only out-and-out Yorkist mayor had been forced on the town. But a great storm upset the Lancastrian plans; Buckingham was defeated and executed, and by the time Henry Tudor appeared in Plymouth Sound the western rebels had fallen back into Cornwall. Henry waited in Cawsand Bay while he took stock; a royal proclamation against him said he had ' a greate Navye and Armye of Straungiers.' Writing about Cawsand a century later, Richard Carew states 'I have heard the inhabitants thereabouts to report that the Earl of Richmond (afterwards Henry the Seventh), while he hovered upon the coast, here by stealth refreshed himself; by being advertised of a straight watch kept for his surprising at Plymouth, hied speedily a shipboard and escaped happily to a better fortune.'

King Richard III came down to Exeter and beheaded three of the western leaders. Others fled. The Courtenays and the Bonvilles had wiped each other out. The Lancastrians predominated now in Devon and Cornwall, and many western gentlemen spent that Christmas in exile with Henry Tudor in Brittany. In 1485, they landed with him at Milford Haven, crushed Richard on Bosworth field, and set the Tudors on the throne of England. After a century of warring dynasties, it was to be many years before the Tudors were to feel secure on the throne and Henry ruled as firmly as Edward IV had before him.

ST ANDREW'S CHURCH

How this restored prosperity is seen in the wave of church rebuilding throughout the west. Plymouth had probably rebuilt the nave of St Andrew's[8] in the early fourteenth century, with the money brought in by the naval activity of Edward III. In 1481 there was a fresh spurt. The town's oldest surviving account book, called 'Thomas Tregarthen's Book' after the mayor of 1480-1, has a Latin inscription on the fly-leaf which declares that the book was started by the decision of Thomas Tresawell, mayor, and his predecessor, Tregarthen. The book, it is written 'appertaineth to the church of St Andrew in Plymouth, started on 24 August 1481, to put in writing all the ornaments of the church as well as all monies belonging to the "reparacion" of the church.' First, is the list of such money as is 'assigned and granted by diverse persons to the making of the south aisle.' The legacies and gifts recorded easily meet the bill from John Dawe, mason, for £44 14s 6d for the materials and labour of building the south aisle, between 1481 and 1485. But, after three pages, the format of the entries changes into what are fairly obviously the churchwarden's accounts.

After 1485, the town's audit book contains entries for money spent on the church; stained glass windows (such windows of this period can still be seen in the churches of Bere Ferrers and St Neot), stones for the north aisle and the tower, and for paving the street by the church stile. Leland, who visited Plymouth in the next reign, writes that 'of late' a merchant of the town, Thomas Yogge, paid for the building of the steeple (steeple, a spire or tower) and the north aisle of the church, and that the town supplied the material. Here is the church starting to rebuild, completing the south aisle, and then in 1485, when Henry Tudor overthrows the House of York, a Yogge comes forward and takes upon his shoulders the main burden of rebuilding the church. His family had long been enemies of the House of York and seem to have suffered at their hands; is this an act of thanksgiving? Yogge's tower still stands, surviving nearly five centuries and a war that destroyed nearly all around it; was it built originally as a monument to celebrate the Tudor accession?

The town was proud of its church and, at the mayor's com-

mand, John Gill preached a special Christmas sermon there in
1486. Soon the mayor's pew was carpeted and two goatskins
were stuffed with flock to make cushions for his pew, gold paint
being used to pick out the town's arms on the cushion covers. A
man from Looe was paid to make a cross and weather vane, with
iron obtained from Plympton. There was music, too; in 1487 a
shilling was paid 'to the old man the singer' to go to Plympton
to fetch songs for the mass.

Probably the merchant's Guild of Our Lady and St George
had always had a Lady Chapel. Now the new south aisle was
dedicated to St George, and the north aisle to St John the Baptist. Apart from the vicar—who had his vicarage just under the
east window, in the corner between St Andrew Street and
Whimple Street–there were three or four chantry priests licensed
to the church. Chantries were common enough, and were priests
maintained by endowment to pray for the souls of certain people.
It was the middle-class equivalent to the rich man's piety in
founding abbeys. At Plympton Erle John Brackley dedicated a
chantry to St Maurice which eventually became the dedication
of the church and altered the town's name to Plympton St
Maurice. At Tamerton Foliot, a chantry was set up for the souls
of the Copplestones of Warleigh. In St Andrew's there was the
Venour chantry, to pray for the family of the man who won the
town's first charter, the Dabernon and Paynter chantry founded
by two merchants to pray for their families, and the Jaybyn
chantry, for which land was given to the corporation on
condition that the revenue was used to pay the stipend of a priest
to say masses at the altar of St John Baptist, in the church of
St Andrew, for the soul of John Jaybyn.

Just south of St Andrew's Church there is still a house which
architectural evidence dates as late fourteenth century, the period
when St Andrew's was being enlarged and beautified. It is still
called the Prysten House, and was clearly built, when the church
was being extended, to serve as the home of the chantry priests.
In 1538, the year of the Dissolution, the mayor and council of

Plymouth made a grant to Sir Thomas Flyte, chantry priest of Jaybyn's chantry, of the 'prysten house, together with the chamber that he now hath both under and above, during his lifetime, without disturbance of any of his fellow-priests there.' The grant was made in consideration of Flyte having paid for the repair of the prysten house kitchen.

Flyte seems to have been long in office, and his name appears in the only two surviving lists of Plymouth chantry priests. In one, he is joined by Sir Keysar and Sir John Nicholas; in another by Sir John Crofts and Thomas Washington. 'Sir' merely marks a priest who had not been at a university. Since Sir Thomas and his brothers moved out, the building has served many purposes from wine store to provision merchant's warehouse, and when the church regained possession the interior was smoke-blackened by long years of bacon-curing. It can only have housed the priests whose name it still carries from about 1490 to 1538, but it could well be not only Plymouth's oldest surviving domestic building but also its earliest school. At Ashburton, the keeping of a free school was a duty specifically laid upon the chantry priest, and though the merchants of Plymouth, who must have been men of considerable education, may have received it at a friary school, a chantry school is much more likely. It is significant, too that, within twenty-three years of the dissolution of the chantries and the friaries, Plymouth found it necessary to establish a Corporation grammar school.

Another social work conducted beside the church, and possibly a joint enterprise by church and corporation, were the almshouses just north of St Andrew's tower. Their age is uncertain, but the wardens were paying rates in the earliest surviving records of the late fifteenth century. A Norman-type archway was preserved when the building was removed in 1868 but it was then thought not to date the building itself but to have been originally part of the church fabric. It may have been a side door of the fourteenth century nave, removed in the 1485 reconstruction and used to embellish the almshouses; in which case it seems that the reconstruction covered the entire group of church, priests' houses and almshouses.

EDGCUMBE AND BROKE

Among the western men who came home with Henry Tudor was Sir Richard Edgcumbe, whose family had sprung from yeoman stock at Milton Damerel and, by marriage, had acquired Cotehele, beside the Tamar. Sir Richard's loyalty to Henry in exile and on Bosworth field was rewarded with high office as Controller of the Royal Household, which made him a rich man. He also became Sheriff of Devon in 1494, and Plymouth made him presents of two sugar loaves, wine, pomegranates and oranges. In the previous year his son Piers had married the last of the Durnford family, the heiress Joan, who brought him all the old Valletort lands at Stonehouse and Maker. Piers was to turn Maker into a park[9] and build the great house that he called Mount Edgcumbe; his descendant is still there as the Earl of Mount Edgcumbe, Viscount Valletort, and Baron Edgcumbe. Plymouth welcomed Piers and his bride with gifts, and the family has played its part in Plymouth affairs to this day.

Another returning soldier was Sir Robert Willoughby de Broke, who became Plymouth's first Lord High Steward. A soldier of fortune, he made himself a landed gentleman by marrying Blanche Champernowne. The Champernownes, originally of Dartington, had acquired the Valletort lands at Modbury by marriage, and Blanche's grandmother was a Ferrers, a family descended from William the Conqueror's chief farrier, whose badge was a horseshoe. Sir Robert was very fond of his new houses at Newton Ferrers, near Callington (his tomb is in the parish church there) and at Bere Ferrers. His arms are still in Bere Ferrers church, bearing the horseshoe of the Ferrers and a rudder, said to signify his appointment as England's first Lord High Admiral.

In 1486, Plymouth officers met their new Lord High Steward at Plympton 'when we made owre benevolence,' and gave him two sugar loaves. That December, the mayor, Thomas Tresawell, went to see him in London 'for ye benevolence'. No doubt this was all concerned with the renewal of the town's charter, for Henry's title to the throne depended on the House of Lancaster; he would not recognise the two Yorkist kings who had pre-deceded him or the confirmations they had given to the charters of the boroughs. So Plymouth had to go back to its original charter of Henry VI, who was fortunately a Lancastrian and who had even been proclaimed king in Plymouth Guildhall during William Yogge's mayoralty of 1470.

TWO REBELLIONS

Plymouth's charter was renewed fifteen months after Henry VII came to the throne, but the new king soon showed himself to be a hard man, extorting every penny he could in taxation. Ex-chequer pressure was such that, in 1495, the town treasurer rode off to see Thomas Yogge at Ashburton 'when he was seke', and next we find Yogge in London on the town's business. The very next entry in the town accounts is a payment for 'Rollyng of the Chartour', which all suggests that Yogge's influence was used to get the charter entered on the patent rolls as a defence against the Treasury.

Cornwall, too, felt the weight of the tax-collectors but, as a royal duchy, could seek no such legal protection. In 1497, taxes levied to defend the Scottish border proved the last straw, and the Cornishmen rose in revolt. The rebels marched as far as Black-heath before being defeated, and there was at least one Plymouth man, Robert Warwick, among them. The Warwick family owned 'a certain mansion, lands, meadow and pasture' in Plymouth.

Perkin Warbeck, the imposter who claimed to be one of the princes murdered in the Tower by Richard III, decided that

Cornishmen were of greater valour than the Scots he had been trying to stir up. So that same summer he landed at Sennen Cove and again the Cornish rose. The rebel army marched through Launceston to Exeter, and though it by-passed Plymouth, the town was much alarmed. A man was sent to Exeter to 'spy tydyngs' and a boat went out to Penlee to speak to Mr Treffry. This second revolt met a bloody end in the villages of east Devon. The King himself spent a month in Exeter to ensure that Cornwall was disciplined, and the Mayor of Plymouth, Thomas Tresawell again, went up to Exeter while the King was there. The Earl of Devon, Lord Willoughby de Broke, and Lord Daubenny were appointed commissioners to receive the submission of Cornwall, and no doubt they were the 'Lord Prince's Council' for whom Plymouth supplied fifteen pence worth of wine at the mayor's house. The town dressed eight men in uniforms of green and white, the Tudor colours, to join Lord Devon's escort in Cornwall.

A more serious danger to Plymouth at this time were the French again, for Henry was supporting Brittany's efforts to keep her freedom. Twice Willoughby de Broke commanded armies in Brittany, and Plymouth strengthened her defences against possible attack. Gunpowder had brought a vital change into warfare; the castle quadrate now covered too limited a field to be effective, and bulwarks and gun-platforms were built along the edge of the Hoe cliffs to command the entrance into the Cattewater. In the town's oldest surviving accounts, for 1486, there is mention of a watchman at Rame beside a fire beacon, another beacon and a bulwark, on the Hoe, and candles bought for the night watch. Moulds were made from which cannon-balls or lead and iron were cast; shot was also made from stone. In the first few years of the sixteenth century the bulwarks were extended and more guns bought, including two from the Spanish, then the best gunsmiths in Europe.

KATHERINE OF ARAGON

Henry VII sought a link with Spain to counter the Franco-Scottish alliance, and to this end, there landed on the Barbican in 1501 a slight, weary girl—Princess Katherine of Aragon. She came to marry Henry's eldest son, Arthur and, when he died, she married the second son, Henry. Perhaps the English temperament made the break with Rome and the dissolution of the monasteries inevitable, but this sad and serious little girl was to provide the spark that set it all off. No one could have foreseen this when the gentlemen of Devon and Cornwall assembled to welcome Katherine; indeed, she was in the care of the Abbot of Compostello, whose cathedral church had been the goal of that pilgrim trade from the town up to half a century earlier. The town had its address of welcome translated into Spanish and Latin, gave the royal household sheep and oxen and wine (Thomas Yogge supplied the claret), and paid minstrels to entertain the guests.

Tradition says that the Princess and her household gave thanks for their safe arrival at St Andrew's[10] and spent a fortnight recovering from their journey at the house of John Paynter, a merchant who had been mayor in 1487. His house was in the angle between High Street and Catte Street, and one wall survives in the garden of a school which is still called Palace Court, the name that ever after attached itself to Paynter's house. The house itself stood four-square about its courtyard until 1880, when it came down to make way for the school; in its last days it was rackrented and verminous. It was never a thieves' kitchen such as the Whitefriars, once the palace of John of Gaunt, became, but both the royal residences of Plymouth came to shabby ends.

Paynter's fine house, the two houses of the Yogge family, and the rebuilding of St Andrew's show that Plymouth was at last recovering from its mid-century depression. In Henry VII's reign, the Plymouth-Fowey customs returns doubled, from £327 to

£647, though depreciation in the value of money, and Henry's more efficient tax collection, must be allowed for. The Exeter-Totnes customs returns trebled, from £515 to £1,615. Plymouth fell from being the twenty-second town in England in 1377 to the thirty-third in the 1520s, while Exeter had gone up from the twenty-third place to fifth. Even Totnes, though smaller than Plymouth, had richer merchants.[11] The wool trade was making these towns, whereas Plymouth handled only the coarser cloth from Tavistock and some from Ashburton. Even in fish, Torbay was yielding more than the old grounds off Plymouth. Tin-mining on Dartmoor had a boom in the early sixteenth century, but as the miners had to dig further for the metal so the waste in the rivers increased. Once again, there were constant complaints about the state of the Plym and the way the miners were silting it up.

The Breton raids of 1403, the cost of rebuilding and strengthening defences afterwards, the loss of ancient trades and the anarchy of the Wars of the Roses had all combined to give Plymouth a bad time for the first half of the fifteenth century, even though the town had become independent. There was some recovery in the second half; the town was able to improve its guildhall and nearly renew its parish church, to support merchants whose houses were fit for a princess and to create the new Looe Street ward, but clearly the recovery did not keep up with that of the rest of the country, or even the rest of Devon.

Stonehouse, by now had grown into a sizeable village. The Durnfords had a manor house at Stone Hall which they had been licensed to fortify. One crenellated wall still remains, though the last 'big house' on the site came down in 1963. Houses lined both sides of Stonehouse High Street and Buckland Abbey had a house where the Naval Hospital now stands. In all probability, the monks built it and turned to Stonehouse as a port from which to ship their products when they lost their rights in Plymouth on its incorporation. The new borough seems to have aroused James Durnford's ambitions, for in 1442, he set up his own court and a pillory in Stonehouse. But Stonehouse, as part of the hundred of Roborough was still controlled by the abbot of Buckland, who made Durnford close the court, remove the pillory, and pay him £20 in compensation. In 1472 Stonehouse, which had been part of the parish of St Andrew's, had its own chapel of St Lawrence licensed for divine worship. This church was removed in the last century to make way for the Royal William Victualling Yard, though part of its tower is the folly in Mount Edgcumbe Park, visible from the Hoe.

The Wise family acquired Stoke by 1428 but they continued to live in their big house at Sydenham, near Lifton, letting the Keyham manor house remain as a farm. In 1525 they relinquished their rights on the northern bank of Stonehouse Creek to allow the new owner of Stonehouse, Sir Piers Edgcumbe, to build a tidal mill at Millbridge. This bridge opened up a new route from Stonehouse up Molesworth Road and down the hill to a ford over the Keyham Creek (which in time gave its name to the modern district of Ford), and so to St Budeaux.

Here the Budockside family was prospering and by 1482 the population had increased sufficiently for them to complain to the Bishop of Exeter that it was unreasonable for them to have to go all the way to St Andrew's for baptisms and funerals, when they could celebrate the other services of the church in their own chapel. The Bishop agreed and gave them the licence they wanted, on condition that they provided a priest's house and a graveyard. Successful yeomen, and merchants of Plymouth moving out into the country were building houses big enough to have private chapels licensed, such as for the Haisendes at Kinterbury and for Roger Boswynes, the seaman.

It was all very pastoral. Leland came over the Saltash ferry and rode over Weston Mill Bridge, down Swilly Road to Pennycomequick and so into Plymouth. 'The ground between the passage of Asche and Plymmouth', he wrote, 'hath good corn but little wod.' Shipbuilding had long since bitten into the big timber; the unproductive coppices had made way for golden barley and oats to feed the new town. The new Mill Bridge was evidence of agricultural prosperity. Was anyone aware, in all this quiet pastoral of waving cornfields, that the world was opening up? Certainly on the Plymouth quayside they must have known that a man named Columbus had opened for Spain a new way to what he thought were the Indies, and that Cabot had sailed from Bristol to a New Found Land. But they could little have foreseen that this opening up of the Atlantic was in time to cover all their fields with close-packed houses.

CHAPTER SIX

THE NEW WORLD

W HEN Turkish wars closed the eastern Mediterranean, western Europe cast around for other routes by which to reach the spices of the East. A Portuguese ship had rounded the Cape of Good Hope by 1487, and Columbus crossed the Atlantic for Spain in 1492. The Atlantic islands, Madiera, the Cape Verdes, the Azores and the Canaries, had already been colonised. Henry VII, who often talked of war with France but wasted little money on it, encouraged Cabot and the Bristol men to cross the Atlantic, but their New Found Land was a cold place and it was some time before its wealth of cod was realised. Henry VIII, however, was no sooner on the throne in 1509 than he was at war with France, and Plymouth, on the edge of the ocean that was exciting men's attention, was soon re-building its bulwarks under the Hoe and buying more guns, for fear that the French would come.

Plymouth escaped being burnt by the French, as Fowey was in 1511, but saw no profit from the war, even though it was being waged in its old stamping-ground of Gascony. The mayor hired a fishing-boat and took 12s 6d worth of chickens out to the Lord Admiral when he came home to Plymouth that year with an unsuccessful army. By the end of the war in 1515, there were formidable defences facing the Sound, set up at considerable expense and named after the alderman or wards who were responsible for manning them, like Thykpeny's bulwark and the Looe Street gun.

A new man moved into Plymouth about this time, William Hawkins. His father was a rich merchant of Tavistock, and his mother an Amadas of Launceston. William was exporting tin and wool (clearly acting as a shipping agent for his father), and importing salt from Rochelle, wine from Bordeaux, Portugal and Spain, pepper from Portugal, olive oil and soap from Spain, and fish from Newfoundland. Not until 1543 is there a payment to the watchman at Rame 'for his comyng hither by nyght when the newfoundland men came yn' but Plymouth ships must have been in the business much earlier. The Bristol links were strong. By 1523 William Hawkins was worth £150 a year, one of the five richest men in Plymouth. Next year he was treasurer of the town (a post then held annually by a member of the council, and a stepping-stone to the mayoralty). The town's income which he handled in the year was £63, less than half his personal wealth. Of the £150, £140 was ventured in trade with Spain. He helped man the bulwarks when French pirates chased an Italian ship into the Sound in 1527. The French captains were brought ashore and detained until they agreed to sail in peace; their ships, meanwhile, being menaced by the guns on the Hoe. When they did go, the Hoe gunners were given a shillings worth of wine, and the Italian 'argosy' paid Plymouth £26 13s 4d in gratitude. That year, too, William Hawkins was accused with other leaders of the town of beating and wounding John Jurdon—'so as to endanger his life'—but no one seems to have been very upset about it.

All this time Hawkins was hearing stories from west European ports, especially Lisbon and Seville, of the riches being brought home from the Guinea coast of Africa, and from the Americas. Plymouth had been trading with Spain and Portugal for a century and more; in fact, so many Englishmen had settled in San Lucar, the outport of Seville, that they had their own church of St George there. No doubt there were Plymouth men among them, and Hawkins himself had probably visited his agents in Lisbon and Seville. In 1530 Hawkins decided to make the venture himself, the first Englishman to trade across the Atlantic. He was between 35 and 40 but Richard Hakluyt, setting down the story years later, recorded :—

> Olde M. William Haukins of Plimmouth, a man for his wise-
> dome, valure, experience and skill in sea causes much esteemed,
> and, beloved of K. Henry the 8, and being one of the prin-
> cipall sea-captaines in the West parts of England in his time,
> not contented with the short voyages commonly then made
> onely to the knowne coasts of Europe, armed out a tall and
> goodly shippe of his owne, of the burthen of 250 tunnes, called
> the *Paule of Plimmouth*, wherewith he made three long and
> famous voyages unto the coast of Brasil. . . .

It was not a difficult voyage for seamen accustomed to running down to the coast of Spain. There they could pick up the
north-east trade winds down the African coast, fair winds and
currents across the narrowest part of the Atlantic to Brazil, and
fair winds up to the westerlies for the straight run home. Hakluyt
records that Hawkins loaded ivory on the Guinea coast, but as it
was also the centre of the 'Guinea grains' trade, as the local
pepper was called, he probably added some to his cargo. In
America, he took on the brazil wood much needed in Europe for
dying cloth (and which gave the country its name). Politically,
the voyage was safe enough for it touched only the coasts claimed
by Portugal, which the French were already raiding, and did not
involve any Spanish lands, which would have upset King Henry's
fostering of his Spanish alliance.

It must have been a profitable voyage for Hawkins went again
in 1531 and again in 1532, and became so friendly with the
natives in Brazil that one chief returned with him, a member
of the crew, Martin Cockeram being left behind as guarantee of
the chief's safe return. Hawkins took the chief to London 'at
the sight of whom the King and all the Nobilitie did not a little
marvaile'; not surprisingly, as he had bones fitted into holes in
each cheek which stood out an inch and another hole in his
lower lip in which was set a precious stone the size of a pea. One
hopes that he was an honoured if incongruous guest on St Lambert's Day in Plymouth that autumn, when William Hawkins
was chosen mayor. Next spring, Hawkins stayed at home but

his ship made the voyage back. The chief died on the way, but such was the word of the English, that Martin Cockeram[1] was allowed to return to his native Plymouth, to live on for fifty odd years.

Hawkins seems never to have made the voyage again himself but continued to develop the trade, re-exporting the brazil wood even to Italy. A Bristol exporter shared a ship with Thomas Cromwell, MP for Taunton and already in the Privy Council. Hawkins was writing to Cromwell seeking royal loans with which to arm his ships; he had three or four in the trade and lost at least one. A clue to the profit of these voyages, which other ports were now emulating, comes from the accounts of the *Paul*, master John Landy, in 1540. She sailed in February with 940 hatchets, 940 combs, 375 knives, 10 cwt of copper and lead arm bands, 10 cwt of lead in the lump, 3 pieces of woollen cloth and 19 dozen nightcaps. The cargo was worth £23 15s 0d and paid export duty of £1 7s 3d (the manufactured goods seem to have been described merely as metal, an early example of customs-evasion). The sole shipper was William Hawkins.

The *Paul* was back on 20 October with a dozen tusks of ivory and 92 tons of brazil wood, valued at £615 and paying duty of £30 15s 0d. For a 250-ton ship, it was a light cargo and there may well have been peppers passed off as ship's supply and other disguised goods. But the profit for a six-months voyage is fantastic; allowing for the cost of wages and victualling, and forgetting what else may have come home, it must have been over one thousand per cent. No wonder Hawkins in 1536 could buy a new house and garden in Kinterbury Street, just below Old Town Street. No wonder either that he was in trouble with the customs. Peter Grisling who had been indicted with Hawkins in the 'affray' of 1527, was the 'searcher', or customs officer. Soon after Hawkins's mayoralty, he and two other merchants, James Horsewell and John Eliot (who had previously been in business at Ashburton, like the Yogges), complained that Grisling was exercising his office, with rapacity and extortion, and making it his main source of income.[2] The battle raged for years, and in 1536, when Horsewell was mayor, Grisling called him 'a naughty heretic knave'.

THE DISSOLUTION

It was a dangerous charge, for 'heresy' then meant opposition to the King's desire to divorce Katherine of Aragon, the dispute that led to the break with Rome. The friars in Plymouth were particularly outspoken against this, and Horsewell had given proof in April 1533 that he was no 'heretic' when he warned Cromwell that 'there be knave friars here that play their part.' The Grey Friars, in particular, were protesting, and Sir Piers Edgcumbe was sent into the town to examine them. He sent the warden, Friar Gawen, to Launceston Castle and put others who spoke ill of Queen Anne Boleyn into the pillory or the stocks. Thomas Mychelson, 'the clerke', was sent to the Bishop of Exeter's prison.

It was abundantly clear that the religious houses were doomed, and up and down the country the abbots and their friends were making anticipatory dispositions. At Stonehouse, the Abbot of Buckland made over all his manorial rights, and probably the abbey building as well, to the Edgcumbes. In 1534, Plymouth was finally relieved of its annual payment to Plympton Priory, which was given instead the advowsons of Blackawton and Ipplepen. The excuse was Plymouth's 'ruen and decay' and though Leland, the antiquarian, who was in the town about this time, writes of decay in the Old Town Ward, it is far more likely that the Prior of Plympton cancelled Plymouth's pension rather than see it bought up like an annuity by some speculator.

The small houses went first. In the autumn of 1538 the 'Lord Visitor in the West', the Bishop of Dover, rode down through Somerset, Devon and Cornwall closing down the friaries. Plymouth took him two days; he dealt with Whitefriars on 18 September and Greyfriars[3] on the 19th. Local officers assisting him

Medieval Plymouth had three friaries. This external wall of the Blackfriars is now an internal wall in Coates's gin distillery in Southside Street. The Whitefriars, remembered by Friary Station, had the view below of Sutton Harbour.

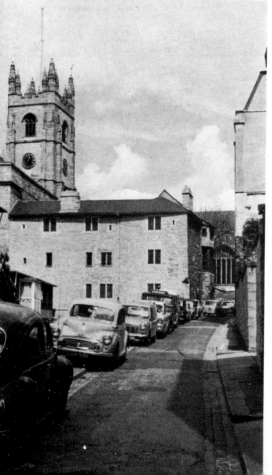

The Greyfriars stood on the site of the modern block of flats looking out over what may be Sutton Harbour's oldest quay and the Parade inlet to the 'South Side'. Left, Fynewell Street running up to St Andrew's Church and the Prysten House, where the chantry priests of the church lived.

were the mayor, Thomas Clowteynge; the mayor-elect, William Hawkins; and the town clerk, James Horsewell. Six brothers signed the surrender of Whitefriars. There was not much in the house, but 211 ozs of silver which had been purloined were turned over to the Visitor. How much had gone and was never returned is another matter. At the Greyfriars next day there was even less; John Morys (who signed as 'Warden of Plymouth') and his seven brothers had been left with what remained in the church, together with the bells and clock in the steeple; the rest had been 'brybeyd away'. There is no record of any of the other friaries in the west clearing out their possessions like this, before the Visitor's arrival and, considering that all the local dignitaries at the time were fighting High Court actions over customs, it suggests a tough and independent town.

The alabaster table which the Visitor found at the high altar in Greyfriars church indicates its wealth, for English alabaster of the time was famous throughout Europe. Table may mean re-table, a long shelf behind the altar with richly carved panels; possibly the altar itself, movable, had also been 'brybeyd away'. What is said to have been the rood-screen of the Greyfriars is today in the parish church of Blackawton, between Totnes and Dartmouth. It is carved with the initials of Henry VIII and Katherine of Aragon, and the Aragon badge of the pomegran-ate. Katherine must have landed on the Parade right in front of the Greyfriars, and the rood-screen would have been a fitting memorial. Some of the friars who risked prison by speaking up for her at the end may even have remembered the tired young girl of all those years before, and perhaps the Abbot of Com-postello had been their guest.

Hawkins and his friends took delivery of the buildings for the King, and Horsewell acquired a lease of the Whitefriars. It was a splendid building at Coxside standing inside its own walls and with an imposing gate; a spire on the church dominated the head of the harbour. In 1546, Gregory and Charles Isham, London speculators in monastic property, bought both the Plymouth friaries, later selling the Whitefriars to William Amadas, a Hawkins cousin. Through marriage, it passed to the Sparkes in 1600 and they were there until 1714.[4] Then decay set in; during the Napoleonic wars the Whitefriars was a military hospital, and by 1830 it had become a common lodging house, as low a den as one could/find with its thieves and beggars gathering of an evening for a communal meal. The last vestiges of the building were swept away with the building of Friary Station and the Roman Catholic Church of the Holy Cross.

The Greyfriars became the 'Mitre Inn', which was entered from Woolster Street through a low-arched doorway. This led into a square courtyard with cloisters on the eastern side supported by twisted or spiral pillars, at the end of which a staircase led to apartments formed out of the church. The building was removed to make way for the Exchange, built in 1813 and destroyed in the 1941 blitz; the last fragments of the Greyfriars were in the 'Ring o'Bells' which was pulled down for road-widening in 1956. Now the Woolster Street flats occupy the site.

The Blackfriars does not appear in any dissolution documents, and must have been closed or given up by the friars some time earlier. The building became town property, was used as a debtor's prison, then let to the Huguenot refugees as a chapel, and eventually became the gin distillery which it still is. Odd, that the one friary for which there is no documentary evidence at all should be the only one to survive.

The great monasteries followed the friaries within six months. The buildings at Tavistock and Plympton became quarries; the lead was stripped from their roofs and the structures soon disappeared. The Tavistock estates were acquired by the Russell family who, enobled eventually as Dukes of Bedford, became a new power in Devon. The Champernownes had Plympton for a time, but the estates broke up. They also bought St Germans in 1541, but sold it in 1565 to John Eliot, the Plymouth merchant. The family are still there, in their house beside the priory church called Port Eliot, and their head is now the Earl of St Germans.

Buckland was bought by Sir Richard Grenville of Bideford, who had been Marshal of Calais. His wife was a Whitleigh, one of a family of landowners who took their name from the manor north of Plymouth, and she brought to him half of Compton and Efford. He settled Buckland Abbey on their son, Roger.

In the years after the dissolution, William Hawkins was accounting to Plymouth for church silver he had sold on the town's behalf; the King did not get it all. Much came from the Greyfriars but there was a chalice from St Katherine's upon the Hoe and another from Our Lady's Chapel at Quarrywell, the site of which is marked by the side turning off Regent Street still known as Ladywell. There must have been a little chapel over a holy well[5] of the kind that still survives in some Cornish villages. The rest of the church silver included silver candlesticks and figures of saints which may have come from St Andrew's; a little ship of silver 'hangying apon Seynt Clers cloth' and a bigger ship of silver gilt, weighing 18 oz, both reminiscent of the Corpus Christi ship.

The money from the sale was spent on gunpowder, and bows and arrows. Much attention was still being given to defence; the butts on the Hoe were in regular use and wine barrels were moored in the Sound for gunnery practice. Henry VIII mapped the defences of the south coast and, in 1539, built round guard-towers at Fisher's Nose to protect the mouth of the Plym, at the entrance to Millbay, and on Devil's Point to cover the mouth of the Tamar. The Fisher's Nose tower and the bulwarks that ran along the Hoe cliffs are now the base of the pavement that runs along from the point to the Plymouth Royal Corinthian Yacht Club house; the irregular pattern of the sea wall still shows the angles of the gun platforms and can be seen by peering over the wall. The towers at Devil's Point also remain, even if the best survivor has been converted by Stonehouse Urban Council into a public lavatory.

THE 1549 'COMMOTION'

These defences were wise precautions, for in 1544 France made peace with Spain and turned her energies against England. Horsewell was Mayor of Plymouth that year and, together with Hawkins and Eliot, he received the King's commission to 'annoy the King's enemies'. It was privateering again, with the problems of enemy cargoes in neutral ships, and a fine line between legality and piracy. The line proved too fine for William Hawkins who was called before the Privy Council when the King was at Portsmouth with the fleet, and sent to prison. Sir George Carew of Antony and Roger Grenville of Buckland Abbey were also there as captain and second-in-command of the *Mary Rose*; when she sank at anchor both were among the 500 men drowned. Eight Plymouth ships, and two from Saltash, were in the fleet. The spell in prison did not mend Hawkins's ways. He was in more trouble when his *Mary Figge* captured some Flemish goods, and again in 1546 when he captured a Breton ship after peace had been signed. No one seems to have thought any the worse of him, and a naval officer, Thomas Wyndham, became his partner after the war and re-opened the Brazil trade. Hawkins himself was summoned to the first Parliament of Edward VI as member for Plymouth, he and Horsewell having previously sat several times in Henry's day.

Plymouth washed the town flag and had a 'trivmphe' for the coronation of the boy king. The following year the town was celebrating victory over the Scots at Pinkie with a banquet for which oysters were fetched from Saltash, and meat and drink 'for them which played the antic'. But the reformers about the new king were at work again; they ordered the removal of all images from the churches and stopped what they regarded as superstition in the services. In that spring of 1547 it moved the men of Cornwall to rebellion, for the third time in half a century.

Plymouth paid 26s 8d to Henry Blase and his company 'when

they rode with Sir Richard Edgcumbe into Cornwall against the rebels there', and bought a dozen bowstrings for them. The country was 'pacified by the gentlemen of the country with small trouble,' says the Black Book, 'but yet certain of the chief of the commons were hanged drawn and quartered.' One execution took place on Plymouth Hoe. In the 1547 accounts are the grisly entries; the faggots and the 'quart of rhede' for the fire, the cost of the gallows, payment to the executioner and to the man who led the horse which dragged the 'Traytor of Cornwall' to his death. His name is unknown, but his head and one quarter were raised on poles over Plymouth Guildhall, and another quarter exhibited in Tavistock.

These dreadful displays were a warning to Cornwall and the border town. Plymouth set about defending St Nicholas's Island (Hawkins, Eliot, John Thomas and Richard Hooper going to London about it) and the town settled down. A priest rode to London about the sale of chantry land. The King's fiddler was paid five shillings and English songs were bought for the choir; Latin may have gone but not music. The Act of Uniformity of 1549, which made the English prayer-book compulsory, launched another rebellion in Cornwall, and in Devon, too.

There was considerable alarm. Old Sir Richard Grenville shut himself up in Trematon Castle with the gentry of east Cornwall; his daughter-in-law had married an Arundell and was living at Clifton, now just a farm beside the Tamar, and she probably brought her son Richard Grenville, into the castle too. A yeoman farmer from Crowndale beside Tavistock, Edmund Drake, who was a relative of the Hawkins, fled to Plymouth and took refuge on St Nicholas's Island; his small son, Francis Drake, with him. The aldermen and councillors of Plymouth stood to their posts in the castle quadrate.

Trematon was captured, the gentlewomen stripped and robbed, old Sir Richard flung into Launceston gaol. The Cornish army moved on to Plymouth, where, says the Black Book, 'The castle was valiantly defended and kept from the rebels'. Efforts were made to defend the town, and guns were dragged from their store at the Guildhall up to the Hoe and to the Maudlyn, some to St Nicholas's Island. But the town was taken. 'Then was our stepell burnt with alle the townes evydence in the same by Rebelles', records the Black Book.

This was all the town records, stored in the tower of the Guildhall. No doubt the relics of the traitor of Cornwall, still on poles over the Guildhall from the year before, infuriated the Cornishmen and led them to set fire to the Guildhall. Fifteen years later the town was to spend £120 on a large new building; in 1568-9 there is a reference to the 'newe gildhall'. It was not until 1959 that the Guildhall burnt out in 1941 was restored; it is not unreasonable to believe that the new building of 1564 was restoring a Guildhall destroyed by the rebels of 1549.

Only four books survive from before this destruction of the town records: Thomas Tregarthen's book, which was probably in the church 'vestry, the Black Book (bought in 1535 as the town's ledger), the current account book (which, like the Black Book, was in everyday use and not with the archives), and Simon Carswell's book, the records of a lawyer who had been the town coroner and who probably had the book in his office. Fortunately, all the vital decisions of the town's earlier history had been copied into the Black Book; without that Plymouth's medieval history would be even more difficult to unravel.

Lord Russell came down with an army to subdue the 'commotion' and took the leaders off to swing at Tyburn. They, and their fellow defenders of the old religion had been too impatient, for with Mary Tudor on the throne in 1553 the Catholic religion was restored. Next year, she married King Philip of Spain, after the Earl of Bedford had sailed from Plymouth to wait upon him, and the Lord High Admiral, Lord William Howard, had been in Plymouth to receive the Spanish envoys. Philip himself landed at Southampton but the Hawkins family is thought to have been busy with ships and escorts in the business and the younger Hawkins son, John, seems to have won King Philip's favour and even a Spanish knighthood. King Philip landed at Plymouth in 1557. Old William sat in Mary's first Parliament but died soon afterwards, and the family business was then divided between his two sons, William and John.

THE SLAVE TRADE

William seems to have managed affairs at home; while John went to sea and had made several voyages to the Canaries before 1560. The old Hawkins partner, Wyndham, was pushing further down the African coast to the Gold Coast and Philip and Mary, sensitive to Portuguese feelings, ordered this trading to stop. But it continued nevertheless, and when Elizabeth came to the throne in 1558 she regarded the Portuguese occupation as so ineffective (as indeed it was) that she refused to recognise it. The French, notably the Huguenots, were raiding this territory, as they were the Spanish mainland round the Caribbean, and these Protestant Frenchmen, seamen of Normandy and La Rochelle, were so beyond their country's control that, when France and Spain made peace in 1559, it was agreed that it should not apply south of the Tropic of Cancer or west of the longitude of the Canaries. There was no peace beyond the lines.

This was the world into which John Hawkins launched himself. He took a house in London in 1559, married Katherine Gonson, daughter of the Treasurer of the Navy, and formed a syndicate of wealthy London merchants to back a new ambitious venture, direct trade with the Spanish colonies. Hawkins was presuming on his favour with the King of Spain and on the fact that he would be providing a service that the colonies badly needed, to overcome the Spanish law that only Spanish ships could trade with their settlements. They were sadly short of labour and Hawkins aimed to take Negro slaves from Africa and exchange them for the produce of Spanish America, so gaining the advantages of a double turnover in one voyage. It was also a natural use of the Atlantic winds, for coming home from the south Atlantic it was easier to move into the Caribbean and pick up the westerlies than to struggle through the capricious wind belt north of the north-east trades.

Hawkins sailed from Plymouth in 1562 with three ships, *Salomon, Swallow,* and *Jonas,* picked up a pilot in the Canaries, loaded three or four hundred slaves in Guinea, and traded them in the smaller Spanish American ports for pearls, ginger, sugar and hides. To demonstrate his good faith, he sent a Portuguese prize under her own captain to Seville, and two cargoes to San Lucar under his second-in-command, Thomas Hampton. But the Portuguese took his ship to Lisbon and the Spanish confiscated the cargoes that reached San Lucar. Hampton narrowly escaped arrest and met Hawkins in Plymouth with the story in August 1563. Hawkins went straight off to Queen Elizabeth who took up his case; he may even have gone to Spain himself to claim his cargoes. But, to King Philip, Queen Elizabeth was a heretic, and the privateers she had licensed in a new war against France were also harming Spanish neutrals.

Undeterred, Hawkins fitted out a new expedition, and this time there were Navy Board officers and men of the Privy Council in his syndicate as well. The Queen herself chartered a Royal ship to Hawkins, the *Jesus of Lubeck,* and told him to sail under Royal colours. Now an extra service was being offered to the Spanish colonies; defence against the French raiders. King Philip had entered into similar arrangements with Catholic Italy in the Mediterranean; perhaps he would do the same in the Atlantic with England. The *Jesus* was an impressive ship of 700 tons, with a massive poop and forecastle, towering over Hawkin's own three little ships, but Henry VIII had bought her from the Hanseatic League twenty years before and long neglect under Edward and Mary had left her so rotten that she had already been condemned once before Hawkins took her. The fleet sailed from the Catte-water in October 1564 and Hawkins demonstrated his honesty towards Spain by sheltering for five days in Ferrol, in northern Spain itself.

He had to do some fighting to collect his four or five hundred slaves in Guinea, and on reaching the Spanish Main found that the colonies had been told not to trade with him. But they needed his slaves, and at port after port the pretext was that they traded with him under threat of violence. On his way home, Hawkins called at the first French colony in America, in Florida. He found the colonists close to starvation and they would have been well advised to accept his offer of a passage home, for, a year later, the Spaniards massacred them all. Hawkins reached Padstow in September 1565, with the *Jesus* in such bad shape that she could not sail round to Plymouth until the following spring. But Hawkins showed a profit of sixty per cent and the Queen gave him a coat of arms with a bound slave as the crest. There was no shame then in slaving.

JOHN SPARKE

Among Hawkins's officers on that voyage was Anthony Parkhurst, who later moved into the Newfoundland trade and, in 1578, was arguing that England should found a settlement there to support the fisheries. Another was John Sparke, whose father had moved from Cheshire to Plympton, and who wrote a graphic account[6] of the voyage. He tells us that an officer was killed at the very start of the voyage, by a falling pulley in Plymouth Sound, and records the renowned order that John Hawkins made to his fleet off Ferrol; 'Serve God daily, love one another, preserve your victuals, beware of fire, and keep good company.'

John Sparke is the first Englishman to mention either the potato or tobacco. Of their first watering-point in the Spanish Main, he says:

> Certain Indians . . . came down to us presenting mill and cakes of bread, which they made of a kind of corn called maise . . . also they brought down to us which we bought for beads, pewter whistles, glasses, knives, and other trifles; hens, potatoes and pines (pineapples?) These potatoes be the most

delicate roots that may be eaten, and do far exceed their parsnips or carrots.

So here, in the very dawn of English exploration, is the traditional picture of bartering on the beach with the naked Indians 'tawny like an olive'. It was not until they were at the French settlement that Sparke saw tobacco for the first time.

> The Floridians when they travel have a kind of herb dried, which with a cane, and an earthen cup in the end, with fire, and the dried herbs put together do suck through the cane the smoke thereof, which smoke satisfieth their hunger, and therewith they live four or five days without meat or drink, and this all the Frenchmen used for this purpose; yet they do hold opinion withall, that it causeth water and fleme to void from their stomachs.

What stories for a boy to bring back to Plymouth. 'The commodities of this land are more than are yet known to any man . . . gold and silver they want not. . . .' He told, too, of a Frenchman who traded a hatchet for two pounds of gold.

After this western voyage, John Sparke seems to have moved into the Russian trade. For most of the century England had been searching for passages to Cathay north-west round America and north-east round Europe, and there were many links between these men and the western adventurers. When the company of Merchant Adventurers was formed in 1555 to develop the trade with Russia—which had been opened, almost as a sideline, through Archangel—Sebastian Cabot, son of the Newfoundland man, became the first governor. The Earl of Bedford was one of the adventurers, and among the names of the first 'assistants' appear those of John Eliot and John Sparke, both Plymouth names.

In 1566, Sparke made his way down to Novgorod, south of Leningrad, in an effort to open up the Baltic trade which the Danes and Swedes were denying to us. Two years later, because he knew Spanish (Hawkins and many of his officers knew the language), he was chosen for a journey from Archangel down the Volga to the Caspian Sea, and thence to Persia in an effort to

break the Portuguese barrier at the mouth of the Persian Gulf
which was closing this route to India. He reached so far south,
bartering Devon woollens for spices, that a companion could
write 'Babylon is from hence fifteen days journey' but it was
hard going. 'Better is it . . . to continue a beggar in England
during life, than to remain a rich merchant seven years in this
country'. Sparke turned back, to be in Moscow when the Tartars
burnt the city in 1571. He was one of three Englishmen to
escape : thirty perished in the fire. After that Sparke came home,
to settle in Plymouth as a merchant and a town councillor. He
may have continued as a local agent for the Muscovy Company,
for they loaded wax, tallow, cables and flax at Archangel for
Lisbon and Spain, and these cargoes may well have been transhipped in Plymouth.

FIGHTING BEGINS

Hawkins kept plugging away at his Atlantic dreams. Of three
ships that sailed (not very successfully) for Guinea in 1566, the
leader was the *Castle of Comfort*, jointly owned by Hawkins
and Richard Grenville. A squadron of four ships was also sent
out by Hawkins under the command of a relative, John Lovell.
Another member of this expedition was Hawkins's cousin, young
Francis Drake. After the 1549 rebellion, his father had gone to
the Medway as chaplain to the fleet, and become vicar of Up-
church there. Around the mudflats and in the tides of the
Thames estuary young Drake had learnt to be a seaman and,
by legend, had been so good a mate that his first master left him
a small coaster. True or not, he was back in Plymouth in 1566,
about twenty-three years old, and sailing in his cousin's ship.
He was already a man of determined ideas for long afterwards
a Welshman, under the pressure of the Inquisition, confessed that
during this voyage Francis Drake had made him a heretic. The
expedition made the usual round trip, Guinea and the Caribbean,
but with no success and Hawkins never again employed Lovell.
Two other captains, Thomas Hampton and James Ranse, together

with Drake, were transferred to a new expedition which Hawkins was already gathering when they returned.

It was an expedition for which John Hawkins had made careful preparations, dining with the Spanish ambassador in London, offering to fight the Turks in the Mediterranean for King Philip, and assuring the ambassador that neither he nor his ships would go to the Indies that year. There was even a story about a fabulous goldmine in Africa, and two Portuguese renegades joined the fleet in Plymouth as pilots. There were four Plymouth ships and two Queen's vessels, the *Jesus of Lubeck* again, and the *Minion*. The *Minion* was only half the size of the *Jesus* but just as rotten; she had been built in 1536.

What Hawkins was really planning is unknown, but whatever it was, Spain was not trusting him. In August 1567, seven ships from the Spanish Netherlands came bowling into the Sound and headed straight for the Cattewater. They made no salute: neither their Spanish flags nor their topsails were dipped. Fearing an attack, Hawkins opened fire from *Jesus* and *Minion* right there in the Cattewater. He 'commanded his gunner to shoot at the flag of the admiral which, notwithstanding, they persevered arrogantly to keep displayed, whereupon the gunner at the next shot raked the admiral through and through.'

The Flemings then went about sharply, and sailed out of the Cattewater to anchor under St Nicholas's Island. The admiral sent protests to the Mayor of Plymouth and was referred to Hawkins, who received him on the quarter-deck of the *Jesus* with an armed guard. Hawkins said bluntly that he was the general of the Queen's ships in the Cattewater and must enforce the respect that was her due. He mollified the Dutchman with presents of beer and poultry, but the squadron remained in the port until the end of September; watching Hawkins, protesting to the Spanish ambassador, and eventually securing a diplomatic reprimand from the Queen to John Hawkins.

Altogether, it was a worrying autumn for Hawkins. A Spanish ship came into the Cattewater with Flemish prisoners aboard, and when some masked men set the prisoners free, the Dutch admiral accused Hawkins of the deed. Hawkins's retort was that it had probably been done by the admiral's own Flemish sailors. Then his Portuguese pilots escaped in a ship to Spain. The Queen again censured Hawkins, but eventually agreed that he should make the usual Africa-West Indies voyage. So, after a service in St Andrew's Church attended by the 400 men of his crews and all his officers, Hawkins sailed at last, on 2 October, the customary time of year for these Guineamen.

A gale scattered the ships and nearly sank the *Jesus*. There was fighting on the Guinea coast, and more trouble when they eventually arrived in the Caribbean with 500 slaves. Real force had to be used, and trade was unsatisfactory. Then a hurricane battered the ships, the old *Jesus* needed repairs, and all the ships wanted food and water for the voyage home. Hawkins put into San Juan de Ulloa, the outport of Mexico city and the terminal point of the *flota*, the fleet that each year took the treasure home to Spain. The *flota* was not due for a fortnight, by which time Hawkins hoped to be away again. It arrived the next morning.

Hawkins was so positioned that he could have denied the *flota* entry. But he had been in trouble the year before for shooting at the Spanish flag in Plymouth and here he was in a Spanish port claiming to be serving the King of Spain. He decided to make terms with the *flota*, and offered to let the Spanish ships in if they would allow him to complete his repairs and leave. A new Viceroy was in the *flota*; he agreed that Hawkins had been trading honestly in the Indies, and accepted his bargain. But once inside, the Spanish attacked the English.

Only John Hawkins in the *Minion*, and young Drake, who had been given command of the little *Judith* during the voyage, brought their ships out. Drake reached Plymouth in January 1569. Hawkins limped into Mount's Bay at the end of that month. William Hawkins had to send a fresh crew down from Plymouth to sail the *Minion*, her own men could go no further. Of 400 men who sailed from Plymouth in October 1567, only

70 came home again. Apart from the lost ships, £3,100 in treasure had been left behind in San Juan.

Robert Barrett of Saltash, a cousin of Drake's, had been Hawkin's flag-captain in the *Jesus*, a man who had been entrusted with all the dangerous jobs, who might well have become the greatest sea captain of the age. With the other prisoners, he was shipped back to Spain and the Inquisition. He was burned at the stake in the market place of Seville. Some of his companions rotted and died in prison there. Six were sent to the galleys, from which Job Hortop escaped after twenty years to come home to his native Plymouth. Paul Horsewell, the eleven-year-old son of John Hawkins's sister[7], was kept in Mexico more or less as a house slave, settled there and raised a family.

About a hundred men who had been set ashore on the north American seaboard, rather than face the voyage home in the *Minion*, were nearly all captured. Anthony Goddard, their leader, was set free in 1571 and got home to Plymouth; three men apparently walked the length of North America to be picked up by a French ship off Cape Breton. Miles Phillips, a boy, escaped to England in 1583. Many who were taken, either at San Juan or from Goddard's party, went to the stake. The Inquisition was more merciful in Mexico than in Seville; these men were strangled first. Others ended in the galleys. The sentences are in the Spanish records: John Moon of Looe, 26, seaman, 200 lashes and six years in the galleys; John Williams of Cornwall, 28, 200 lashes and eight years in the galleys; Robert Plinton of Plymouth, 30, 200 lashes and eight years in the galleys. As the report leaked home to Plymouth, so the bitterness grew. San Juan de Ulloa was the turning point; it was war from thenceforward.

THE PROTESTANT FLEET

Times had indeed changed while John Hawkins was away on that 'troublesome voyage'. The Prince of Orange had launched a Protestant rebellion against Spain in the Netherlands. Mary,

Queen of Scots, had fled to England and was a prisoner, but still a threat to the English throne as a Catholic alternative to Elizabeth. The Duke of Alva was leading a Spanish army in the Netherlands, and a squadron laden with treasure to pay his soldiers had been dispatched from Spain.

Huguenot privateers from La Rochelle chased these treasure ships into Fowey, Plymouth and Southampton, in the autumn of 1568. William Hawkins, who was then mayor of Plymouth, had a ship sailing with the Huguenot privateers under licence from the Prince of Condé, their leader; while another privateer was Henry Champernowne of Modbury, nephew of Sir Arthur Champernowne of Dartington, Vice-Admiral of Devon. The ship that came into Plymouth Sound anchored off Saltash, as far from the privateers waiting in the Channel as she could get, and her captain was persuaded to unload her cargo for greater safety. William Hawkins and Sir Arthur Champernowne supervised the unloading, and sixty-four cases of silver coins were taken to Plymouth Guildhall for safe keeping.

Spain accused the English of seizing her treasure ships, and retaliated by seizing all English ships and goods in the Low Countries. Elizabeth ordered the seizure of all Spanish ships in her harbours. William Hawkins heard that his brother had been killed in Mexico, and sent anxious inquiries to London. Elizabeth, discovering that the money for the Spanish troops had actually been borrowed by Spain from Genoese bankers, treated with them and had the loan transferred to herself. The day after John Hawkins crept into Mount's Bay, Sir Arthur Champernowne set off for the Tower of London with the treasure from Plymouth Guildhall, riding away up Lipson Hill with an escort of fifty horses, fifty foot soldiers and artillery.

Denying Alva his pay-chests was a major victory for the Protestant fleet in the Channel. It was becoming a religious battleground with the Huguenots in rebellion against the Catholic monarchs of France, the Calvinist Dutch fighting the overlordship of Spain in the Low Countries, and Protestant England on their side yet not wishing openly to antagonise France or Spain. Elizabeth was very conscious that they could in turn organise religious rebellion against her.

When that Spanish treasure ship was chased into Plymouth there were believed to be fifty Huguenot privateers in the Channel, thirty of them English. William Hawkins had the biggest stake in the fleet; he was virtually the commander-in-chief and Plymouth the main base of their operations. Helping the French Protestants had an honourable background; Devon men had helped to defend Le Havre in the first French war of religion, Humphrey Gilbert, of Dartmouth, had been wounded there, the twin brothers, Nicholas and Andrew Tremayne of Collacombe, near Tavistock, killed.

Four young cousins who had sought adventure by helping defend Vienna when the Turks overran Europe—Richard Grenville, Henry Champernowne of Modbury, Philip Budockshide of St Budeaux and his brother-in-law, William Gorges, from Somerset—now joined forces with William Hawkins. The Budocksides were coming up in the world. Apart from marrying Sir Arthur Champernowne's sister, Roger Budockside had rebuilt his house at Budshead early in 1560, and largely rebuilt (or at least provided the land) for the re-building of St Budeaux parish church on its present site. Perhaps the old church with its tower and three bells was too near his manor house, or he disliked the parishioners invading his privacy. Some of the stones of the old church seem to have been used in the new; it was planned for the new prayer-book with no chancel and no doubt the altar was well out in the nave. Roger's son Philip became his uncle's partner in the *New Bark*.

Philip Budockshide held letters of marque from the Prince of Condé. In 1569, the privateers chased a squadron of Flemish ships into Plymouth Sound. They were sailing under the Spanish flag and carrying goods from Morocco; sugar, molasses, and ostrich feathers. 'Barbary hulks', the records call them. Flying the Queen's flag Philip Budockshide sailed out to tell them that there was a general stay of shipping, that the Queen's ships were outside and they could not escape. He placed four men aboard each and brought them up off Saltash. That night his men descended upon them and stripped them; three he actually sailed right over to La Rochelle. Richard Grenville was in the business, too, and in the late 1560s (after he had sold his grandmother's land at Compton) he shared the *Castle of Comfort* with William Hawkins. It was a ship that managed to get into more scrapes and more Admiralty Court wrangles than any of the western privateers.

Another name now turned up, one that was later to stand in the first rank of Elizabethans; Martin Frobisher. An orphan from Yorkshire, he had first gone to sea with Wyndham when that partner of old William Hawkins had re-opened the Guinea trade in 1540. By 1563, Frobisher was in Plymouth, a Hawkins captain. That year he brought in five Frenchmen; the next year he took a ship which was carrying tapestry for King Philip himself, and that landed him in Launceston gaol. But he married a Launceston girl, and thereafter was as much West Countryman as Yorkshireman. He was privateering in the *Mary Flower* in 1565, and at sea under a Huguenot commission the next years. In 1569, he held the Prince of Orange's commission, but again had a spell in prison, which does not appear to have harmed his career as, by 1572, he was in the Queen's service in Irish waters.

The State papers are full of the screams of those who suffered from these marauders. In November 1568 the 'Rochellers' brought sixteen French prizes into Plymouth to sell their cargoes. In December, the *Marseilles*, obviously a Frenchman, was stripped in the harbour, and in January 1569 certain English pirates brought three Flemish and one Spanish vessel into Plymouth, divided their rich cargoes, and sold them. The Spanish ambassador complained that the marauders in the haven of Plymouth were being favoured by friendship at the Court. In March another Plymouth pirate with a crew of 200 took a Flemish ship into the Cattewater, stripped it, and put the crew ashore on the Barbican. They were left to beg at the door of St Andrew's, and would have starved had not a countryman living in the town kept them for several days. One of the men heard an Englishman say what a fine ship the *Brielle* would make for Admiral Hawkins.

John Granger plundered the *Pelican of Normandy* in the Cattewater, and three of the crew were slain. Bernard Grave of St Malo was imprisoned in his own ship by a Plymouth pirate and William Hawkins, who was ordered to rescue him, kept the ship for himself. They were pirates to Spain, privateers to the Huguenots, and very welcome in the eyes of the Queen. Plymouth was fighting her war for her.

In 1569, the Prince of Orange brought the Catholic Flemings and the Calvinist Dutch together to fight the Spanish, and began issuing letters of marque to his own people and to the English. When driven out of the Low Countries, these Dutch Sea Beggars made Dover their base. There was another Huguenot force operating from the Solent under Pourtault de Latour; he was killed in the spring of 1569 and Jacques de Sores, who had been in command of a Hawkins ship, took over the Solent leadership. The three Protestant squadrons became international, each a mixture of English, French and Dutch in ownership, leadership, and crewing. Plymouth must have been a more polygot port than ever, and with so many Dutchmen in harbour (and there had been Dutch residents since 1436) it is no wonder that Plymouth became the traditional English home of gin.

No wonder either that Plymouth needed more quay space. In 1572, says the Black Book, 'the kaye on southesyde, whereof the southe ende adjoneth to the Barbygan ynderneath the Castell, was Builded by the towne vnder full sea marke, and Contayneth in lengethe one hundred and Thurtie Foot and in Bredthe fourtie and fower foot'. It is still there, although it has doubled in length.

This was the far-from-peaceful England to which the men of San Juan de Ullua returned. For them there was little peace either side of the lines now. Drake, for instance, was packed straight off to London to tell his story, and that spring of 1569 was probably an officer in a naval squadron, escorting a convoy of English ships past the Spanish Netherlands to a new trading point in Europe, Hamburg. He was back that summer and married Mary Newman in the new church at St Budeaux. Legend makes her a Saltash girl, but there are many Newmans in the St Budeaux registers and one would expect a girl to marry in her own parish church.

The Newmans had strong links with the sea; a Harry Newman had served in the San Juan de Ulloa voyage, and in 1560 Mary's elder sister, Margaret, had married a John Bodenham whose son, Jonas, later became Drake's right-hand man. Probably John Bodenham, now Francis Drake's brother-in-law, was related to the Roger Bodenham who called at Plymouth in 1550 on a Levant voyage. Marrying and settling in Seville, he traded from there to Barbary and made one voyage to Mexico, and was still living in San Lucar in 1580. It gave Drake an odd but close link with those Anglo-Spanish merchants, and a valuable source of information.

While Drake was getting married, John Hawkins seems to have been leading an English fleet to restock La Rochelle and bring home all the Huguenot plunder they could not sell in France. Among it, there were even French church bells, whose bronze may well have gone into the new guns for the defence of Plymouth. Sixty ships made up the convoy, of which eight were owned by William Hawkins. Later that year, Henry Champernowne and Philip Budockside took a company of local gentlemen down to aid the 'Rochellers', and that jaunt gave a first taste of war to another Devon youngster, Walter Ralegh. Budockside never came home. Philip's father, Roger, died four years later and the St Budeaux estates passed to William Gorges.

In 1569 there were rumours in Spain that one or both of the Hawkins were at sea, and in the following year John Hawkins was putting up to the Council in London a plan to capture the Spanish *flota* on its way home from San Juan de Ulloa. It would have been the perfect revenge but he wanted Royal ships with him to avenge the insult of 1568 to the Queen's ships. He had his own strong fleet at Plymouth and a Spanish spy in Plymouth reported its numbers, strength and arms in detail to the Spanish ambassador. All told, it amounted to 3,170 tons, 1,585 men, and 406 guns.

But the Queen preferred to keep all her ships in home waters; there were too many threats from Scotland and Alva. John Hawkins heard news of some of his men being in prison in Seville, and set to work to secure their relase. He began to bargain with the Spanish ambassador, and even entered into a plot with him whereby, in return for his men, he would aid an English rising in favour of Mary, Queen of Scots. By early 1571 he was offering to turn his Plymouth fleet over to Alva, and leave the Channel mouth open to invasion. His intermediary was George Fitzwilliam. He had been captured at San Juan; now he had won his release and through the Hawkins plot—he was even professing to be a secret Catholic—he gained the release of a score or so of Hawkins' men.

John Hawkins had won his main objective; at the same time he had wormed himself into the full Spanish plan and was telling Burghley all about it. The leader of the English plotters, the Earl of Norfolk, was arrested and executed, but the Spanish still did not discover John Hawkins's double game. Even when the Spanish ambassador was told he was *persona non grata* and sent packing, Hawkins went with him to the coast. It is a strange business for a Plymouth MP, as John was in 1571, to be engaged in—real cloak and dagger, complete with invisible ink and all the trimmings.

After this Ridolfi plot something had to be done to smooth relations with Spain, superficially at any rate, and to mollify France. Both were complaining bitterly about the Channel privateers. So, in 1572, John Hawkins was commanded, together with William Winter, an officer of the Navy Board, to order out all the privateers from the harbours of the eastern Channel, and to warn the English of those ports to give them no further aid. It seems a strange order to give to a man whose brother was the privateer admiral of the other half of the Channel. The Sea Beggars made no argument. The Solent squadron sailed up to join the Dover force, and the two squadrons sailed east to capture Brill, on the Dutch coast itself. A little later they took Flushing, and were never turned out. Their war against Spain was now being run from their home country. Did John Hawkins just order them out, or did he, on the Queen's behalf, plan just this very move with the Dutch commanders? After all, Sir Humphrey Gilbert, who had sat with John Hawkins as Members of Parliament for Plymouth in 1571, was in the Low Countries in 1573, fighting with the Dutch Protestants against the French and Spanish Catholics.

The French massacre of the Huguenots on St Bartholomew's Day 1572 cut their strength to nearly nothing. They were reduced to La Rochelle, and a Plymouth expedition under Henry Champernowne failed to help them. Nevertheless, they hung on, and patched up a kind of peace with the Catholics. Elizabeth made a second gesture of friendship towards France and Spain, and her navy cleared the Channel of such privateers as were left. The *Castle of Comfort* stayed in the privateering business with a French captain, which brought both William Hawkins and Richard Grenville into trouble. William and John went on buying cargoes in Plymouth from privateers, and lost ships about their legitimate business to privateers elsewhere. But privateering in the Channel was fading out as a respectable business. The Hawkins ships were in a more legitimate trade, reaching even down to Genoa, in Italy. John continued as MP for Plymouth and was more and more concerned in national affairs, finally succeeding his father-in-law as Treasurer of the Navy in 1577. His fellow MP for the town was Edmund Tremayne, of Collacombe, whose younger brothers had died at Le Havre. Tremayne eventually became Clerk of the Privy Council, an important link at Court. William remained in Plymouth, mayor in 1578 and again ten years later. The two brothers ran the town mills at Millbay and built a new weigh-house.

But the war with Spain was not over. The privateering moved away from the Channel to the Atlantic, and Plymouth continued to be its base. The Hawkins brothers were still deeply involved, but the leadership passed to their young cousin, Francis Drake.

CHAPTER SEVEN

WAR WITH SPAIN

NEITHER Plymouth nor the Hawkins brothers forgot San Juan de Ulloa. Nor did young Francis Drake. He had seen John Hawkins's attempts at peaceful trade come to naught on the Spanish Main, and was resolved to try different ideas. Late in 1570 he sailed in a Hawkins ship, the little 25-ton *Swan*, probably under Huguenot letters of marque. It was a voyage of reconnaisance, on which only one or two merchantmen were captured to feed his men and pay his way.

Drake wanted more than commerce-raiding. His goal was the main treasure route. The treasure came up from Lima, the capital of Peru, through a peaceful Pacific where only Spanish ships sailed, was transferred by land across the narrow Isthmus of Panama and, heavily guarded, was shipped again from Nombre de Dios for Spain. In that winter of 1570-71 Drake established a secret base in the Gulf of Darien, between Panama and South America proper, where he buried some stores and made friends with the Cimaroons—escaped Negro slaves who lived in their thousands in the jungle of Panama—before returning home.

At Whitsun 1572, he sailed again in a Hawkins ship, the 72-ton *Pasco*, with his younger brother, John, in command of the *Swan*. Another brother, Joseph, was with them. Only one man, John Oxenham of Plymouth, was over thirty. At his Darien base he found pinned to a tree a note from another Plymouth captain, John Garrett, warning him that the Spanish knew of his base. Drake fortified it, and stayed on. A little later, Captain James Ranse of Plymouth, a friend of earlier voyages, arrived and agreed to join him. They nearly captured Nombre de Dios itself, but such a raid was too much for Ranse, and he went home.

Drake stayed on in a new base, raiding towns and ships. John Drake died while attacking a ship, Joseph Drake of a fever. When the plate fleet came in to Nombre de Dios, Drake marched inland to try and intercept the mule train. A drunken seaman ruined the ambush but, from a tree on a high ridge, a Cimaroon guide showed Drake the Pacific. He was the first Englishman to gaze upon that ocean, and he prayed to God 'to give him life and leave to sail once in an English ship in that sea'.

With a Huguenot ship, he made another raid on a mule train carrying the Peru treasure, and brought it off after hairbreadth escapes. But his ships by then were so rotten that he first had to capture two Spanish craft to bring him and his treasure home. When these two strange craft reached Plymouth it was Sunday morning, 9 August 1573. As word went round, the congregation ran out of St Andrew's to welcome him, leaving the parson preaching to an empty church. Only thirty men of the seventy-four who had sailed came home, but they brought with them £20,000 of gold and silver. An equal share had gone to France; Spain, in modern values, was a million pounds the poorer.

But the Queen was looking for peace with Spain, and though privateers followed Drake he, himself, had to disappear. Two years later he is recorded as serving the Earl of Essex in Ireland, and he may have been running convoys from Plymouth to Ireland all that time. Bigger projects were under discussion in Devon. Sir Richard Grenville, who was busy turning Buckland Abbey into the mansion that it is today, was proposing to round South America, find the unknown land believed to exist in the south Pacific, colonise it (the first English talk of colonisation), and return round the north of America. William Hawkins, Piers Edgcumbe, Grenville's half-brother Alexander Arundell of Clifton, and several cousins were in the scheme. But the Queen would not approve, fearing that the plan might upset Spain. At the same time, Sir Humphrey Gilbert had a project to open the north-west passage, and as this would not upset Spain, Martin Frobisher was sent off in command in 1576. He brought home lumps of ore from the islands between Greenland and Canada, and as everyone thought they contained gold there was a rush to invest money in his second voyage. For this, in 1578, he had fifteen ships, and embarked forty-one miners at Plymouth. He got as far as Hudson Strait but found no north-west passage, and though he came home loaded with ore, there was no gold in it. Interest in the north-west passage slumped, and Frobisher's stock with it.

AROUND THE WORLD

Drake had come back from Ireland in 1576 and proposed a voyage very similar to the one that Grenville had not been allowed to make. He formed a syndicate of Court people, unlike Grenville's West Country syndicate, and as Spain was becoming more menacing, the Queen was now less averse to upsetting her.

Drake went down to Plymouth to prepare for his voyage and there found his old lieutenant, John Oxenham, planning a voyage of his own. Later that year, Oxenham sailed for Panama and, after hiding his ship, crossed the isthmus he had explored with Drake, built a pinnace, and became the first English sea captain to sail the Pacific. The unarmed Spanish ships were easy prey, and Oxenham began to hide hoards of silver. But he made no hurry to get away. Had he, perhaps, arranged to wait for Drake, and was this a part of the plans they had made in Plymouth?

Life in the town was much as usual. The English had given up the privateering business but the *Castle of Comfort* had brought a Breton prize into Cawsand Bay the year before and the Hawkins family were 'ransoming' Huguenot prizes. London merchants were financing Guinea voyages out of Plymouth. Ships were still sailing to the Caribbean, eight Hawkins vessels and half a dozen others in 1575. In 1576, John Horseley, from Dorset, brought a little ship into Plymouth laden deep with silver and gold from Darien. Apart from Oxenham, a dozen Caribbean voyagers had left Plymouth in 1576.

Drake did not get away until November 1577 and, officially, he was going to trade with the Turks at Alexandria. He had five ships[1] and 160 men. Thomas Moon, who had been his ship's carpenter in 1572, was in command of a pinnace, and others with him included Drake's brother, Thomas; a young cousin, John Drake from Tavistock; his nephew William Hawkins (son of the second William) and a John Hawkins, of uncertain relationship. It was a rough autumn, and within a few days the ships were back in the Cattewater, with the *Pelican*, the flagship, dismasted. They were away again on 12 December. Then there was silence.

Sir Humphrey Gilbert sailed the next November with a bigger squadron but was back in February, having been mauled by a Spanish fleet. Captain Sharpham and Mr Fortescue sailed about the same time with five large ships, planning a settlement on the coast of Brazil, but it came to nothing. Then, in June 1579, one of Drake's captains, William Winter, struggled into Ilfracombe.[2] Drake had scrapped two of his smaller ships, lost another in a storm, and executed an officer, Thomas Doughty, for mutiny. Winter's own men had mutinied in the Straits of Magellan, because they had not signed for such a voyage, and he had been forced to turn back. News began to leak through Seville to Plymouth that Drake was on the Pacific coast of South America, marauding at will. There were fears that, in his fury, Philip might declare war on England, but he was too busy planning to take over Portugal, which he did in 1580.

Then in October of that year some fishermen off Rame Head were hailed by a homeward-bound ship: 'Is the Queen alive?' Drake was back.

He anchored under Drake's Island and remained there while messengers rode to London to tell the Queen of his return. Drake had raided the major Pacific ports of Spanish America, from Valparaiso to Callao, without firing a shot, and had stripped treasure ships until his own craft (now renamed the *Golden Hind* in honour of the crest of his patron, Sir Christopher Hatton) could hold no more. He had heard of the capture of John Oxenham and had pleaded for his release in a message to the Viceroy of Peru (it was in vain, for Oxenham and his officers were hanged in Lima a year later). He had followed the coast of North America[3] until cold and fog had forced him to give up hope of the north-west passage, and come home through the East Indies. There he had made a treaty with a sultan who had fallen out with the Portuguese, and found room for six tons of spices and a drinking-cup made of a coconut shell which, mounted in silver, is now in the wardroom of H.M.S. *Drake* at Devonport. He had exposed Spain's weak flank, opened a door to the Indies, had sailed round the world. Magellan had also done this but he had died on the voyage, whereas Drake was the first captain, and the first Englishman, to make the circumnavigation.

While he waited under Drake's Island for the Queen's reaction, his wife, Mary, rowed out to him with the Mayor. No doubt William Hawkins went out as well, but Plymouth was an unhealthy town that autumn. The plague had killed 600 people and even mayor-choosing was done on the windy heights of Cattedown for health's sake.

The messenger to London returned with instructions that Drake was to put his treasure into Trematon Castle (his own share he put in the care of an old friend, Christopher Harris of Radford, in the old house at the head of Hooe Lake). He was then to go to London to report to Her Majesty in person. Prudently, he loaded six packhorses with gold and jewels, and the Queen talked to him in private audience for six hours. How much treasure he brought home is unknown, estimates vary between returns of £14 to £47 for every pound his backers invested, and from a whole year's revenue of the Crown to £2½ million of modern money. Drake himself was rich beyond dreams, the most famous seaman of England, and henceforth the Queen's chief adviser on maritime matters. He sailed the *Golden Hind* round to Deptford where

Elizabeth knighted him on his own quarter-deck. All London trooped to see his ship and she was hauled out near Deptford as a showpiece, as we have since kept *Victory* at Portsmouth, until she rotted away on the beach.[4] Pieces of furniture made from her timbers were afterwards guarded as precious relics.

In Plymouth, as throughout the country, Drake was a national hero. His town house[5] was at the top of Looe Street, just across the road from the Guildhall, in the very heart of the town. Most townsmen must have passed his door daily, and when in the town he must have been as familiar a figure as anyone. For a time he was the tenant of Thorn Park, the long-vanished manor house whose site is now covered by Hyde Park School. Richard Grenville, conscious of an ancestry dating back to the Conqueror and of having propounded the very plan Drake had carried out, could not bear to live in the shadow of this upstart and flung off back to Bideford. He sold Buckland Abbey, which he had just finished converting into the great house it still is, to Drake's friend, Harris, and John Hele, a rising young lawyer, for £3,400. He could hardly have known they were acting for Drake, but it now became his country house.

In 1581, Plymouth elected Sir Francis as mayor. He put the councillors into red cloaks like the aldermen, and set up a compass on the Hoe. But national affairs largely occupied him, and with Leicester, Burghley, Walsingham and Hatton, he set up a syndicate to develop his trade links with the East Indies. Ships were assembled at Plymouth under the command of Edward Fenton, John Hawkins's brother-in-law. Young William Hawkins was second-in-command and another boy-veteran of the circumnavigation, John Drake, commanded a small ship called the *Francis*. Their orders were to reach the Moluccas by way of the Cape of Good Hope but when they were in the south Atlantic young Hawkins and Drake persuaded Fenton to go the other way, only to find that a strong Spanish force was guarding the Straits of Magellan. Spain was determined not to be caught a second time. The expedition broke up and came home,[6] with Hawkins in irons. John Drake decided to stay in South America, and joined other Englishmen who were already living beside the River Plate.

COLONISATION

Francis Drake, the Hawkinses, and the sea captains of Plymouth, had all been brought up to sea-faring, trading and fighting. But the gentlemen of Devon, with their university educations and their experience of colonisation in Ireland, saw further ahead. To them, it seemed better to stake a claim in America rather than merely to steal the fruits of Spanish labours. Grenville's 1576 project had talked of colonising, and in 1578 his cousin, Humphrey Gilbert, obtained letters patent from the Queen to take possession of lands not 'possessed of any Christian prince . . . and to inhabit or remain there.'

He made his first attempt, in Florida, that same year. It failed, but one of his captains was his half-brother, Walter Ralegh, who had to do some hard fighting before he got back. Gilbert sent another ship across in 1579, but the main attempt did not take place until 1582, when five ships and 260 men sailed from Cawsand Bay, landed at St John, Newfoundland, and claimed it for the Queen. They then turned south but on the uncharted coast of America the flagship was lost with a hundred men and all the stores. There was no alternative but to sail for home, with Gilbert in the smallest ship of all, the ten-ton *Squirrel*. He would not shift to a larger vessel : 'We are as near to heaven by sea as by land,' he shouted across the waters, and was last seen, before *Squirrel* foundered in an Atlantic gale, calmly sitting on deck reading a book.

His half-brother, Ralegh, inherited his colonising charter and brought in his cousin, Sir Richard Grenville. They sent out two survey ships in 1584 under Captain Philip Amadas of Plymouth (a Hawkins cousin) and Arthur Barlow. On their return, Ralegh named the country they had surveyed Virginia, in the Queen's honour (he was her favourite at the time), and was knighted in reward.

The following year Grenville—since the Queen would not be parted from Ralegh—took out from Plymouth the first party of Englishmen to settle in America. They set up a colony at Roanoke, with Philip Amadas as second-in-command. On the way home, Grenville captured a Spanish ship which, he told Walsingham, contained only sugar and ginger, forgetting to mention the hides, cochineal, gold, silver and 600,000 ducats which were also in her hold. A contemporary letter said the ship was 'worth a million' and Ralegh hastened to Plymouth to help Grenville keep an eye on it.

Drake's wife, Mary, died in January 1582 and she was buried in St Budeaux churchyard. Childless, she had had only a year as Lady Drake and mistress of Buckland Abbey; how much of her twelve years of married life, while her husband ranged the world or was busy at Court, did she spend with her mother at the Newman home at St Budeaux?

Drake, that year, was urging a new plan which the Queen approved but would not let him carry out. Like Ralegh, he had to stay close at hand. So, in November 1582, seven ships sailed from Plymouth under William Hawkins with his brother's son Richard, only 22, as second-in-command. The scheme was to win over the Portuguese islands in the Atlantic to Don Antonio, the exiled claimant to the throne of Portugal which Philip had seized. Hawkins went to the Cape Verde islands where Portuguese treachery led to a number of Englishmen being murdered. Hawkins lost heart in the scheme, sailed first to Brazil and then to the Caribbean. He dredged up oysters for their pearls off the island of Margarita, but all the time he was really waiting for the treasure *flota*. No records survive of what happened, but he came home with treasure, hides, and sugar as well as pearls, and that year the flagship of the *flota* was reported at Seville as missing.

The Hawkinses, Ralegh, Drake, and most of the Court, then put their money into another plan to open the East Indian trade but it never materialised. The Duke of Parma was sweeping across the Low Countries, leading a Catholic army intent on crushing Protestantism in Europe. Elizabeth had to help, though she still refused to declare war. John Hawkins proposed that the western men should take letters of marque from Don Antonio. In 1584 the Queen gave Drake her own commission to sail to the West Indies, and then held him back. He spent some of the time getting married again, to Elizabeth Sydenham, daughter of a landed gentleman of Somerset.

DESCENT ON THE INDIES

Philip himself gave Elizabeth the excuse she needed to take action. The Spanish harvest had failed and English merchants were invited to send in grain. Then, when the ports of Spain were filled with English ships, they were seized and their crews flung into prison. The barque *Primrose* escaped from Bilbao and came home with the story. So, in September 1585, Drake took to the sea again, the first time for five years. He sailed from Plymouth Sound, flying his flag in the Royal ship *Bonaventure*, with Frobisher as his vice-admiral in another Royal ship, and accompanied by nineteen private ships. There were old shipmates among their captains, Thomas Drake, Thomas Moon and Richard Hawkins, as well as over 3,000 seamen and soldiers.

A week before they sailed, Don Antonio came into the port. 'The kinge of Portingall arived at Plymouth the 7th Daye of September verye poore & was Driven from his cuntry by the kinge of Spaine ii years before, & was relieved by the Quenes majestie, & was sente for by her majestie to the Corte, where he was Condocted with 50 horses or more.' So the Black Book records, while legend says that he was entertained both by Drake and the Edgcumbes.

Excitement was high as the expedition prepared to set out;

even the Queen's new favourite, Philip Sidney, had ridden down
to Plymouth to join the fleet. The Queen commanded him to
return and told the mayor, John Sparke, to arrest him if he did
not instantly comply.

Drake sailed for Vigo in northern Spain, sacked the town,
and after freeing English ships and crews, watered his fleet and
stocked up with green vegetables. He remained in Vigo for eight
days, and then moved on to the Cape Verde islands and took over
Santiago. Here a ship's boy was murdered and, remembering
the murders of three years before, the town and two others were
burnt to the ground. Drake sailed on for the West Indies and
captured the two chief Spanish cities there, San Domingo and
Cartagena, in brilliant operations. John Sparke sent word from
Plymouth to London that Drake 'runneth through the country
like a conqueror.'

Among the Plymouth men who died was Tom Moon, Drake's
former carpenter and later an officer in the *Golden Hind*. He
had led the boarding party over the rail of the first treasure ship
in Valparaiso harbour, shouting 'Down dog' in Spanish to the
first seaman he met on her deck. He had gone up the beach at
Cartagena before dawn with the first landing party, and had been
killed in the first fight. For fourteen years he had been at Drake's
elbow, reliable, brave, and loyal.

Drake took a ransom from Cartagena as he had from San
Domingo (though not as much as he wanted) and sailed on.
He called at Roanoke where the colonists had come through
their first winter. It had been a hard time, and Grenville was two
months overdue. Drake gave them a choice of supplies or a
passage home. They decided to leave, and when Grenville arrived
a fortnight later he found his first colony deserted. After much
searching for them, he left another fifteen men in their place,
and they were never heard of again. On his way home, Grenville
sacked the Azores, and reached Plymouth to find Drake's stature
greater than ever after his 'descent on the Indies'. King Philip's
financial credit was ruined, and Drake was now a European

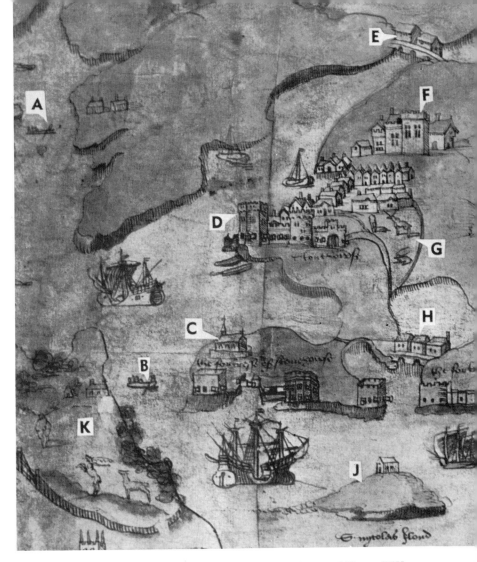

Stonehouse from the map on which the new defences of Henry VIII were shown. A, Saltash ferry; B, Cremyll ferry; C, St Lawrence's chapel; D, manor house; E, Mill bridge; F, Buckland Abbey's house in High Street; G, deer park; H, Sourpool mills; J, Drake's Island; K, Mount Edgcumbe park.

Plymouth from the Henry VIII defence map. A, the Barricades; B, St Katherine's Church; C, the Castle Quadrate; D, Blackfriars; E, St Andrew's Church; F, Greyfriars; G, Market Cross; H, Guildhall; J, Whitefriars. What at first glance is a jumble of houses is in fact a fairly accurate picture map.

figure—*El Draco*. 'Truly,' wrote Burghley, 'Sir Francis Drake is a fearful man to the King of Spain.'

Drake spent the summer of 1586 ferrying reinforcements to the army in Netherlands. Sir Walter Ralegh sent two pinnaces off from Plymouth in June, the *Mary Sparke* and the *Serpent*. They captured the governor of the Straits of Magellan and brought him home prisoner; off the Azores, they tackled a treasure fleet of twenty-four ships, including two 1,000-tonners and, though beaten off, they still had a rich haul of ivory, hides, and brazil wood. Jacob Whiddon, Thomas Drake, and Richard Moone of Saltash were in this dashing little expedition. Their three deeply-laden prizes reached Plymouth six hours ahead of them, and when they themselves came in: 'wee were received with triumphant joy, not onely with great Ordinance then shot off, but with the willing hearts of all the people of the Towne, and of the Countrey thereabouts; and we not sparing our Ordinance (with the powder we had left) to requite and answer them again.'

On July 21 Thomas Candish, a Suffolk gentleman who had been with Grenville when he set up the Roanoke colony, sailed from Plymouth for the South Seas. Three days later, three ships commissioned by the Earl of Cumberland came into the Sound, joined up with some others (including Ralegh's *Dorothy*) and they, too, sailed on 17 August, on Drake's old route, with Robert Withrington in command. They met a lot of trouble in South America, but one odd capture was a Portuguese account of the New World with records of Drake's 1572 raid on Nombre de Dios, Oxenham's forays in the Pacific, and a graphic account through enemy eyes of the efforts the Spanish had made to catch Drake on his circumnavigation. It recorded that, in all, Drake had taken from the coast of Peru 1,390,200 ducats of silver and 150,000 ducats of gold, apart from precious stones and plate.

At Buenos Aires, Withrington heard that John Drake, the young nephew of Drake who had stayed behind there in 1582, had been captured, but was alive and in good health. He had been shipwrecked, and after having been held prisoner by the Indians for a year, had escaped, only to fall into Spanish hands. At first, he kept secret his relationship to the great Sir Francis, but a Portuguese pilot who had met the circumnavigator recognised him. Withrington reached Plymouth in 1587 to tell Drake that his nephew was being sent to the Inquisition at Lima. It is doubtful if Drake ever heard of him again but, in fact, he was set free in 1595, though forbidden to leave Peru. As escape was almost impossible, he probably married, as did other English released prisoners, and settled there. At the end of the last century there was a noble family called Drake del Castillo in Spain who claimed descent from the great admiral.

But while Withrington failed, as Fenton had failed, to get through the Magellan Straits, Thomas Candish succeeded, and made a prosperous voyage, even though it did involve less pluckings and more fighting than Drake's. A Plymouth man, William Stevens, was killed on the Pacific coast. Candish made his major capture off California and came home by way of the South Sea Islands, the Phillipines, the Java Sea and around the Cape of Good Hope.

SINGEING THE BEARD

While these voyages were starting in the summer of 1586 John Hawkins had been cruising the Channel with a fleet in case the Spanish sought revenge for Drake's descent on the Indies. That winter reports began to reach England that, in every port of Spain, the 'enterprise of England' was going forward. The long struggle, the undeclared war, was coming to a head. Philip had resolved to crush England and a mighty fleet was to be his weapon.

Drake was ordered to form a counter-fleet at Plymouth. The Navy contributed the *Elizabeth Bonaventure* (she had been his flagship in 1585), *Lion*, *Dreadnought*, and *Rainbow*. John Hawkins had been in charge of the Navy Board since 1577 and these new ships were the fruits of his experience at sea. They sat lower in the water than those of earlier design, and were better seaboats, being faster to windward and steadier in a sea. Unlike their predecessors, they were not designed to serve as floating battlefields for soldiers but as artillery platforms from which to sink the enemy by gunfire. Hawkins, in fact, had created the battleship, and Drake was the man to demonstrate how they should be used. London merchantmen, Plymouth ships, and Levanters, long used to forcing their way through a hostile Mediterranean, joined him until he had thirty ships.

Drake had clear instructions; he had permission 'to distress the enemy ships within the harbours', to stop the Spanish flotillas from joining up, to halt their supplies, and to intercept the *flota*. But he feared that the Queen might still change her mind as she had before, and he was bursting to be off. '. . . the wind commands me away. Our ship is under sail . . . Haste. From aboard Her Majesty's good ship, the *Elizabeth Bonaventure* this 2nd April, 1587', he wrote from Plymouth.

Hardly had he cleared the Sound when messengers came clattering into the town with new orders for him. He was not to enter forcibly into 'any of the King's ports or harbours . . . or do any act of hostility upon the land'. Hawkins sent a pinnace after Drake with the Queen's new orders but they never caught up with him. The pinnace captured a prize worth £5,000 instead; no doubt Hawkins had privately briefed her captain.

On Wednesday 19 April Drake sailed into Cadiz and smashed the galleys defending the harbour. In one day his new ships ended the age-old ascendancy of galleys over sailing ships in confined waters. He burnt or removed some thirty vessels amounting to 10,000 tons of shipping. He came out on the Friday morning, after having treated a port of Spain like some small West Indian town. Then, anchoring under Cape Sagres, he captured the castle that had been Prince Henry the Navigator's headquarters, and stopped all coastwise shipping, confiscating their stores and burning the staves they were bringing round from the Mediterranean for supply barrels. That did more harm than the Cadiz raid, for when the Armada did sail it had insufficient casks and most of them were of green wood.

Next Drake anchored off the mouth of the Tagus, and when the Marquis of Santa Cruz refused to come out and fight, he ran south to the Azores and captured a carrack homeward bound from the East Indies. She was the *San Felipe*, and her cargo of calico, silk, carpets, taffetas, sarsanets, lawns, indigo, pepper, cinnamon, maize, ebony, saltpetre, and a casket of jewels, fetched £114,000, the richest prize yet taken and the first East Indiaman. 'It taught others' wrote Hakluyt, 'that carracks were no such bugs but that they might be taken. . . .' Her charts and sailing-directions opened up to England the secrets of the East Indies.

Drake brought this treasure ship into Plymouth Sound on 26 June, 1587, and sent her up to Saltash to be unloaded under the care of Sir John Gilbert and Sir Francis Godolphin. All England buzzed with the stories; Drake had singed the King of Spain's beard and reduced his credit in Europe to its lowest ebb. No wonder that two judges of circuit went out of their way 'of pleasor to see the Town and harborough'.

But Drake also had his troubles; in his domineering determined way he had refused to hold conferences of his captains while at sea and when his vice-admiral, William Borough, had protested he had charged him with treason, court-martialled him, sentenced him to death, and brought him into Plymouth a prisoner. Eventually Borough went back to his job at the Admiralty and the argument died away; he was even given a ship again the following year but it never left the Thames.

THE ENGLISH FLEET

It was war now, and Spain was still preparing her fleet. That winter, the Lord High Admiral, Lord Howard of Effingham, was at Chatham with John Hawkins and Frobisher, watching the

Low Countries. Drake was in Plymouth, building up a fleet of thirty ships and, by January, had over 2,000 men under his command, just about the population of Plymouth itself. His orders, once again, were to ravage the Spanish coast, and he worked night and day to fit out his fleet. Then the Queen changed her mind and told Drake to pay off half his men. Nevertheless, he continued equipping his ships and in February heard that the Marquis of Santa Cruz, who had refused his challenge at Lisbon, had died. The Marquis of Medina Sidonia, who had tried to rally the land defences of Cadiz against him, was the reluctant new commander of the Armada.

Grenville was fitting out five ships at Bideford for Virginia, but was now ordered to take them round to join Drake. They arrived in early May, with Grenville's second son, John, in command of one, but Grenville himself went back to Bideford. Drake had been preaching to the Queen the basic naval dictum of seeking out the enemy on his own coast. She was sufficiently impressed to order Lord Howard to leave only a small squadron in the Thames and to sail his fleet round to Plymouth.

At eight o'clock on the morning of 23 May the Lord High Admiral approached Plymouth; eleven great ships of the Navy with eight pinnaces, sixteen great ships of London with four pinnaces, seven ships of the Lord Admiral's and twenty ships from the Channel ports. Drake led his thirty ships out to meet them, sailing three abreast. Howard in *Ark Royal* was flying the Royal Standard and a vice-admiral's pennant; Drake in *Revenge* an admiral's pennant. As the ships came abreast both struck their pennants; Howard sent his vice-admiral's pennant in a pinnace to *Revenge* and the entire fleet came into the Sound with Howard as admiral and Drake flying a vice-admiral's pennant. The office of Lord High Admiral was hereditary; it was only fitting that a great noble should hold the office.

Howard and the biggest navy ships anchored in the Sound, and the rest in the Cattewater. Drake was under St Nicholas's Island. John Hawkins, who for so many years had striven to prepare this fleet, was able to leave his Medway dockyard in June and join the fleet as rear-admiral. His brother William, now over 70, was appropriately enough mayor of Plymouth that year, and Anthony Goddard, who had been captured after San Juan de Ulloa, was treasurer of the town. Richard Hawkins commanded the Queen's ship *Swallow*, and the mayor's son William had the *Griffin*.

Apart from the Admiral, Lord Thomas Howard, the Earl of Cumberland and Lord Sheffield, there were no noblemen afloat. Nor were the country gentry, like Ralegh and Grenville, at sea; their place was with the county militia forces in case the Spanish landed. There are some county names in the fleet, such as that of John Harris and Tristram Gorges in the little *Advice*, John St Leger, Humphrey Sydenham, Ambrose Mannington and Thomas Chichester, but they were either younger sons out for the sport or men like Grenville's son John, and his cousin James Erisey (who had married a Carew of Antony), who followed the sea as a profession.

For this was, essentially, a fleet of professional seamen. The Queen's ships were commanded by sea captains of long experience; Sir William Winter; Edward Fenton, John Hawkins's brother-in-law; Luke Ward, Hawkin's vice-admiral of 1585; Thomas Fenner, Drake's flag captain of 1585; the other Fenner brothers, Robert Crosse, Ralegh's captain Jacob Whiddon; John Davis, a Gilbert man from the Dart with several Arctic voyages to his credit. Frobisher's lieutenant was an Eliot, and Drake's lieutenant was his first wife's nephew, Jonas Bodenham.

In the twenty-four ships listed as 'merchant ships appointed to serve westwards under the charge of Sir Francis Drake' there were many Plymouth names: William Sparke, John Tranton, Thomas Cely, James Founes, John Yonge, John Grisling. Plymouth surnames also crop up in many of the ship's names. There was a general stay upon shipping; no doubt every Plymouth ship and every captain of the port was serving in the fleet; better, if nothing else, to be on the Royal payroll than idle.

There were some famous ships in the fleet. The Lord Admiral's flag was in the *Ark*, built the year before by Walter Ralegh and sold by him to the Queen, and variously known as *Ark Ralegh*, *Ark*, and *Ark Royal*. Lord Cumberland was in the *Elizabeth Bonaventure*, Drake's flagship in the Indies and at Cadiz. Drake had the *Revenge*, one of John Hawkins's best, launched at Deptford in 1577. John Hawkins himself had the *Victory*, and it was typical of the man that he chose not a new ship but an old one that he had rebuilt, to demonstrate his faith that they were as good as any. He was right enough. *Victory* had been launched in 1561, and had been rebuilt as a low, fast galleon in 1586. She was to be rebuilt again in 1610, to serve as flagship both to Blake and Monck, and was wearing an admiral's flag when she finally went aground fighting the Dutch and was burnt by them in 1666. For a wooden battleship, an active life of 105 years is astonishing. Frobisher had the biggest ship of all, the unconverted *Triumph* of 1,100 tons, twice the size of Drake's *Revenge*.

Apart from the Queen's ships, there was also a strong force of London merchantmen, including tough vessels like the famous earl's *Galleon Leicester* and the Levanter *Edward Bonadventure*, which in 1591-93 was to be the first English ship to make the voyage to India and lead to the formation of the East India Company. It is noticeable that the London ships were bigger than the western vessels, indicative of where the centre of trading had moved.

All English ports were required to provide some ships, furnished at their own cost. From the west, Bristol sent four, Bridgwater one, Lyme Regis two, Weymouth two, Exeter and Topsham three, Plymouth two (the *Charity* and the *Little John*), Saltash one (the *John Trelawny* under Thomas Meek, who had been round the world with Drake), Fowey and Looe one.

How did Plymouth manage to feed and water so great a fleet? Howard's first letter to Burghley declared 'there is here the gallantest company of captains, soldiers and mariners that I think were ever seen in England. It were pity that they should lack meat. . . .' In another letter he wrote, 'I know not which way to deal with the mariners to make them rest content with sour beer.' Victualling ships were constantly coming in from other ports to supplement the local efforts.

In his winter fleet Drake had had 2,900 men in Plymouth, and when the other squadrons joined him in May there were 9,500 men. In July, Lord Howard and John Hawkins sent an estimate of costs to Burghley. Of £6,000 already sent, £5,500 had been spent, and another £19,570 was needed at Plymouth. In September, James Quarles, the chief victualling officer, set out his accounts for 300 days, 1 December 1587 to 20 September 1588. Victualling and ship's stores alone, without pay, came to £21,155. A significant item was 'victualling on shore at Plymouth, at 6d per diem, £2,222 6s 0d. This must have paid for the 1,000 soldiers that were in the fleet, and arithmetic suggests that apart from the 9,500 seamen, the 2,000 inhabitants of Plymouth had these 1,000 soldiers billeted on them for three months.

It was a stormy summer, and it was just as well that it was not fine and hot. The big navy ship *Elizabeth Jonas* came in with Howard in May, and 200 of her crew of 500 were dead within a month. Lord Howard had the survivors put ashore, the ballast taken out, and the whole ship fumigated with fires of wet broom. He brought the crew up to full strength with new men, 'very tall and able as ever I saw' but by 10 August, after the Channel fighting, the infection had broken out again and Lord Howard had to send her into reserve at Chatham. The fighting was not such as to cause heavy casualties but, by the end of the summer, there were few ships that had not lost a third of their crew or more. Lord Sheffield's *Bear* had fallen in strength from 500 to 260, Frobisher's *Triumph* from 500 to 325, and Drake's *Revenge* from 250 to 176. Even John Hawkins, with his great reputation for looking after his crews, lost 150 of his 400 men in *Victory*. 'The companies do fall sick daily', Hawkins wrote to Burghley.

THE ARMADA SAILS

The fleet had assembled in Plymouth just in time. A week after Howard came in, Medina Sidonia led the Armada out of Lisbon, on 30 May. Foul winds pushed him as far south as Cape St Vincent, and when he did at last struggle north a gale hit him off the northern corner of Spain. Most of the fleet took shelter in Corunna but a few ran north to the appointed rendezvous in the Isles of Scilly. Howard had spent two days watering his fleet in Plymouth and then put out to patrol the mouth of the Channel. But the storm that hit the Armada drove him back into Plymouth.

Then on Saturday 22 June, when ten victualling ships came into Plymouth, word came that on the Thursday a Mousehole boat had sighted large ships off Mount's Bay with red crosses on their sails, and had been chased back into harbour. More reports came in on the Saturday and the Sunday; there seemed to be two Spanish squadrons in the mouth of the Channel.

Howard sailed again on the Sunday, taking with him the victualling ships and the provisions they had not yet trans-shipped to the fighting vessels. But Medina Sidonia had already sent a pinnace to recall his scattered ships to Corunna, and Howard found nothing. Drake slipped round Ushant into the Bay, but still the sea was empty. The English fleet stayed in the chops of the Channel, with Drake pleading all the time for a descent on the Spanish coast where the Armada must be. Finally, Howard agreed and on 7 July the whole might of England sailed for Spain. Halfway across the Bay another gale hit them, and on 9 July they were forced to turn back.

The fleet was in Plymouth again on 12 July, leaving only fast pinnaces to patrol the Channel approaches. Gale damage had to be repaired, provisions made up, and the ships watered again. It was a hectic time, with old Mayor Hawkins taking charge of the shore work, beaching the ships that needed cleaning and caulking, driving his men on the Cattewater beaches by day, and working through darkness by the light of flaming torches.

The gale that drove the English back to Plymouth brought the Spanish out of Corunna. Medina Sidonia, his fleet rewatered and revictualled, sailed on 12 July, the very day Lord Howard had regained Plymouth. On Friday 19 July he was sighted off the Lizard by Thomas Fleming, a relation of John Hawkins's wife, who was in a pinnace named *Golden Hind*, after Drake's great ship. Fleming reported his sighting to the admiral at Plymouth on the afternoon of that Friday.

Legend says that Howard and Drake, together with all their senior officers, were playing bowls on the Hoe, that Drake stopped, wood in hand, to listen to the news and then bent to play his shot, exclaiming, 'We have time to finish the game, and beat the Spaniards afterwards.' The story is fully in keeping with everything about Drake, the bravado, the refusal to be rushed, the joke in the hour of danger, the need to keep men calm and free from panic. And bowls, after all, was a Plymouth game; a 1584 town record talks of 'playing at booles' and a Spanish jibe set down in 1625 says 'we caught you playing at bowls.'

Moreover, the fleet was ready. Two days before, John Hawkins had written to Burghley: 'the four great ships are in most royal and perfect state . . . the strength of the ships generally is well tried.' Howard wrote the same day saying he had heard that the Spanish fleet was ready to leave Corunna, that the royal ships were in good shape, Drake and his ships ready; and that all would be in three or four days.

So when at three o'clock on that Friday afternoon, Drake heard that the Armada was off the Lizard, he knew there was no more to be done for the ships. The light south-west wind blowing the Spanish slowly up the coast was also blowing straight into the Sound, which meant that the English would have to be warped out, towed by their seamen rowing the ships' boats. But that could only be done on the ebb tide, of which there was only an hour or so left, not enough to take the ships far. Only after

high water at eleven that night[7] could the fleet move; time enough
to finish his throw, indeed the game, to keep everyone calm and
for all the officers to be aboard in ample time to make ready for
sea.

When the tide is ebbing in Plymouth Sound the tidal current
outside is setting up-Channel, but close around Rame Head a back
current sets westwards. So, as the English fleet warped out behind
their boats, pushed along by the tide, they could pick up the
back current under Rame to slip them into Whitsand Bay. Six
hours of ebb to get them all round Rame, then six hours of west-
going Channel current to help them west past Looe. 'Although
the wind was very scant,' wrote Howard on the Sunday, 'we
first warped out of harbour that night, and upon Saturday turned
out very hardly, the wind being at south-west : and about three
o'clock in the afternoon descried the Spanish Fleet, and did
what we could to work for the wind (ward), which by this morning we have recovered.'

In fact, it was Drake and the local ships who slipped inshore
of the Armada; Howard and his big ships chose the risky man-
œuvre of sailing across the bows of the Spanish fleet and then
beating to westward. John Davis in *Black Dog* was Howard's
pilot and one of the greatest navigators of the age, but Dartmouth, not Plymouth, was his home port.

That Sunday, Mayor Hawkins and Mr Darrell, the port
vitualling officer, wrote to London as well. 'The Spanish fleet
was in view of this town yesternight. . . . Since which time we
have certain knowledge, both by certain pinnaces come from his
Lordship, also by plain view this present morning, that my Lord,
being to the windwards of the enemy, are in fight, which we be-
held.'

So on Sunday, 21 July, was fought the battle of Plymouth. It
ranged from nine in the morning till three in the afternoon, with
three hours of heavy cannonading. The windward gauge was
decisive; with their nimble ships, the English would close the
Armada inshore rearguard, hammer away with their guns, and

fall back out of reach of the towering Spanish ships. Recalde, the rearguard admiral, was hulled several times and his foremast splintered. He sent for help to Don Pedro de Valdes, who was commanding the Biscayan squadron just ahead of him. Don Pedro fouled two ships in turning back, finally losing his bow-sprit, foremast and maintopmast. The *San Salvador* partially blew up and was eventually taken as a prize into Weymouth. That night, off Bolt Head, Drake cut out and captured Don Pedro's limping ship, the *Nuestro Senora del Rosario*.

Sailing with Drake as a volunteer was Nicholas Oseling. He had been a merchant in Spain for many years and was also one of Walsingham's chief agents there, moving about from port to port watching the Armada preparations and sending intelligence to London. Captured, he seems to have bribed his way out of prison and got back to England, where Lord Howard wrote of him as 'one adventuring his life in so many ways in Her Majesty's service'. Even in battle, our chief secret service man in Spain could play his part, and he interrogated the prisoners from Don Pedro's ship, as he did other prisoners during the long struggle.

Drake sent his prize into Torbay, with Jacob Whiddon in Ralegh's *Roebuck* as escort. The Spanish crew were imprisoned in Torre Abbey, the ship taken round to Dartmouth, and Drake in due course was the richer by Don Pedro's ransom. He was the third senior officer of the Armada, and this capture was the only rewarding prize. Frobisher, who saw much hard fighting with no such reward, was furious. He was overheard to say that if he did not have his share he would make Drake 'spend the best blood in his belly'. Frobisher also complained that Drake had extinguished his stern lantern, which was intended to guide the fleet, and had left his comrades floundering while he took his prize. But no one else makes such a complaint; Frobisher was always unlucky and always jealous of Drake.

So the Spanish fleet was edged away up Channel, always harried by the English but never quite able to get to grips with them. The weather gauge which had been captured by that use

of the tides out of Plymouth was decisive. At last, the Spanish
ships anchored among the sands off Calais, hoping to join forces
with the Duke of Parma. At midnight on Sunday 28 July, fireships were sent in and scattered them.

Legend credits Drake with the fireship plan, and certainly
five of the eight fireships were Plymouth vessels. These were
Drake's own *Thomas*, John Hawkins's *Bark Bond*, William Harts'
Angel, Captain Yonge's *Bear Yonge*, and the *Bark Talbot*. Plymouth men sailed them down on the Spanish fleet, lit the fires,
touched off the cannons, and then took to their boats. At night,
with a tangle of sandbanks to leeward, the Spanish fleet had either
to stay and burn or else cut their cables and take their chance.
At first light on the Monday morning the English ships, with
Drake in the lead, stormed in to the attack. This battle of Gravelines was the greatest of the campaign. Of the 124 Spanish ships
that had anchored in Calais roads the English could only count
86 on the Tuesday morning and these were streaming away northwards, broken and defeated.

Howard followed them with the main English fleet until a
severe storm that brought no comfort to the scattered Spanish
forced the English to sail south again. 'We left the enemy so far
to the northwards as they could neither recover England nor
Scotland', wrote Drake to the Queen. It had been a long-drawn-
out struggle and everyone was exhausted. Drake finished another
letter to Walsingham on 8 August, his always bad scrawl getting
more and more illegible; 'your Honour's most ready to be
commanded but now half-sleeping, Fra. Drake.' Ralegh and
Grenville, fresh men, were sent to sea with a small squadron to
ensure that the Spanish did no harm on the Irish coast. The
main fleet could then pay off, the naval ships returning to winter
quarters on the Medway and the merchantment going back about
their business. The men were in even worse shape than their
officers. Only one English captain, Lucas Cocke[8] of Plymouth,
and some 200 men died in the actual fighting, but plague had hit
the ship's companies hard and, through the Queen's parsimony,

the men were put ashore penniless round the Thames as the royal ships paid off. Drake and Hawkins fought hard for the men's rights and argued about their pay; in 1590 they took the lead in founding the 'Chatham Chest', the forerunner of all naval charities.

The Spanish fleet was in even worse straits. Only fifty or sixty ships ever got back to Spain. It is estimated that they lost 5,000 men at Gravelines alone. One Spanish supply ship, the *San Pedro Mayor*, quite lost after wandering round Scotland and the west coast of Ireland, came back into the Channel to be wrecked on 28 October in Bigbury Bay. The following January, a Hamburg ship, the *Falcon Blanco Mayor*, which had got back to Lisbon, was sailing home again when she was captured in the Channel and brought into Plymouth.

Finding her way home through the storms that decimated the Armada was the *Desire*, in which Thomas Candish was completing his voyage round the world. He had sailed from Plymouth in July two years before with three ships; one had been burnt in the south Pacific for want of crew, the second had disappeared off California. *Desire* was the third ship, and Candish the second sea captain, to make the circumnavigation. On 3 September, they heard from a Flemish hulk of the 'overthrowing of the Spanish Fleet, to the singular rejoicing and comfort of us all'; six days later, 'after a terrible tempest which carried away most of our sails . . . we recovered our long-wished-for port of Plimmouth.'

CHAPTER EIGHT

THE SECOND AND THIRD ARMADAS

A LL through the winter of 1588, in spite of the general rejoicings and the thanksgiving in St Paul's Cathedral for
the defeat of the Armada, the English commanders were
aware that Spain had been hammered but not beaten. In November, John Gilbert, as a Vice-Lieutenant of Devon, wrote that
he had heard Medina Sidonia was back in Spain, and that a new
expedition against England was to be prepared. He had ordered
Dartmouth, Plymouth, and the Cornish ports not to carry any
fish to France, as the Spanish were buying up victuals there for
their fleet.

Various counter-measures were advanced. Sir John Hawkins
(he and Martin Frobisher had been knighted by Lord Howard
during a lull in the Armada fighting) wanted to keep six warships blockading the Spanish coast. The bills were now coming
in for the Armada and, compared with Cadiz, it was clearly
cheaper to fight on the enemy coast. The bill from Plymouth
for those five fire-ships alone was £3,650. Drake wanted a direct
assault on the Spanish coast, and he was supported by a soldier
friend of Irish days, Sir John Norris, 'Black Jack', now Marshal-
of-the-Field of the Queen's Army in the Netherlands. As joint-
commanders,[1] they planned to capture Lisbon and restore Don
Antonio to the throne of Portugal. Dutch ships would join them,
and cavalry and artillery would be brought from the Netherlands.

Drake in *Revenge* started gathering the forces in the Downs,
but the Dutch ships, the cavalry and artillery, never turned up
and he sailed down to Plymouth early in 1589. Norris came in

with a squadron of royal ships, and the names of the two commanders brought in further support. Soon they had twenty ships,
2,500 seamen and 11,000 soldiers—a rough crowd mostly veterans from the brutalities of fighting in the Low Countries and
Ireland. The stormy summer was followed by a stormy winter, and
the sailing date of 1 February was twice put back. Food was running short. Plymouth and the West had been scoured bare, and old
William Hawkins was at his wit's end to victual an expedition
already eating its campaign stores.

Twice the fleet put to sea, and twice it put back. Norris wrote
to Burghley saying that unless the Queen victualled his soldiers,
he would have to turn them ashore to forage for themselves. With
their numbers swollen to 20,000 this was unthinkable, and the
Queen agreed to feed the fleet until it sailed. There were eighty
ships now. To add to the Queen's displeasure, her new favourite,
the hot-headed Earl of Essex, emulated the Sidney of five years
before, and ran away from Court to join the fleet. He did manage to get to sea, one of the ships picking him up in Falmouth.

By mid-April, the whole expedition was launched. Drake and
Norris spent a fortnight capturing Corunna, ignored the Armada
ships still in the Biscay ports, and sailed for Lisbon. The mouth
of the Tagus was still too well defended for frontal attack, so
the army was landed north of the river. The soldiers marched
to the walls of Lisbon but they had no siege artillery, were short
of food, and rotten with plague and the results of over-drinking
in the sack of Corunna. They fell back on their ships and, when
Vigo was stormed on the way north, only 2,000 soldiers were fit
to go ashore. By June, the expedition was back in Plymouth.

The Queen was furious that her orders (the usual mass of instructions) had not been carried out. The men from the expedition, on the other hand, thought they had not done so badly.
Anthony Wingfield, a soldier, wrote: 'In this short time of our
adventure we have won a town by escalade, battered and assaulted
another, overthrown a mightie prince's power in the field, landed
our armie in 3 several places of his kingdon, marched 7 dayes in

the hearte of his country, lien three nights in the suburbs of his principall cite, beaten his forces into the gates thereof, and possessed two of his frontier forts. . . .'

It was more than the Armada had done in England. What was even more important, the fleet had taken sixty Hanseatic League ships off the Spanish coast, replenished their own supplies and stopped the vital supply of masts, ropes, copper and tallow needed to refit the Spanish fleet.

The Queen was not to employ Drake at sea again for six years but he was busy in public life as the leading citizen of Plymouth and as a Member of Parliament. The war went on but followed a new pattern on the lines suggested by Sir John Hawkins. The Drake raids had led Spain to spend a lot of money improving the defences of the Indies, so the new plan was to hover about the Azores seeking to intercept the homeward-bound *flotas*. There were still the emulators of Drake seeking to reach the Pacific through the Magellan Straits or the Indies round Good Hope, and new money was coming into the business. Merchants from Barnstaple and Exeter were in it, and more and more of the big London houses. An increasing number of expeditions fitted out in the Thames, but nearly always Plymouth was the final point of departure. London men sent the *Richard of Arundell* off from Plymouth in December 1588 for the south Atlantic, and she was back in Cawsand Bay the following December.

While Drake was on the Spanish coast in 1589, George Clifford, Earl of Cumberland, was in Plymouth with the Queen's ship *Victory*, collecting a squadron. Cumberland had inherited his title in 1569 as a boy of eleven and been made a ward of the second Earl of Bedford, Drake's godfather. He had married his guardian's daughter but she left him when she found him having an affair with a lady of the Court. Cumberland rapidly spent his family fortune and turned to seafaring to recoup. He had financed Withrington's 1586 expedition, and commanded the *Elizabeth Bonaventure* against the Armada. Lord Howard sent him to the Queen at Tilbury with news of the Gravelines victory, and ever afterwards Cumberland wore the Queen's jewelled glove in his hat.

In this 1589 foray, he took three French ships in the Channel, passed Drake homeward-bound from Lisbon and, in the Azores, took a Portuguese ship full of sugar and brazil wood, and finally a West Indian ship said to be worth £100,000. He sent this last prize home under the command of a friend, Christopher Lister, who had long been a prisoner of the Barbary pirates, but she was wrecked in Mount's Bay and Lister was drowned.

Cumberland was not alone in the Azores that summer; there was a small ship called the *Drake*, some ships of Walter Ralegh's under John Davis, and a Weymouth ship. So alarmed were the Spanish in the Azores that they unloaded the West Indian fleet there until one quay was covered with chests of silver—over five million pieces of eight, apart from gold and pearls uncounted. Frobisher was roaming the islands too, but his bad luck persisted, and the best prize he sent home in that rough winter of 1589 was wrecked on Eddystone. In August of that year, John Chudley (who had been a volunteer in the *Ark Royal* against the Armada) sailed from Plymouth for the Pacific, but after six weeks of struggling against headwinds to get through the Straits of Magellan, he finally turned for home, one of his ships being wrecked off the French coast.[2]

THE HOE FORT

William Hawkins died at Plymouth in the autumn of 1589. He was seventy, and worn out by the strain of helping to fit out four major expeditions in five years. He may have been a boy on his father's first trans-Atlantic voyage of 1532, and in his time he had seen the opening up of the New World. His younger brother, John, had taken a year's leave from the Navy after the Armada, but now he came back into service.

Spain was building a big fleet of new ships to escort her *flotas*, ships built on the English model, a tribute to the work of John

Hawkins. Through the winter of 1589 John Hawkins prepared to go to sea, for it was feared that this new Spanish ship-building presaged another Armada. The alarm in Plymouth was such that : 'the towne uppon this late reporte was strucken with such feare that some of them had convaied their goods out of the towne and others, no doubte, would have followed if they had not been stopped by the cominge of Sir Francis Drake who, the more to assure them, brought his wife and family thither.'

This is from a letter which the Mayor, John Blythman, and Drake wrote in May 1590 to the Queen asking for financial help in building a fort upon the Hoe. The joint authority is interesting. For centuries, the mayor had been captain of the castle quadrate and commander in time of war, and Drake had held this office as Mayor in 1581. But at the end of his term of office, his successor, Thomas Edmonds, petitioned the Crown that Drake should be made captain of the fort and island. No confirmation of the petition[3] exists but from that time Drake did exercise a vigorous lead in Plymouth's defences, and county lieutenants sent to him their returns of soldiers available for Plymouth.

St Nicholas's Island had been fortified in 1549 and more money spent on it between 1573 and 1583. The barricades under the Hoe had been strengthened, and Sir Arthur Champernowne, Vice-Admiral of Devon in the 1570 'cold war' with Spain, had set up his headquarters in the island; it was the key to the whole harbour rather than the castle quadrate, which only guarded Sutton Pool. This letter to the Queen reports thirteen pieces of ordnance on the Hoe, four on the castle towers ('which is of no strength'), and twenty-three on the island, but most of them borrowed. The island defences had been built up, and armour stored there for 350 men. On May Day ('as their custom in every yeare') the town had paraded at least 1,300 men on the Hoe and, from that day forward, Drake had ordered that there should be kept watch and ward every night as if it were a garrison town :

Of which watch every Master in his tourne as captain is to have the charge and to watch with them himself until midnight, and then to be relieved by his deputie, who shall be a man of like substance and truste. This watch did Sir Francis himself beginne on Friday laste.'

And from that day the name of Drake's Island[4] gradually ousted the old term of St Nicholas's Island. That letter was written in May 1590. In June, the Duke of Parma invaded France from the Low Countries and a Spanish force captured Port Louis at the mouth of the river Blavet in southern Brittany. By August, Spain had a squadron of ships there, by October an army of 3,000 men. It was a threat to our shipping routes, and to the West Country. Plymouth did not wait for the Queen's help; the Black Book for that year records:

'The northwest tower of the Castell was covered with leade, and 7 brass piecs (guns) were placed yppon the iiiior Castells. This yere likewise were the platteformes (for guns) at Hawe tymbred, the gate a cocksyde wch is to be shutte everye neight was newe made, and the greatte platte forme by the gate att Iland, and the wall neere the same contayninge 257 fote was nowe newly made. Mor bought two demy-colverines and two (w)hole colverines of Iron and mounted them at the barbigan and bulwerkes.'

The platform by the gate at Drake's Island is still there. Clearly, the old town walls were patched up and an extension made at the eastern end to enclose Breton Side, advancing the wall from Martyn's Gate to Cockside.

GRENVILLE'S LAST FIGHT

Hawkins had been ready for sea in the spring of 1590 but the Queen would not allow him to leave the coast uncovered. He did take a squadron down the Spanish coast later in the year, and Frobisher went to the Azores, but they had missed the first treasure fleet. Spain halted the rest for the year. In April 1591, three ships sailed from Plymouth for the Cape of Good Hope and India. Only James Lancaster in the *Edward Bonadventure* reached

Ceylon and the East Indies, where he tried to plunder the Portuguese ships, but his crew were in such low health that they compelled him to turn back, only to be wrecked in the West Indies and the survivors brought home in a French ship. In August of that year, Candish left Plymouth with Ralegh's *Roebuck*, the *Desire* under John Davis, and a ship of Adrian Gilbert's, intending to repeat the voyage round the world. But they came to grief in the Straits of Magellan, Candish died at sea, and Davis just managed to limp back to Ireland.[5]

By 1591, Spain had accumulated two years' treasure in the Caribbean and was desperate for it. She sent out a fleet of her new ships 'in the English style' to bring it home, with another fleet to escort them back from the Azores. England knew of these moves and sent Lord Thomas Howard off to intercept. Ralegh was to have been his vice-admiral but, though he sent some ships, it was Grenville who took his place. Cumberland was in Plymouth with them fitting out a squadron of his own. They were away in the spring, and for three months cruised round the Azores with little profit.

By the time the *flota* sailed, having lost one or two ships to English raiders, the English fleet in the Azores was hard hit by sickness. They tried the old device of putting men ashore on the island of Flores, to recover, free from the pestilent air of the ships. They expected the *flota* to appear from the west; instead, they were caught by the escort fleet from Spain, fifty-five ships strong. Cumberland managed to send a pinnace to warn Howard and he sailed with six fighting ships and six supply ships, just in time to get to windward of the Spanish. Grenville in Drake's old flagship, the *Revenge*, was last away, too late to weather the Spanish fleet. For a day and a night Grenville fought, then, mortally wounded, he ordered the last of the powder to be used to sink the ship. The master refused, and surrendered. Grenville was carried to the Spanish flagship, where he died. the *Revenge*[6] went down in a great storm that sank some seventy Spanish ships as well.

So passed another of the great sea captains, two years after William Hawkins. Richard Grenville had grown up on Tamarside, inherited estates at Efford, made Buckland Abbey into a dwelling house; if not a Plymouth man, he was a close neighbour.

At home, a government engineer, Robert Adams, was surveying Plymouth and consulting with Drake and Sir Arthur Champernowne on the town's defence needs. John Sparke, the mayor, sent off their report in February 1592, with a map made by Adams. They recommended a fort on the Hoe to cover the bulwarks from land attack. It would cost millions to environ the town with a royal strength ('for nature hath commandment of it') but it could be protected with a wall and ditch from sudden surprise.

On 30 May, 1592 Queen Elizabeth signed letters patent declaring that Plymouth was an ancient port, of frequent resort by her Navy and by merchants, and was to be made defensible by enclosing it with a ditch, wall, bulwark and other defences towards the sea, according to a plan made upon view of the town by skilful persons. She was not willing that the inhabitants should be burdened with the cost, as it would benefit the whole country, so there was to be a tax upon all pilchards exported, a grant of £100 a year out of the customs of Devon and Cornwall, half the forfeitures from carrying prohibited wares, and 'as many as have had relief from Plymouth, special persons are to be appointed to receive benevolence from them.'

Sir John Burrough, Ralegh, and Frobisher were in Plymouth preparing for a Panama raid, but they were so long delayed by head winds that they decided to try the Azores again. Cumberland already had a squadron there. No *flota* came their way but they did fall in with a Portuguese squadron from the East Indies and made the biggest capture of the whole war. The 'Great Carrack', as she is always called, was the *Madre de Dios*, laden with jewels, spices, drugs, silks, calicoes, carpets, ivory, ebony, Chinese porcelain—all the riches of the East. She was said to be worth

£150,000. The Hawkins ship *Dainty* first sighted her, Burrough in Ralegh's *Roebuck* played the main part in taking her, helped by a Queen's ship, three of Cumberland's ships and a Caribbean privateer. The seamen plundered her all night, and when the motley fleet returned to Plymouth sailors were laden with pearls and selling porcelain dishes for sixpence. Sir Robert Cecil was sent down from London to supervise her unloading at Dartmouth, and while seven miles from Exeter he could 'smell the loot on sailors making for London'. Sir Walter Ralegh had been recalled by the Queen before the ships set out and imprisoned for his affair with Elizabeth Throckmorten; now he had to be released and sent to help because the sailors would listen to him. Drake, too, was called in, and Richard Hawkins. The western ports had a spree unparalleled in their history. Only Frobisher was unlucky again; he had not been in at the capture.

Small wonder that Spain was angry, and in February 1593 John Sparke was urging the Privy Council to hurry over the Plymouth fortifications, as the inhabitants were much alarmed by reports from Spain threatening to burn it in the next summer. 'Many inhabitants are abandoning the town and cannot be persuaded to stay for the defence thereof.' Robert Adams came down in May and sent off a plan showing that work was in hand on the fort. The work was going slowly because 'the hardness of the rock has been extremely painful' and more money was wanted. 'The town had good will and small means, and there is less hope of the cold charity of their small fellow-feeling neighbours.' Local records show that four gates were also set up round the town in 1593, so it seems that a start had been made on turning the improved medieval defences into the stronger walling of the Adams plan.

That summer, Richard Hawkins put to sea. He had built a ship on the Thames, which his mother named the *Repentance* but the Queen herself rechristened the *Dainty*, for the express purpose of following Drake's route round the world. (She had been in the Azores the year before.) Now, after one false start from Plymouth in which a storm nearly cost him his new ship, he was finally away in June 1593. When he sailed, he saluted the crowds on the Hoe with trumpets and gunfire, to which the town replied. It was to be a long farewell, for though Richard Hawkins became the third Englishman to complete the Magellan passage, he was captured in the Pacific. Spanish naval power was not to be caught a second time: Hawkins had ten long years in Spanish prisons before he saw Plymouth Hoe again. Perhaps, in Lima, he even saw his distant cousin, John Drake, but while John never left Peru, Hawkins was eventually transferred to Seville and finally won his freedom.

Cumberland was in the Azores in the summers of 1593 and 1594 but the war was moving nearer home. The Spanish troops broke out of Port Louis and established a strong position threatening Brest. So, in 1594, a military expedition formed up in Plymouth, under the joint command of Frobisher and Norris, to deal with the threat. Drake held himself in reserve in Plymouth (he was back in royal favour and busy at Court again) and the Queen ordered that 500 men should be ready to move into Plymouth for its defence, if needed. The army was landed in Brittany and the Spanish strength broken, but in the fighting Frobisher received a mortal wound. He was brought home to Plymouth to die; on 22 November 1594 his entrails were buried in St Andrew's Church and his body taken to St Giles Cripplegate, in London. This blustering, rough-tongued Yorkshireman who fell out with so many of his comrades, who saw so much of the fighting and so few of the rewards, alone died in his adopted home port.

But it was increasingly clear that Spain's strength lay in the flow of treasure from America, and so long as it came in every year she could rebuild her ships and her armies as fast as they could be broken. Attacks on her coast and blockades in the Azores were winning battles but not the war. Drake's original plan of striking at the source of her wealth seemed to be the best after all.

There was a belief, too, that Spain had found a new source of treasure, as rich as her original conquests in Mexico and Peru. William Parker of Plymouth, who had been with Drake in the 1587 raid on Cadiz and became one of the most successful privateers in the Caribbean, had several years earlier brought back stories of a new city of gold, El Dorado, in Guiana. The ports of Spain were buzzing with similar stories. Ralegh's imagination was fired; he sent Jacob Whiddon to prospect in 1594 and himself sailed from Plymouth in 1595. With him were John Grenville, who was killed in Guiana, John Gilbert, a Gorges from St Budeaux, Jacob Whiddon, and a company of West Countrymen. The same year, two other expeditions sailed from Plymouth under Sir Robert Dudley and Sir Amias Preston. None of them found El Dorado, but they had their successes, in common with the swarms of privateers from half the ports of England who were pin-pricking away at the wealth of Spain.

DRAKE'S LAST VOYAGE

In 1595 a more determined effort was set afoot. Sir Francis Drake and Sir John Hawkins were off to sea again, in joint command of a major raid on the West Indies. They began to assemble their fleet in April; six naval ships, twenty-one merchantmen, including many Hawkins ships like the *Salomon* which, a few years before, had been captured by Barbary pirates. They had between 2,500 and 3,000 soldiers under Thomas Baskerville. Spanish intelligence was good, and to upset the English plans galleys from Port Louis raided the Cornish coast. They kept a respectful distance from the forces at Plymouth but they threatened Scilly, appeared on the north Cornish coast, captured a Cornishman off the Manacles, and then landed troops at Mousehole. That village, Paul Churchtown, Newlyn and Penzance, were all burnt. The Cornish levies were hastily summoned to march against the invaders, and Drake sent ships round from Plymouth to cut them off. At the first sight of this opposition the Spanish disappeared. This was closer home even than anything in Armada year, and the Queen (as Spain no doubt intended) was loth to see Drake and Hawkins sail and leave the coast unguarded.

Plymouth, too, was worried about its unfinished fort. The money was slow in coming in, the neighbouring gentlemen were not anxious to make benevolences (however much they profited from Plymouth's prosperity), and the fishermen avoided the pilchard tax as much as they could. There were fears, too, that a professional soldier was to be appointed governor, and two visits of Sir Ferdinando Gorges, a cousin of the St Budeaux family and a successful young soldier in the Netherlands, had not helped to allay this suspicion. Plymouth even offered to pay for the completion of the fort if they could have a royal grant, an annual allowance, and Sir Arthur Champernowne as governor.

News that the Spanish *flota* flagship was lying dismasted in Porto Rico finally persuaded the Queen to let Drake and Hawkins sail. Other news had also come in; Hawkins' son, Richard, was a prisoner in the Pacific. It was an added burden for John Hawkins to bear; he was now 63 and his joint-admiral was attracting so many men anxious to follow the magic name that they already had more men than rations. Drake was 50; it was 27 years since they had first sailed together for the Spanish Main. Drake had been the junior then; now he had equal rank, and greater fame.

For the last time, on Thursday 28 August, the two cousins sailed out of the Cattewater and under the Hoe, no doubt to the sound of guns and trumpets and the town waits. Overnight, they anchored in Cawsand Bay and on the Friday stood out to the south-west. Baskerville in the *Hope* struck upon the Eddystone but came clear; already the voyage had that Friday-sailing smell.

An attempt to land in the Canaries did not come off, but enabled Spain to warn the Indies of their approach. Five of Spain's fast new warships were sent in pursuit, and, off Dominica, they captured the *Francis*, of Hawkins' squadron. Sir John fell ill; 'his sickness began upon newes of the taking of the *Francis*.' He took to his bunk in the *Garland* on 2 November and never left it again; he died as the fleet anchored off Porto Rico on 12 November. The Spanish guns thundering defiance at the English fleet were his death knell, a fitting final tribute for this Plymouth man, the creator of the Elizabethan navy which established English sea power. In the same cannonade, a round shot went through the quarter-deck of the *Defiance* and took the very stool from under Drake as he sat at supper. Two of his officers were killed, including Brute Brown of Tavistock, an Armada volunteer.

This was a new, well-defended Main. Three million ducats were ashore in the strongest fort and, though Drake could burn the ships in the harbour, he could not take the town. He sailed on to capture Rio de la Hacha, and Santa Marta, and Nombre de Dios, without reward; on an alerted coast the Spaniards had emptied the smaller towns and would not even ransom them. So Drake burnt them, and sailed on. Off Rio Captain Yorke of the *Hope* died, and Thomas Drake took command. Sickness was rife, and soon Jonas Bodenham had to take over the *Adventure*.

From Nombre de Dios, Baskerville marched the soldiers across the isthmus for Panama, the treasure centre of the Pacific. It was Drake's old dream. But there were forts on the road now, and Baskerville was back, much mauled, within four days. Drake sailed west for a lonely island where he careened and watered his ships; he had not been in these waters for twenty years but it was the stamping-ground of his youth. He was having no great success but he had gone on longer, and lost more men, before his luck had turned in 1574. But the sickness was still in the fleet and it was an unhealthy coast, still called 'Goffo de los Mosquitos'. Captain Plat died at the island and Drake himself 'began to keepe his cabin, and to complaine of a scowring or fluxe.' They sailed back for Porto Bello, the town Spain was building twenty miles west to replace Nombre de Dios, but Drake was dying of dysentry. He signed his will on 27 January, making one alteration; Sampford Spiney went to his nephew Bodenham, who was at his side.

In the early hours of 28 January 1596, Drake asked

his servant to put his armour on him, that he might die like a soldier. 'He used some little speeches at or a little before his death, rising and apparelling himselfe, but being brought to bed againe within one hour died.' It was four o'clock in the morning, Drake lying dead in the great cabin of his flagship *Defiance* as she led a mixed squadron of Queen's ships and Plymouth ships along the coast of Panama. That afternoon they anchored in Porto Bello, from which, in spite of the fine new fort, all the people had fled. With the whole fleet assembled, and to the sonorous cadences of the new prayer-book, the greatest Elizabethan seaman was committed to the deep, in death as in life lying athwart the treasure route of the New World. He was not to lie alone; the following day Captain Josias of the *Delight*, Captain Egerton, Abraham Kendall, and the chief surgeon, James Wood, all died and shared Drake's grave. Seamen lie with him too; for at the next muster the fleet had but 2,000 men left, and three ships for which there were no crews had to be scuttled.

With Baskerville now the admiral and Bodenham commanding Drake's *Defiance*, the fleet sailed for home. In the Indies, they met twenty ships, part of the sixty-strong fleet that Spain had sent to deal with them, and beat them off very creditably. Scattered by storms, they were back in Plymouth just after Easter.[7] Thomas Drake had brought home his great brother's drum, and hung it in the hall of Buckland Abbey.

After Drake and Hawkins had sailed, it was clear that Plymouth needed a permanent garrison and commander. Strode of Plympton and Harris of Radford had orders to supervise the completion of the fort, and on 6 September Burghley made a note that Sir Ferdinando Gorges was to take charge of it. Gorges came to Plymouth in October and seems to have been accepted. The mayor was James Bagge,[8] a Weymouth man who had moved to Plymouth the better to operate his financing of Caribbean privateers. He wrote to the Privy Council about Gorges, welcoming 'a gentleman of his worth and experience amongst us in these dangerous times.'

Three days later, there were reports of more galleys at Port Louis and, on Gorges's advice, forty men were put into the island under the command of Anthony Goddard and Ingrim Barker. But Gorges was not going to relinquish his governorship of Brill until his Plymouth commission was signed, and he went back to the Netherlands. On the night of 14 March a Spanish pinnace sailed into Cawsand Bay, and landed twenty-five men armed with muskets, who fixed barrels of gunpowder to the doors of five houses. They fled at the first shot of the villagers, who then extinguished the burning fuses. This finally convinced the Queen; she appointed Sir Ferdinando 'captain or keeper of the castle or fort lately built and fortified near Plymouth, and captain of St Nicholas's Island.' Gorges was back in London on 3 April for orders, and in Plymouth on 12 April. A fortnight later, Captain Troughton came into the Sound in *Bonaventure*, the first to return of the Indies squadron, bringing the news that both Drake and Hawkins were dead.

Plymouth was jumpy with invasion scares and spy stories. The previous December a suspected spy had been taken out of a London ship and notes in his possession were found to relate to the new fort. These had been sent up to Robert Cecil, but he was one of Cecil's own agents. In June 1596, a suspicious character was reported riding to London, a little man of swart complexion wearing a black doublet of uncut velvet and sea-green velvet hose. He had talked of a plot to seize the new fort at Plymouth and hold it against all England. All London was seached in vain for him.

Gorges was not helping; he brought to Plymouth the arrogance of a garrison commander in a foreign town. Two months after his appointment, he wrote to the Privy Council complaining that the town council had been discussing defence and had sent a sergeant to summon him to them. He 'scorned such a manner of sending for and made answer that if Mr Mayor and his brethren had anything to say he prayed them to come to his lodgings.' This broke up the council in a great fury and the mayor came to tell him that he did them a great wrong 'in so foolish and so braving a manner'. Gorges wanted a commission 'sufficiently ample to exclude all cavil or contradiction of so ignorant and stubborn a people.'

This was Gorge's version. The mayor also wrote to the Privy Council complaining that Gorges refused to let the civil authority arrest his soldiers for felony or debt, and that when the deputy town clerk, John Hele[9] had been sent with a message, Gorges had impressed him and sent him to the island as a soldier. The town asked for his release, for relief from billeting soldiers, and for the old right of mustering the townsman.

In the end, the Privy Council called both parties before them, and ruled that justice, the old castle, the townsmen, and shipping were all matters outside Gorges's jurisdiction, but that the town and its equipment should be at his command when the enemy threatened.

The arrogance of Gorges is explained by his background. Of ancient lineage, he had started soldiering in the Low Countries in his 'teens, had served under Norris in Drake's Spanish raid of 1589, been with Essex helping the Huguenots in the siege of Rouen and had been knighted in the field for bravery. He had gone back with Essex to the heavy Netherlands fighting and had become governor of Brill while still in his twenties. He was just 30 when he came to Plymouth. But after the initial disagreements he learnt that a different standard of behaviour was required in an English town. He bought a house at Kinterbury, just below Saltash Passage, invested in Caribbean privateers, and settled down.

His old commander, the Earl of Essex, was in Plymouth when the ships came home without Hawkins and Drake. Spain had captured Calais and a counter-stroke was wanted. A major expedition was forming, a hundred ships under the Lord High Admiral, with Ralegh as the leader of one squadron. Essex, no longer the runaway courtier of 1589 but now Earl Marshal of England, had 2,000 trained and disciplined soldiers from the

Netherlands. The force was quickly prepared, secretly and swiftly assembled, and sailed out of the Sound on 3 June 1596 to strike Cadiz like a bolt from the blue. Ralegh forced the inner harbour; Essex hurled his troops ashore on the western sandpit of the port; the two rival favourites of the Queen's fighting like heroes as they raced to be first into Cadiz. They held the town for a fortnight. Medina Sidonia burnt his ships rather than allow them to be captured and thirty-six vessels went up in flames together with 12,000,000 ducats' worth of cargo. Philip lost forty fighting ships as well, including the ship which had crushed Richard Grenville at Flores. The town was systematically looted and then burned; after that the splendour wanes. In the looting it was every man for himself, and when the fleet got back to Plymouth it was the story of the 'Great Carrack' over again. The great men had their hoards, and every seaman was bartering with London hucksters in the inns and on the quaysides around Sutton Pool.

MORE ARMADAS

That autumn, Philip gathered together what was left of his fleet and sent a second Armada against England in revenge. But the season was too far gone and the Biscay storms spread-eagled his fleet and sank twenty out of the thirty ships he had left.[10] But the alarm had been raised in Plymouth, where Gorges and the new mayor, Humphrey Fownes, checked the town's defences and barricaded the land approaches.

As soon as the weather began to improve in 1597, Lord Thomas Howard, Essex and Ralegh were again in Plymouth preparing the counterstroke. They assembled forty-two ships and 6,000 soldiers but again weather held them up for months, forcing them to eat their voyage supplies. Then sickness developed, and after one fruitless attempt to get to sea Essex paid off most of his soldiers. When the fleet did finally get away, it made little more than a gesture off Ferrol before heading south for the Azores and the Spanish treasure ships. Even then they found

themselves at the wrong end of the island when the *flota* did
appear, and although William Monson gave chase with a few
ships the Spaniards managed to gain safety under the guns of the
islands. A prisoner in one of the Spanish ships hit by Monson's
gunfire was Richard Hawkins, who was being brought from his
captivity in Peru.

Deciding that England was now wide open to him, Philip
scraped together every ship he had and sent off his third Armada,
136 ships strong. Their orders were to make for the mouth of
the Blavet, pick up the Port Louis galleys, and then, after making
a feint at Falmouth, to land 8,000 men in longboats west of
Plymouth and capture the town from the landward side. There
was a report from Spain that Plymouth had been 'bought for
50,000 crowns'. With the English fleet at sea, Gorges drew 500
men into the completed fort on the Hoe, and into the island. As
it happened storms scattered the Spanish from Lizard to Blavet
and Essex reached Plymouth first. When his ships appeared
off Rame Head that October they were taken for Spaniards
and people in Plymouth barricaded their houses, ready to fight
street by street if need be. The alarm spread throughout the
country, and even Parliament was prorogued. Plymouth furiously
strengthened the Hoe defences and flung up timber gun-emplace-
ments on Mount Batten; it cost the town an extra rate the next
year.

Essex wanted to be off to sea again in pursuit of the
Spanish, but was ordered to stay in Plymouth and take
charge of its defences. The Queen's old fears had actually
come true; her fleet away and the Spanish on the coast. But
there was no need to chase the Spaniards; storms soon broke
up their fleet and never again were they to menace the western
coast. Philip made peace with France in 1598 and gave back
Port Louis and Calais. But his war in the Netherlands went on;
English privateers still raided his convoys in the Channel and
his ships in the Caribbean.

By now, Gorges had a regular garrison at Plymouth, consisting

The high altar of St Budeaux Church, where Sir Francis Drake was married. Built in 1563, it is the first Plymouth post-Reformation church. There is no screened sanctuary and the two aisles are the same length as the nave. Below, the demolition in 1964 of Budshead House, which was rebuilt by Roger Budockside at the same time as he rebuilt the parish church on the hill above.

Part of the Adams map of 1592 sent to the Privy Council with proposals for new defences at Plymouth. It is the first properly surveyed map of Plymouth with much detail; the roofed market cross can be seen and the Guildhall with its tower beside it; at the junction of North Street and Breton Side is the oak tree known in the next century as 'Great Tree' and the century after as 'Old Tree'.

mainly of Low Country veterans, and told Essex in November that, as there were not enough lodgings on the island, he had billeted his soldiers in Plymouth and Stonehouse, and was sending out a guard each night. By the following year the strength of his garrison had increased to 200 men. No doubt his high standing with Essex helped him in Plymouth, while his national reputation was such that he was appointed sergeant-major to the army which Essex took to Ireland in 1598. He was back in Plymouth that autumn, but in 1601 he was implicated in Essex's plot against the Queen. Plymouth raised money to help his defence, and he not only kept his head but was back as governor by the end of the reign.

Soon after his first appointment to Plymouth, Gorges sent a map of the fort to London. It shows the bulwarks along the cliff-top in great detail, and a path leading up from them to a sallyport. The path is still there, and there is a granite gate of the same shape as the one in Gorges drawing in the present Citadel wall. The plan of the Citadel follows a regular geometric pattern all round until it reaches the Drake fort; it then takes the shape of the fort and, clearly, the 1595 walls were incorporated in the Citadel of 1666. Inside are a number of granite gateways carved with the same details as the sallyport; obviously pieces of the Elizabethan building used again.

Hoegate, the last town gate to be demolished, stood late enough to be photographed, and the same characteristics appear in its granite archway. No doubt it was one of the four new gates of 1593, carved by the same mason as the fort gateways. But how much stone wall was added to the town defences is incalculable; it proved difficult enough to raise the money for the Hoe fort and the probable answer is that after the Coxside extension had been completed and the key points walled, the rest was left in its 1590 'improved medieval' condition.[11]

After Spain had seized our wheat ships in 1585 the English Government had issued 'letters of reprisal' to private citizens and these licences were used by professional seamen, merchants, and the Court gentry to continue their plundering right up to the time King James I made peace with Spain upon his accession. Seeking only private gain, they worked singly or in ever-shifting alliances out of Plymouth and half the ports of England, a constant stinging scourge to Spain. Sir Anthony Sherley left Plymouth in May 1596 with a mixed company that occupied Jamaica's only settlement and, in March of 1598, Cumberland led a fleet of twenty ships out of Plymouth on an expedition which ended in the capture of Porto Rico. Early in 1601, Sir Richard Leveson left Plymouth with a fleet that met the Spanish *flota* in the Azores but was not strong enough to attack it. However, he had better luck when he sailed back to Portugal, cut an East Indian carrack out of Cezimbra roads and brought her safely home to Plymouth.

All these were amateur adventurers, and the leading professional in the business at the end of the war was William Parker of Plymouth. After serving with Drake in the 1587 Cadiz raid, he found enough money to buy his own ships, with which he captured Puerto de Caballos in the Honduras in 1594 and a second time in 1595, and Campeche in Mexico. In November 1601, sailing from Plymouth with five little ships and only 208 men, he captured Porto Bello itself in a raid worthy of Drake. The town was the new Atlantic terminal of the treasure route, and though Parker missed the main bulk he managed to collect 10,000 ducats. He refrained from sacking the town and released his prisoners. Then, before departing, he brought his ships up 'somewhat to the eastward of the Castle of Saint Philip under the rocke where Sir Francis Drake his coffin was throwne overboard'—the last salute to Drake from a Plymouth Elizabethan. Today, the ships in and out of the Panama Canal pass only a few miles to the northward and pay no attention at all. Parker was the most distinguished of the last Caribbean privateers; he may or may not have been mayor of Plymouth (there is a conflict of dates), but certainly the captain of one of his ships, Robert Rawlyn, was mayor in 1620.

In 1603 Queen Elizabeth died, James I made peace with Spain, and the long war was over. Declared or undeclared, Plymouth had been fighting it for over thirty years, fitting out ships and victualling fleets. Her streets had been filled with sailors, and her warehouses and merchants regularly enriched with the captured treasures of the Indies. The town was going to feel the pinch of peace, though the economic centre of the business had, for some years been passing to London.

The foundation of the East India Company in 1600 was a direct result of Drake's voyage and his treaty with an Indonesian potentate had provided the legal basis for the early voyages. These had started from Plymouth; now the company was founded by London merchants and their ships sailed from the Thames. A John Hawkins appears in the original list of men granted the East India patent, and William Hawkins III sailed in the company's third expedition of 1608. He lived for four years in the emperor's court at Agra, near Delhi, and took an Indian wife, but died in 1613 on the voyage home. William Parker sailed as vice-admiral for the company in 1617, only to die in the east. Just as Plymouth had launched the American trade, so it was her enterprises which opened up the long association with India.

The leading sea captains, the Hawkinses, Drake, Parker and so many more, were Plymothians by birth or adoption. The leading gentlemen were also linked with the town; Grenville had a Whitleigh grandmother; the mother of both Ralegh and the Gilberts was a Champernowne, descended from the Valletorts, and the Budocksides and Gorges were Champernowne cousins. Behind them were the Plymouth merchants: Trelawny, Amadas, Fownes, Sparkes, and Treville. The story of Elizabethan England is very much that of Plymouth; at no other time since has the town contributed so much to England's history and it left a great mark upon Plymouth itself.

CHAPTER NINE

THE ELIZABETHAN EXPANSION

FROM old Master Hawkin's first trans-Atlantic voyage of 1532 to the end of the Spanish war, Plymouth's prosperity had grown steadily, and the town with it. The greatest growth came (as always) at the end of the good years and, over the period, the town very nearly doubled in size. The main addition came on the South Side, the area now called the Barbican and wrongly regarded as the oldest part of the town. In fact, it is an Elizabethan suburb, and a good two centuries younger than the area north of Notte Street.

The quay at the Barbican was built in 1572 to serve the Protestant privateer fleet; ten years later steps were constructed where the Mayflower Pier now is to enable seamen to reach their boats at low water. In 1584 a new street leading towards the new quay was paved, and this was undoubtedly Southside Street. It had started life as the pathway to the castle, but was probably fully lined with houses before the roadway was paved, even though it was not named Southside Street until 1591. The little streets branching off on either side to the waterfront and to the Hoe, were all created about this time, as shown by the number of late-sixteenth-century houses they contained until the demolitions of this century. Only one of these streets is documented; an entry in the town accounts for 1584 shows four shillings paid 'for convaienge of the water over the Southeside Kaye thatt rennes from Mr Sperkes newe streate.' New Street is still there, sloping downhill to the quay, the Elizabethan houses that John Sparke built still standing. Sparke's energy, which sent him travelling from the Caribbean to Russia, survived into his later days, for here he emerges as the town's first known speculative builder.

The open space between Looe Street and Vauxhall Street was

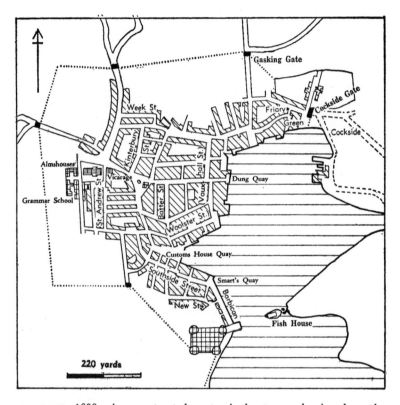

PLYMOUTH 1600. *A reconstructed map of the town, showing how the expansion of the Elizabethan prosperity spread over the South Side and east towards Cockside (although the map shows rather too many houses in this area). The street names shown occur in documents of the sixteenth century. The wall is still guesswork, though probably about 1590-1595 the medieval wall was restored for most of its length with modifications near the Castle and an extension eastwards to bring Breton Side within the walls, involving the new Gasking Gate in North Street and the Cockside Gate. Probably the Whitefriars walls were incorporated in the defence perimeter; Adams recommended that the Whitefriars spire should be demolished as it would be an advantage to an attacker; for that reason he left it off his map of 1591 but the spire did survive another century and more.*

filled up, Looe Street was largely rebuilt (some of the houses again survive) and much rebuilding was done in High Street. Several of the now-demolished houses boasted rich plaster ceilings, as did the 'Ring o' Bells' at the corner of Vauxhall Street and Woolster Street. In 1574, the new guildhall had 'sylynges' set up; no doubt in the same ornamental style. Other contemporary ceilings can still be seen in the great hall of Buckland Abbey and, rescued from Saltash, inside the doors of the City Museum.

About 1580, the Greyfriars site was developed apart from the 'Mitre Inn' round the cloisters. A doorway which is still preserved in a Woolster Street garage once graced the Mayor's House, where the town held formal banquets in the seventeenth century and which later became the mayoral stores. The house is believed to have belonged to William Page, the 'merchant of Plymouth' whose murder[1] was of such national interest that Ben Johnson and Thomas Dekker wrote a play (now lost) called 'Pagge of Plymouth'. In his dotage Page had married Ulalia Glandfield, daughter of a Tavistock tradesman, after her lover, George Strangwidge, had gone off on the Cadiz expedition of 1589 and been reported killed. But George came back, and he and Ulalia hired two villains to murder the old man in his bed. Another accomplice was Ulalia's maid, and all five were hanged at Barnstaple Assize (moved there because of plague at Exeter) in 1591. The episode had all the bloodcurdling qualities of an Elizabethan melodrama; even the judge, Glanville, said to be a relation of Ulalia's, was so horrified that he never sat upon the bench again.

The town was beginning to spread northwards, where Treville Street was named after a family trading with the Mediterranean and North Africa. Further north again, Week Street was first mentioned in 1585, and houses were being built at Friary Green, at the Coxside gate, in 1587. All these new houses had pleasant gardens at first (Thomas Doughty, whom Drake executed on the circumnavigation, is said to have plotted in Drake's own garden in Looe Street) but they were filled by cottages very quickly for apprentices and servants. There was such building in Drake's garden in 1587, and the foundations of the cottages can be seen in the gardens behind New Street.

The harbour that produced all this prosperity was also taking its modern shape and becoming lined with wharves. Many of them were not open quays as now, but had warehouses on the water's edge into which cargoes were directly unloaded. The largest warehouses, built round a central courtyard, were called palaces. Smart had a 'pallais' on Smart's Quay (now the fish market) and a dock was dug alongside it in 1598. The Parade inlet was lined by the New Quay, and Hawkins's or Customs House Quay. The Elizabethan customs house, with 1586 carved on a lintel, is now a bookmaker's office on the Parade.

Many of these warehouses and new quays were built out over the harbour bed and limited the water area; the Parade inlet was so reduced at this time. It also led to much litigation with the Crown (which claimed the seabed as royal property) in the seventeenth century. The medieval Sutton Wharf was continued with a dung quay at the bottom of Looe Street (where probably the street sweepings and stables refuse were dumped for removal by barge to fertilise the fields). William Weekes built a quay at Coxside, in the north-east corner of the harbour, where John Sparke had his quay. Sparke also provided a cellar for 'strangers goods' in 1578, and the 'long seller adjoyninge the Crane Quay' served as a bonded warehouse. There had been a crane quay by 1519; by the end of the century there seem to have been at least two cranes.

Another pointer to the growing population is the provision of a gallery in the north aisle of St Andrew's Church in 1596. Church attendance, after all, was then compulsory.

Maps appear as important sources of information, and three generations of the Spry family served the town as painters, artists, and map-makers. In 1546, John Spry painted a drum and 'made a plott'; next year he made 'a plotte of the haven'. Robert Spry was active by 1570, when he painted both the maypole and 'the ball at Mr Mayor's'. Equally cryptic is an entry for 1580 when Robert painted 'a picture of the Turk on Mayday', but he was not above painting targets either. In 1584 he made a map (see opposite page) which was sent to the Privy Council with a Water Bill. Lord Burghley was the chief man of the Council; his son was the first Lord Salisbury[2] and this map is still (like John Spry's 1547 map of the haven) in Lord Salisbury's library at Hatfield House.

THE COUNTRYSIDE

Robert's leat map is on too small a scale to afford much information about the town itself, but there are some details, such as the fire beacons on the Hoe, at Pennycross (hence Beacon Park) and on Roborough Down. Roborough village is marked by a 'Greate crosse', and the Buckland Monachorum turning by 'Broken Crosse', obviously the crosses which still mark the remote Dartmoor roads then marked the road out of Plymouth.

All the great houses of the neighbourhood are shown with the names of their owners beside them. The Harris family had been at Radford since the reign of Henry V; John Harris was a sergeant-at-law (the highest rank of barrister) in Henry VIII's time), and Christopher Harris was MP for Plymouth in 1583 and a friend of Drake. Strodes had been at Newnham since the middle of the fifteenth century. Parker, at Boringdon, was a member of a new family from north Devon which, in the next century, moved to Saltram and took the title of Morley. Drake is shown as residing at Buckland Abbey, his friend Rous at Halton beside the Tamar, and Arundell (Grenville's step-father) further down.

The Copplestones had been at Warleigh since the Wars of the Roses, and had in them the blood of the Hawleys of Dartmouth. An unhappy legend of Elizabethan times says that the head of the house murdered his godson outside Tamerton Church on a

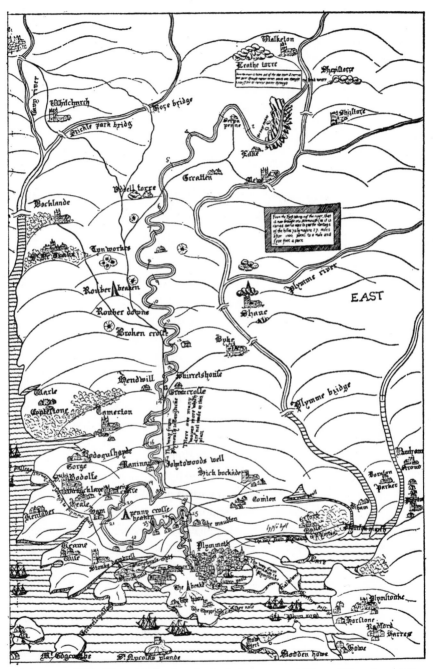

SPRY'S PLOT, 1584. *The map showing the projected course of Plymouth's water supply, sent to Lord Burghley in 1584.*

Sunday. Though he bought a pardon by selling much of his land it was felt that justice was done when he died without sons and his lands passed through daughters to the Elfords and the Bamfields. The Copplestone Oak, still standing outside Tamerton Foliot Church, is said to have been the scene of his crime.

Gorges is shown as living at Budockshead, and Wise at Keyham. The principal Wise residence was at Sydenham, near Lifton, and though they owned Keyham from 1428 they paid little attention to the estate.

These were all old county families, but the map shows a new development, the new country gentlemen. Ham, for example, was an old possession of Plympton Priory; now it was a Trelawny home. A younger branch of this important Cornish family had moved into Plymouth, made a fortune as merchants and, though still active in the town, had moved out again to set up as country gentry as well. Kinterbury, Manadon, and Pennycross were undergoing similar development. The Spry map does not reach south of Plymouth; had it done so it would have shown Wembury House, built in 1592 as the most magnificent mansion in Devon, with a gatehouse big enough to house any ordinary family. The builder was John Hele, one of the numerous family which originated at South Hele farm, near Cornwood, and became extensive landowners. John Hele, born in 1540, became a lawyer and did much business for Plymouth. By 1592, he was the town's recorder, and a sergeant-at-law.

For information on Plymouth there is the map which (reproduced facing page 193) Spry helped Adams, the architect of the defences, to make in 1591. The town accounts show it was a careful job; Robert Lampen, a builder of St Budeaux, was called in to help 'take the levell of the ground', and surveyor's tapes and other instruments were bought. The wall which Adam proposed is the main feature; how much of it was built is another matter but the gates certainly were. In the centre of the harbour entrance is the built-up island which served as a defence against both sea and enemy; on it, is the fish house where pilchards were cured.

The streets are accurately mapped and identifiable. At the junction of High Street, Buckwell Street and Whimple Street there is a building with a tower, which must be the guildhall, and beside it there is a drum-shaped edifice that must be the market cross, of the lantern type best represented in the south of England today in Salisbury. The town records of 1564, covering the rebuilding of what is most likely the guildhall, mention the purchase of a dozen moorstone pillars and contain a note that 'the forefront of the market-house was made this year.' The following year's accounts mention the leads of the market cross and leads can only mean a roof. In 1611, after a new guildhall had been built covering the site both of the old guildhall and the market cross, the 'morestone pillars of the Market Crosse' were sold to James Bagge, the mayor of 1595. Whether Plymouth had a covered market cross[3] before 1564 is uncertain, but it provided not only a roof for trade but also an assembly point for civic occasions.

Stonehouse is shown on the map with its own quay (first mentioned in the time of Henry VII) at the end of Newport Street. The name explains itself, and the quay is probably part of that which now lies just south of Stonehouse Bridge. Houses had spread from High Street up the slope of Chapel Street, which was the road to St Lawrence's Chapel as well as to Cremyll Ferry.[4] 'The waye from Stonehouse to Tavistock' is marked along the line of modern North Road. The crenellated manor house wall (part still survives) goes right across the road to the ferry, with an impressive gate, to join a deer park on the shores of Sourpool.

There are more payments to Spry, the painter, in 1594 and 1595, but the only surviving map is a 'plott of the forte and of the hawe' of 1595, which is clearly by a different hand and probably the work of Robert Spry junior, who was still working for the town in 1621. What happens to the other Robert, probably his father, is uncertain, but the St Andrew's registers for August 1591 record the death of three daughters of Robert Spry. Only plague could so decimate a household; the father may well have

moved out of town with his remaining family and his death may
be hidden in some neighbouring village registers. Young Spry's
1595 map has a most spirited rendering of the old castle and,
beside the plan of the new fort, there is what looks like a circular
dining-table. It must be the compass Drake set up in his mayoralty, with the points of the compass marked on the flat top and
a revolving spindle which could be used to take the bearing
of ships in the Sound. The 'spille' or spindle was repaired in
1585.

DRAKE'S LEAT

The growing population and the large fleets all made heavy
demands on the town's water supply. There was, early on, a
water course to take supplies from the Sutton farm stream to the
quaysides, for the 'cunditt' was mended in 1495. 'Conduit' is used
both to describe a gutter for conveying water and for the small
buildings from which water gushed from a pipe at bucket height,
but these early references must be to simple gutters. A well on
Southside, whose pump was mended in 1549, was useful to shipping, and William Hawkins made a new conduit in 1570, probably to serve the privateers' new quay.

The local water sources were soon inadequate, and in 1560
the town paid 26s 10d to 'Mr forsland of bovy and his company
for vewinge of the ground wherebei freshe water myght have
byn brought unto the towne'. Mr Forsland was a tin-streamer
of importance, accustomed to carrying water long distances over the
Moor in leats. A fresh survey was made in 1577, this time costing
52s 5d, but still nothing happened; legislation was needed and
Elizabeth did not call many Parliaments. But Plymouth was obviously prepared; the next Parliament met on 23 November 1584
and the Plymouth Water Bill had its first reading on 21 December. The preamble set out the need to water Her Majesty's ships
in the port, and the difficulty experienced by mariners who often
had to go a mile or more to fetch water. Clearly, large fleets ex-

hausted the local supplies and parties of seamen had to be sent to the brooks flowing down to Pennycomequick and Lipson. The second reason was the danger of fire, the third the need to scour the harbour. There was nothing in the bill about water for the townsmen, and its full title was 'An Acte for the Presvacon of the Haven of Plymowth.'

The bill was sent upstairs to a committee which included Sir Francis Drake (his first Parliament, as MP for Bossiney, a village near Tintagel) and Mr Edgcumbe, the member for Liskeard. It completed all stages and received the Royal Assent on 29 March 1585. Plymouth now had authority to tap the headwaters of the Meavy and bring the water to the port by a leat, or open water-way. The town wasted no time. The justices of Devon (sitting in quarter-sessions, they exercised the functions of the modern county council) came down to view the course and were well entertained. Spry made his map of the route and this was sent to the Privy Council.

But that spring our wheat ships were seized in the Spanish ports; Drake made his descent on the Indies; the cold war turned hot and it was not until after the Armada and the counter-Armada the following year that the water project began to move again. The vast fleets assembled year after year since 1585 must have emphasised the need.

Robert Lampen planned the course of the leat in detail, and his brother, James, seems to have taken charge of the work, with William Stockman and John Stevane as his foremen. The work began in December 1590 and the water began to flow on 24 April 1591. The leat was seventeen miles long, a simple ditch about six feet wide and two feet deep. Not until a century or more later did it get its modern hard floor and cut granite sides. The head weir is now covered by Burrator Reservoir (for Plymouth still takes its water from the same point). Around Yennadon, the ground was so rocky that a wooden trough carried the water over the ground. Surplus boards were given to Walter Elford, whose house at Langstone is also drowned by the reservoir. Drake, out of favour with the Queen and free to turn to local affairs, was the moving spirit; Plymouth gave him £200 to pay for the actual construction and £100 out of which to compensate the owners of land through which the leat passed. The town had other expenses; messengers to Drake at Buckland; wine and milk at the Church House, Meavy (forerunner of the 'Royal Oak' inn); wine and meals for the justices on their inspections.

Then there was the celebration on 24 April when the water first flowed to Plymouth. Messengers took invitations to Drake at Buckland and Mr Harris at Radford, the mistresses rode out, wine and provisions were assembled, and four trumpeters were sent out on hired horses. It is not hard to translate the bare accounts into a picture of the mayor, Walter Peperell, and the ex-mayor, John Blythman, riding out with the aldermen and councillors and their wives to Head Weir, and there meeting Mr Harris, the MP, and Sir Francis. There were presents to the Lampen brothers, and to the foremen, and a gift to the rector of Meavy. No doubt he blessed the enterprise, the trumpets were sounded, the sluice was opened and the water began to flow down to Plymouth, where it was greeted with gunfire and the company entertained to dinner.

There is an old legend that Drake rode to Plymouth on a white horse and that the water flowed at his horse's tail. Like many legends, it may well have a foundation in fact. Water can only be let into a dry leat slowly, otherwise it scours the bank, and the actual head of water is little more than a trickle, moving at walking pace. If Drake and all the local dignitaries had been at Head Weir for the opening, and a dinner awaited them in Plymouth, it would have been natural for them all to have ridden down over Yennadon and Roborough Down to Plymouth, keeping pace with the water. The leats that are still earthen ditches make excellent horse trails, and one can well imagine Drake, with his gift for the right gesture, jumping his horse down into the leat and, indeed, letting the water flow behind at his horse's tail. It is a splendid picture; the men and women in their best clothes, bright with the panache of the Elizabethans, the trumpeters, the jingling harness of the horses, all riding down to Plymouth through the flaming yellow gorse of an April day, with the greatest living Englishman at their head and the water at their heels.

Drake has been accused of making money out of the leat. He may, indeed, have shown a profit on his contract, for he even fought his national wars on a joint stock basis, but it was nevertheless, his energy which produced the water supply, and Plymouth gave him credit for it. The Black Book for 1590 records :

> This yere on the—daye of December Sr Fraunces Drake Kneight beganne to bringe the Ryur Meve to the towne of Plymmouthe wch, beinge in length about 25 miles, he wth greate Care and diligence effected, and brought the Riur into the towne the xxiiijth day of Aprill the next after psentlie after he sett in hand to Build sixe greast milles, the two at wythy in Eckbuckland pish, thother 4 by the towne, the two at wythy and the two next to the towne he fullie fynished befor michelmas next after, and grounde Corne wth theym.

The mills had been included in the authority of the Act by the Parliamentary committee of which Drake was a member, and he has been charged with lining his pocket in this respect, too. But corn must be ground, fleets need bread as well as water, and the Sourpool, which for so long had driven the manor mills, was drying up. Drake bought them from the Hawkins family and they ceased work in 1592 when the Sourpool[5] was 'made drie for a meadow'.

The Widey mills[6] were at Crownhill. Thence the leat made a great circuit round Pennycross, came across the west side of Mutley Plain and around Houndiscombe Road to drive the first town mill at Drake's Reservoir in Tavistock Road, the second where Cobourg Street leaves the Drake Circus roundabout, and the other two in what was called Mill Lane. Thence it flowed into Millbay (it never did scour Sutton Pool), and parts of the leat still carry storm water from the lower parts of Plymouth.[7]

The new mills upset the other mill-owners in the district and a bill was presented to Parliament in 1592-3 seeking to have them closed. The bill was killed by a committee of which Drake was chairman, and though this has been seen as his final villainy in the business, it may simply have been he was aware that his new mills were closer to the ships than those at Weston Mill, Lipson Mill, or Egg Buckland. This same committee passed two other bills, one of which empowered Stonehouse to cut a leat for a water supply. It was a lesser enterprise than Plymouth's and merely involved tapping a small stream at Tor (the Houndis-combe Brook, which flowed down to Pennycomequick). Boundary stones still mark this water supply, and the long-disused reser-voirs beside Peverell Park Road are remnants of a later century.

The other bill was for 'the inning of Plympton Marsh', the first work of reclamation at Marsh Mills. This reduced the width of the Laira and made it possible in 1618-19 for Long Bridge to be built over the Plym, so saving travellers the discomfort of the Ebb Ford or the devious route over Plym Bridge.

Once in Plymouth, the water was piped, and the town accounts for 1592 show bills from Moore, and another plumber from Totnes, and for nearly five tons of lead 'for to conveye the water'. A great frost in the winter of 1607-8 burst many of the pipes. For the ordinary townsfolk, there were conduits built about the town, little stone buildings[8] with pipes from which the water gushed. The Guildhall and wealthy citizens were directly con-nected to the supply; Peter Silvester paid 30s and Mr Kympe 15s in 1593 as water money. In 1602, the Corporation ordered that no one should pipe water into his house without prior per-mission; by 1608, thirty-eight houses were connected.

PILCHARDS

During the years that Plymouth was struggling to get enough water there was also trouble over what was really the town's staple diet, fish. Early in her reign, Elizabeth not only enforced

A view across Sutton Harbour of the Barbican, the 'new quay' of 1570, and its one surviving Elizabethan house. Below, Pier Cellars, the little Elizabethan harbour between Penlee Point and Cawsand which stole nearly all Plymouth's pilchard trade around 1590.

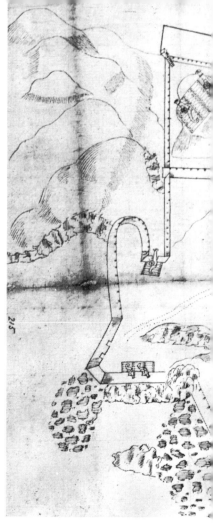

The Hoe Gate, built about 1594, rebuilt in 1657 and destroyed in 1863, contained this arch remarkably similar to that in the south wall of the Citadel (below) and shown in the map on the right.

Ferdinando Gorges's picture map of the Elizabethan fort on the Hoe; note from the photograph (right) that the south gate and its approach road still survive and the even older bulwarks are now under the roadway. These walls of the 1666 Citadel incorporate the walls of the earlier fort.

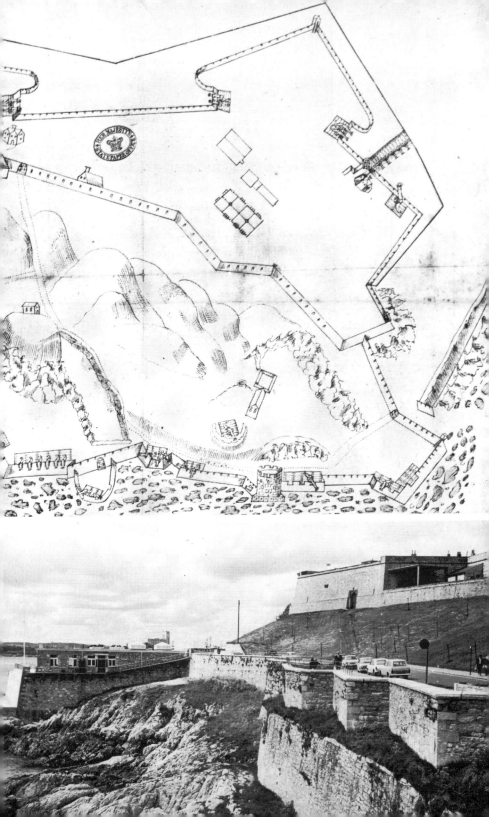

Survivals of Elizabethan expansion: the back of the New Street houses (above) and Looe Street (below) running down to the harbour.

meatless days but made them three a week, Wednesdays, Fridays and Saturdays. By encouraging the fishing industry, she built up the nation's reserve of seamen. Increased demand led to greater production, and seine-netting developed, with three or four boats to a net and half-a-dozen men to each boat. The merchants moved in to develop export markets and, by pressing fish in hogshead instead of the old curing, they were able to catch the oil that ran out of the barrels—train oil—and market that, too. These merchants built cellars from Penlee Point to Picklecombe, close to the fishing grounds and clear of the congestion of Sutton Pool. Next, they began dealing in 'futures', selling the next season's fish before they were caught, and by 1578 the people of Devon and Cornwall were petitioning against this 'big business'. They complained that the fishermen were getting poor wages and that now nobody could buy fish to eat. Dr Rowse suggests that behind this petition were really the Plymouth merchants who were feeling the pinch of competition from Cawsand.

While Drake was mayor in 1581, the council forbade the selling of pilchards before they were caught, and in 1584 they ordered fishwives not to sell at prices fixed by the merchants. That year Plymouth went to the Privy Council and complained that the cellars at Cawsand were a great hindrance to the trade of the town. In 1588 the towns of Plymouth, Millbrook, Saltash and Stonehouse joined against the merchants of Cornwall. The Privy Council decreed that no more cellars should be made at Cawsand, that two-thirds of the fish should be taken to Plymouth, and that no Londoners or people from outside Devon and Cornwall should have cellars at Cawsand. Clearly, bigger men were moving in.

There were more such orders in 1589, and commissioners, Drake among them, were appointed from the two counties to enforce them. But exporting fish had always been good business and in the end both the Government and Plymouth, failing to halt the trade, turned it to good account. An export duty was levied on all fish exported from Devon and Cornwall to pay for the new defences of Plymouth. The merchants did their best to defeat this duty and in 1595 were taking their catches to Fowey, where the exporters refused to pay taxes to help Plymouth. That year, a letter to Sir Robert Cecil complained that there were two million fish in Plymouth, and every ship was claiming that they had caught them off Newfoundland. Nevertheless, the fish tax did raise £1,327 for the fort, of which £877 came from pilchards. Plymouth men moved into the Cawsand business, too, and certainly Richard Treville was operating from there by 1597.

The tiny harbour of Pier Cellars, built for this business between Cawsand and Penlee Point, is still there, though the cellars have now gone. There were cellars, too, at Polhawn, Sharrow Point (Whitsands) and Port Wrinkle. The little harbour built there in 1605 is half-ruined, but the cellars remain on top of the cliff, a high wall about a rectangle lined with sheds open to the central square and surmounted by lofts. It is hard to believe that from Port Wrinckle's little harbour boats made voyages to Ireland, but still of a summer's night one can see the lights of the pilchard fleet strung across the bay from Looe to Rame.

The other little towns which joined Plymouth in this pilchard battle had their foreign trade, too. The *Speedwell* of Millbrook was trading to Ireland in these years, the *Margaret* of Saltash to San Lucar, and the *Judith* of Stonehouse was in the Newfoundland fishing-fleet. Millbrook had eighty houses, a mill, forty ships, and helped, like all the neighbouring towns, to feed Plymouth.

There were a hundred English ships in the Newfoundland business, and half of them were Plymouth-owned. On 23 September 1595, there were fifty Newfoundland ships in Plymouth, all waiting to unload their catches, and French and Flemish ships waiting to take them.

LIFE IN THE TOWN

In these strenuous times the Town Council had also to cope with the social work previously done by the churches. There had been an almshouse just west of St Andrew's tower, certainly as early as 1450 when a chapel was dedicated. It may have been rebuilt in the church rebuilding of 1485-1500. As the town's oldest charity it attracted many legacies which made it the owner of a number of fields and houses. The mayor and corporation became the trustees and administrators after the Dissolution.

When, in 1561, the Town Council resolved to fill the educational gap created by the closure of the chantry school, the Almshouse chapel became the new school and the apartments over it were the lodgings for the first headmaster, Thomas Brooke. For an annual stipend of £10 he was to 'freelye teache all the children native and inhabitaunt . . . gramer and writinge.' The mayor, John Eliot, the aldermen and councillors all made donations, as did many other citizens and neighbours of the town. A wall was built around the school and furniture made for it. Bell, Gill, Westlake and Mintern succeeded as schoolmasters until 1584, when William Kempe, a Cambridge Master of Arts, was appointed. He wrote a book on education dedicated to William Hawkins, and another, *The Art of Arithmetic in Whole Numbers and Fractions*, which he dedicated to Francis Drake. Written in Latin, it included a poem praising Drake for bringing in the water. Kempe was one of the first people in the town to pay a water rate and, even more important, he was the town's first-known author. His period of office also saw the town's first grants towards university education—'1583, vjs. viijd. given to a scholar to brynge him to Oxenforde.'

Physicians and surgeons appear in the records, and they must have had a hard time in those insanitary days when the plague was an annual visitor. The town paid for burying the dead poor, and paid compensation for fumigation, burning bedding, and the costs of a form of isolation. The burying of a 'neger' on Cattedown and the removal of a 'molato which laye about the streete' shows that coloured men were not uncommon. Indeed, the St Andrew's registers show several, men and women, as servants, and a number of births are recorded.

Sturdy beggars who would not work were sent on to the next parish. Thomas Edwarde and Vincent, the town criers, regularly had this job. In 1596, Edwards carried a lame man to Compton in a barrow, and a woman distracted of her wits to Plympton; Vincent took a 'lame and impotent man' to Plymstock. Like their predecessor, Ballemay, they removed 'fackebons' and 'hores' to Compton or Stonehouse. Often the women were punished first, tied to the tail of a cart and whipped through the streets, with a boy walking in front beating a basin. In 1589, there was a 'whippinge of six hoares'; no doubt the army of Drake and Norris waiting to sail for Spain had its camp followers. In 1589 sixpence was given to a poor woman who had been 'carted' and fourpence paid 'for caryenge her awaye'. Was it compassion or an over-brutal whipping?

John, the drummer, beat the alarm about the streets for sterner occasions; a bagpiper led the beating of the bounds in 1589. A St Andrew's cross was carved on the Stonehouse boundary stone that year, and the castle carved on many of the stones the next year; clearly the present arms of St Andrew's cross and the four castles were generally accepted. Householders were required to put out 'candles and lanterns' to light the streets.

The boys still had a day out on Freedom Day. In 1592, there was sixpence for a woman misused by the boys of her apples and basket on St Matthew's Day (21 September); the next year there was 18s 7d for wine, fruit and cake on St Matthew's Day, and for the boys' spoil in the market. There was a new bell on the Hoe, and in 1594 nearly £300 was spent on other bells, presumably for St Andrew's Church. Drake and Hawkins gave a broken gun towards the cost, and perhaps that metal is still in the St Andrew's bells. It would be appropriate enough, because for centuries a special peal was rung each year on the Saturday before 25 July, and on the Sunday the mayor and corporation marched to church in their scarlet robes to give thanks for 'the great deliverance' from the Armada.

Plymouth was still a country town with roaming animals, and, in 1594, a man was fined 10s for killing Joseph Gubbe's pig in the street. But one odour had been removed in 1582 when the 'fumynge howses within the Towne putt downe'. One imagines they were the cellars where the fish were smoked, removed away from the houses. That year, too, the ale stakes (good wine needs no bush) were put down and signs set up. So from that time we have inn signs, although the 'Pope's Head' which was at the top of Looe Street, above what is now the Arts Centre, is named in 1573. Apart from the 'Mitre' on the Friary site in Woolster Street, there were the 'Turk's Head' in St Andrew's Street (where the 'Abbey Hotel' now is), the 'Rose and Crown' and the 'Old Four Castles' in Old Town Street. All were Elizabethan buildings which were pulled down in the last century, but whether they were always inns is unknown. The only inn now in a building of that age is the 'Minerva' in Looe Street.

Maybe, one of them was the base of 'Russell the Post', and 'Peter the Post' (named in 1591). Some idea of the speed of the mail is given by the inscription on the outside of letters at Hatfield House, sent from the town to Lord Burghley. The date, time and town were written down when the letter was handed from one postman, riding as hard as his horse could go, to the next. A typical example left Plymouth at 11.30 am on 23 September 1595. It was at Ashburton at 1 pm, Exeter 4.30 pm, Honiton 6.45 pm, Crewkerne 10 pm, Sherborne midnight, Salisbury at 6.30 am, Andover 9 am, Basing (stoke) at noon, and Staines at 5 pm. Burghley would have it in London within 36 hours.

In 1600, Plymouth was granted a new charter by the Queen which clarified the town's legal rights. It made the ex-mayor a justice in addition to the mayor and recorder, gave the town the right to a prison and excluded the town from the authority of the justices of Devon. By making the mayor clerk of the market, it gave him control of trading in the town. A dispute about Saltash's rights in Sutton Harbour was satisfactorily settled and the two mayors twice dined together in Stonehouse in celebration.

The Town Council was obstreperous from time to time; James Bagge and Richard Hawkins were fined in 1591 for being late on St Lambert's Day, mayor-choosing day. Joseph Gubb (the pig owner) made offensive speeches at the 1601 mayor-choosing, and there were more fines when John Harris and the captain of the watch, John Battersbie, came to blows in the Guildhall, in front of the mayor.

The week before Christmas 1602, the Black Book records that 'Sr Richard Hawkyns knight, who was taken in the south sea by the Spaniardes in the vioadge he beganne in Maye 1593, came home after he had been prisoner.' Here was a ghost from the past, a Hawkins back in Plymouth, a link with the great ones. But the Black Book's next entry was to mark the severance of a far larger link with the past :

> Queene Elizabeth departed this mortal life at Richemonde the xxiijth daie of Marche in the morninge, and that same daie by nyne of the clocke James the Kinge of Scotlande was pclaimed in London to be oure king of England, and the last daie of the same moneth his Majie was proclaymed at the Markett Crosse here in Plymouth to be kinge of Englande, whiche pclamation was reade by Mr. Sargent Hele our late Queenes Sargent at lawe, and was pclmayed by John Lupton our Towne Clarke, at whiche tyme here was greate trivmphe with Bondfiers, gunnes, and ringinge of bells with other kinds of musicke.

The old Queen dead; it must have seemed impossible; she had been on the throne for forty-five years, and most of her people could remember no other Sovereign. It was not just the end of a reign; it was the end of a dynasty. London knew of the Queen's death, and of the new King, on the evening of 24 March. Plymouth heard the proclamation on 31 March.

Perhaps it is fitting that this proclamation was the last great event at the old Market Cross—that granite pillared, open-sided lantern surmounted by a cross which, for so long, had been the heart of the town. Three years after this proclamation, it was pulled down to make way for a new guildhall. But this could not be known to those people of Plymouth standing round on that March morning in 1603, listening to old Sergeant Hele reading out the sonorous phrases in his lawyer's voice, their eyes, maybe, wandering up Whimple Street to the church tower, or down to the blue water and the ship's masts at the bottom of Looe Street, or down High Street to the Parade and the new warehouses. Maybe some of them sucked at little clay pipes or wore hats they had obtained by barter from the Indians; they knew that far side of the Atlantic better than London or even Exeter, and Scotland to them was just another foreign country. They, who had known only the Tudors—Welshmen who had become more English than the English—could not know that the Scottish Stuarts would have stiffer necks, that one would have to be broken before they could settle down together, that the old despotic days of the Sovereign and his ministers was over, that the rule of Parliament was in sight.

What were they cheering, as the bells of St Andrew's rang out, the guns roared, and the bonfires blazed up on the Hoe? They could not know that the war with Spain which they had waged for thirty years and more, was finally over. They might have realised that they had brought the Spanish Empire to bankruptcy. They could not know that they had made England a European power, that they had already ensured that North America would be an English-speaking and Protestant country, that they had written a great page in history. They could not know, that morning around the Market Cross, that they were standing at a great dividing point in Plymouth's history.

ACKNOWLEDGMENTS

It is an odd thought that of the five histories of Plymouth published so far, three authors, R. N. Worth, Henry Whitfeld, and R. A. J. Walling, were professional journalists; while C. W. Bracken originally wrote his history as a series of articles for the *Western Evening Herald*. As a journalist, I am honoured to follow them and owe much to them all; not least to Charles Bracken who was my headmaster at the Corporation Grammar School and first opened my eyes to old Plymouth.

Worth, first in the field, made an extensive search of the municipal records and his will always be the major source book. Llewellyn Jewitt, a month or so behind, had access to a diarist and materials that have now disappeared. Whitfeld, at the turn of the century, used the State papers but quotes no authorities; he also dealt with Devonport as well as Plymouth. Bracken depended extensively on Worth, but did much research in specialised fields. Walling paid little attention to the early days, but has much of value from the period of his own long life.

I have been influenced by the new approach to local history pioneered by Professor W. G. Hoskins, our leading Devon historian. He taught me to walk the ground and use the maps of all ages, and not just to pore over archives. I have also tried to blend the streams of political, economic and physical development into one chronological flow; at times this becomes difficult but often the interplay of events makes their development clear. In places, my conclusions disagree with those of my predecessors; I am not claiming superior knowledge but a number of developments in historical research were not available to them.

My acknowledgments and gratitude for help must go to many people. Professor Hoskins read the chapters critically and spent many hours with me discussing the problems; the faults are still mine but he guided me around many pitfalls. Mr A. A. Cumming, the Plymouth City Curator, and Mr W. Best Harris, the City Librarian, made me free of their establishments and refused me nothing. Mr James Barber, the assistant curator and archaeologist, read the prehistory and his medieval excavations have (apart from some alarms) been of much help. Mrs Marian Beckford of Plymouth Local History Library, Mr K. D. Holt, the City Archivist, and Mr Edwin Welch, his predecessor, lent their professional knowledge cheerfully. My colleagues, Mr Frank Booker and Mr Kenneth Doble, read dirty typescripts and Mr John Ryan and Mrs M. Emptage turned them into clean copies. I have been helped in the Devon Record Office and Exeter City Library, by the Marquis of Salisbury's librarian, Miss Clare Talbot, and by the curator of the Royal Institution of Cornwall, Mr H. L. Douch. Dom John Stephan and Mr Edward Hyams answered queries patiently; Mr Richard Pearse, of Tywardreath, made me free of his extensive studies of medieval port records and some early aspects of Plymouth's development; Dr H. J. Hewett, of Saltash, was equally generous with his great knowledge of the Black Prince and the wine trade. Mr William Jackson, of the Plymouth city engineer's department, helped with his knowledge of underground Plymouth. Mr Michael Lewis, late Professor of History, Royal Naval College, Greenwich and President of the Society for Nautical Research, guided me to the sources of Elizabethan maritime history.

It was Mr Ernest English, for twenty years secretary of the Plymouth Guild of Social Service, who first set me on this task and applied the spur when needed. The ideas had long been simmering; he brought them to the boil. My printer, Mr R. E. Harvey Brendon, of Messrs Clarke, Doble and Brendon (whose grandfather first published R. N. Worth), maintained the heat and my publisher, Mr David St John Thomas, gave the final pressure. There are many, like Mr Malcolm Spooner, who helped in argument; many I have missed and to whom I apologise.

Finally, it would not have been possible without the understanding and patience of my family and above all my wife, who in the end set to work as well to produce the pictures and vital help with the index.

NOTES

The main sources are the many papers by R. N. Worth in the *Transactions of the Devonshire Association* and the *Plymouth Institution*. The most detailed summary of them, with some new interpretations, is contained in an unpublished history of Plymouth by Dr Margaret Lattimore, held in typescript by Plymouth Central Library.

Notes

1. At one period in the Ice Age the sea-level was much higher than it is today, and raised beaches can be seen in the Hoe cliffs just west of the Royal Corinthian Yacht Clubhouse, and in West Hoe quarry.

2. Sir Joseph Banks, the naturalist, was in Plymouth in 1776, waiting to sail for the South Seas with Captain Cook, when a cave containing bones was found in the limestone caves at Stonehouse. In 1812 when quarrying began at Oreston for limestone with which to build the Breakwater, Sir Joseph wrote to the Superintendent, Mr Whidbey, asking him to watch for any caves or bones. The first find, in 1816, was described by Sir Everard Home in the *Transactions of the Philosophical Society* in 1817. More bones were found during the century at Mount Wise, Stonehouse, Pomphlet and Oreston; but none was identified as of human origin until 1887 when Burnard, Leak and Alger bought Hill's Shipyard at Cattedown to extend their manure-works and quarried back the cliffs to expose the famous Cattedown Cave. R. N. Worth and Robert Burnard began excavations and their finds were detailed in the *Trans. Plymouth Inst.* of 1887 and lodged in the Athenaeum Museum, only to be largely destroyed in the Blitz of 1941. So no modern scientific tests have been applied.

3. 'Shute Park, north of the Public Central School site, and Hampton Shute take their names from streams which flowed through the town to Sutton Pool.' C. W. Bracken, *The Book of Plymouth* (1938), p. 46.

4. Mount Batten finds date from 1832. Knowledge of the site suffers from its having been investigated in the pioneer days of archaeology, and Mr T. V. Hodgson, the Plymouth Borough Curator who looked after the finds made when the RAF Station was being built during the First World War, was a sick man who never completed his report. Mr James Barber has since collated the finds but many have disappeared over the years.

5. *Ancient Trackways of Devon*, G. B. Grundy, *Arch. Journal* (1941-2), records the north Devon route. The Roman road north of Dartmoor is slowly winning acceptance, the Teign Bridge route has been explored by Comdr. and Mrs Woolner (*Trans. Devon. Assn.* 1954 p. 211 and 1959 p. 149).

6. The late Canon G. H. Doble's *Saints of Cornwall* are the major source
    books for St German and St Budoc. J. Brooking Rowe in his *Parish
    and Vicars of St Andrew's* (*Trans. Plymouth Inst.* 1873-6), maintained
    that the pre-1566 church at St Budeaux was near Lower Ernesettle Farm,
    that the farm buildings were on the chapel walls and that the site was
    known as the churchyard. Before the marshes were reclaimed, this site
    would have been on the exposed main bank of the Tamar, and may
    be the priest's house and cemetery of 1482.

7. Before the Second World War there was a stained-glass window in
    Pennycross Church depicting the boy martyr. Brooking Rowe (*Trans.
    Plymouth Inst.* 1873) quotes a tradition that the church is older than
    St Andrew's. Worth dates the church from the fourteenth century; G.
    W. Copeland and Masson Phillips (*Ancient Buildings of Plymouth*, 1956)
    believe it to have originated as the fifteenth-century chapel of Penny-
    cross; in 1535 it was the chapel of Pennycross Barton, Ham and
    Manadon. But in 1869 the plinth of a Norman font was found, usually
    evidence of an ancient right to baptism, and cannot have been part of
    the font brought from St Budeaux in 1820 by the Rev C. T. Collins-
    Trelawny.

CHAPTER TWO   Saxons and Normans

Principal authorities: For the Saxons: W. G. Hoskins' *Westward Expansion
of Wessex* (Leicester University Press, 1960), his *Devon* (Collins, 1954) and
Devon and its People (Wheatons, 1959). For Domesday Book and the Nor-
mans: the Rev O. J. Reichel's chapter in the *Victoria County History of
Devon*, papers in the *Trans. Devon Assn.* and specially the extra volume
for 1930, *The Hundreds of South Molton and Roborough*. William the
Conqueror's castle building: H. R. Watkin's *History of Totnes* (1917).
Compton: R. N. Worth's paper on *The Tithing of Compton Giffard* (*Trans.
Devon Assn.* 1896).

DOMESDAY BOOK: W. G. Hoskins has advanced the theory that the villeins
were farmers, the bordars smallholders, and the serfs literally slaves working
for the lord of the manor, and that one can often find the number of farms
in each manor to match the number of villeins. Applying that to the Plymouth manors, and the method indicated in the caption to Map No 4 of
establishing the boundaries, a tentative picture of all the manors can be
drawn. The Domesday Book also gives the value of the manor in 1066 and
in 1086, which gives a clue to their prosperity.

The Plymouth manors, dealing first with those settled from the sea, are:

TAMERTON FOLIOT (originally Tambretona). Value 60s rose to 100s. Mainly
arable, one wood 1½ miles by ¼ mile, probably the modern Porsham Wood.
The manor was probably on the knoll now shared by the church and Cann
House, and had seven slaves and a saltworks. There were sixteen farmers
and six smallholders; the old farm names are Belliver, Horsham, Warleigh
(the look-out place on the Tamar), Haysend, Pound Cross, Southway, Ash-
leigh, Coppers, Webbers, four Broadleys and Witsun (all names recorded
before 1400). Looseleigh (the clearing in the woods for the pigs) appears
in 1498 but must be older; Clittaford, Trehills and the three Coombes are
all old names.

STOKE (Stoches). 40s to 70s. Manor at Keyham (now lost under Barton Avenue) with five slaves, fifteen cows, twelve swine, 160 sheep and forty goats. Two acres of woodland, twelve of pasture, sixteen farmers and four smallholders. Few farms can be traced, but Ham, Higher and Middle Swilly, Pennycomequick, Ford (a Nicholas de la Forde in 1238), Upper and Lower Stoke are probables.

EGG BUCKLAND (Bochelanda). 50s, no change. Manor near church, ten slaves. Saltworks, the only packhorse in the district, three cattle, seventy sheep. 200 acres of woodland, probably Glen Holt. Ten farms and eight smallholdings. John Austen of 1333 took his name from the farm; there was Mainstone (1201), Bowden (1321), Pool and Frogmore (1572), Shallowford (1623), Thornbury, Deer Park (near Efford), Doidges, Goosewell, Cressbrook, Estover and Rock.

KING'S TAMERTON (Tanbretona). Part of the area, Saltash Passage, was in the Honour of Trematon and part of Cornwall until 1895. Value 1086 20s, manor possibly at Barne Barton, small with one slave. Six farms and two smallholdings, likely farms East and West Barne, Gubb, Weston Mill, Kinterbury (first mentioned 1330) and Moor Farm.

SUTTON (Sutona). One slave, fifteen sheep (probably grazed on the short turf of the Hoe, where Lambhay means sheep-enclosure). 20 acres of pasture. Four farmers and six smallholders, identification beyond likely.

ST BUDEAUX (Bucheside). Value 30s. Woodland 1½ miles by ¼ mile, traces still on south side of Budshead Creek. Four slaves. Five farms, probably including the three Ernesettles (1281) and Agaton (1333).

LIPSON (Lisistona). Value 20s, fell to 10s. One slave, six cows, twenty-eight sheep and thirty goats on demesne, probably Lipson farm which was across the road from the modern 'Penguin' inn. Four farms and three smallholdings; to fit in this amount of land, Lipson must extend south of Lipson Creek and probably down to the edge of Tothill Creek. The farms might be Higher Lipson, Laira, one now lost under Connaught Avenue, and Little Saltram (Salisbury Road School stands on the site). The Orthopaedic Hospital occupies the site of three small farms, Mount Gould, Higher Mount Gould and Lower Mount Gould, which acquired these names after the Civil War and might be the three smallholdings, isolated at the end of the peninsula.

LEIGHAM (Leurichestona). 10s. One slave, two farms, eight acres of wood, three of meadow. Until the 1966 plans for a new housing-estate invaded the manor, it was still as it was in 1086, between the Plym and the Forder Valley with the Plym Bridge–Egg Buckland road as its third side, with just Leigham, the manor-house beside the river, and two farms, Higher and Lower Leigham. Even the woods and meadows remain. Worth and Bracken tried to fit this manor in between Lipson and Sutton, but the ownership descent alone justifies Reichel's identification.

STONEHOUSE (Stanehus). Poorest and smallest of all the Plymouth manors, there was one farmer who paid 5s. The manor-house must have been on the Stone Hall knoll (the last 'big house' was demolished about 1964), probably on the Roman villa site.

EFFORD (Elforde). Value 10s, improved to 20s. Two slaves, three farmers, one smallholder; twenty acres of woodland (probably the tangled hills behind the 'Roundabout'), two acres of meadow, and a fishery worth twelve pence, probably a salmon-fishery, with traps built across the Plym mudflats. Before World War II, there were three farms in a group at the top of Efford Lane, Efford, Little Efford, and Higher Efford, with Manor Farm a little to the east. These are, no doubt, the demesne and three villein farms of Domesday, with the smallholder perhaps down at Crabtree running a ferry when the tide made the Ebb Ford impassable. Efford Warren, looking down on the Forder Valley, was very likely an early introduction of the Norman owners where rabbits could breed and be trapped well away from the farms.

COMPTON (Contona). 30s. Two slaves, five cows, two pigs, fifty-two sheep. Twenty acres of woodland. Within two or three centuries Compton swallowed up Lower Mutley and the manor-house moved from Compton village to Thorn Park in Mutley, on the site now occupied by Hyde Park Road School. Six farms, four smallholdings.

MUTLEY (Modlei). There were two manors of this name, both small and only worth 5s each, in the valley of the Houndiscombe Brook. This flowed into the head of Stonehouse Creek at Pennycomequick, but forked at the present junction of Dale Road and Central Park Avenue, the southern stream coming down from Mutley Plain and the northern from the Venn Estate along the edge of Central Park. From this stream, another came down Oxford Avenue, the back of Giffard Terrace Road, and through the Old Cemetery, and this third stream divided the two manors. Tavistock Road was the eastern boundary. The present Hyde Park Road and Weston Park Road ran through the heart of the two manors, and was called Mutley Lane; a very ancient route to Pennycross and Honicknowle.

South Mutley had two farms which can be identified as Houndiscombe Farm (near the site of the Royal Eye Infirmary) and Tongue's Land, now Mutley Barracks. The Tongue's Land name slowly degenerated into our modern Townsend Hill: Ford Park was one of the fields.

Northern Mutley. Ten sheep, one farm, and two smallholdings. The manor-house and farm must have been just north of St Gabriel's church; the two smallholdings were probably Upper and Lower Venn, out in the far corner of the manor. Venn means 'rough ground' and much of this area was open moorland until quite late. This manor became part of the tithing of Weston Peverell and, when it was built-up, the new suburb took the name of Peverell.

WIDEY (Wide). Worth 10s, three slaves, seven cows, two pigs and forty sheep on the demesne at Widey, and South Widey probably the one villein farm. The name means 'withy' and came from the withies or willow-trees growing around the spring which was the heart of the manor and, flowing down to Egg Buckland, formed the boundary with Compton. There was half a league of woodland, three furlongs wide, which must have filled the river valleys north and south of Widey. Linketty Lane, still rustic, winds through the heart of the manor. Widey Court was built by the Hele family out of their late Elizabethan prosperity.

MANADON (Manedona). Across Tavistock Road from Widey; it was worth 20s in 1066 and only 12s 6d twenty years later. Nearly all arable, with one slave on the demesne, three farms and a smallholding. A country house was

built at Manadon in 1567, and in the next century the Harris family re-built and turned the whole estate into parkland, obliterating the old pattern.
WESTON (Westona). Across the Ham Brook from Manadon, and stretching south to the Saltash road, west to Weston Mill. Increased in value from 10s to 30s; three slaves, fifteen cows, ten pigs, 180 sheep and sixty goats. The manor-house, Pennycross Barton, was beside the church and demolished in modern times; the one farm may have been Tor, and there was one small-holding. The Peverell family, which added the suffix to Weston, were descended from an illegitimate son of William the Conqueror (Chas Worth, *Devonshire Parishes* Vol. II, p. 219).
BURRINGTON (Buretona). The name means the 'boor's, or peasant's' farm, a very small manor worth 10s with three farms packed into it; they must have been very small. Before industry changed the pattern there was Bur-rington itself, with a small farm close by; then Burrington Farm and Burra-ton Farm a little removed; the manor and three farms. The name, and the cramped little farms in the heart of the uplands, strengthens the Celtic idea.
HONICKNOWLE (Hanenchelola). Another small manor, worth 10s, with two slaves on the demesne, and two farms.
WHITLEIGH (Witeleia). Again two manors of the same name, neatly contained between the streams flowing down to Tamerton Creek. East Whitleigh, held in conjunction with Widey (from which it was only separated by Tavistock Road), doubled in value from 5s to 10s, was in three smallholdings with a large wood—Whitleigh Wood—which is still there, much cut about. West Whitleigh had one slave at the manor tending one cow, twenty-seven sheep and sixteen goats; there were two farms. Before the post-war housing estate changed the pattern, it was still clear; West Whitleigh House had Whitleigh Farm to the east and West Whitleigh Farm to the west; the manor with its two farms.
COLERIDGE (Colrige). In 1066 waste; by 1086 recovered from the charcoal burner's woods and worth fifteen pence.

Notes

1. St Katherine's Church is first mentioned in 1370 in Bishop Brantyng-ham's Register, vol. 1, folio 10. St Andrew's appears as a parish church in the Taxation of Pope Nicholas IV, 1288-91, along with Stoke Damerel, Tamerton, and Egg Buckland.
   Hoe, means 'high place', and is a limestone ridge that ran from Mount Wise, above the Tamar, through Stonehouse, the present Hoe, Catte-down, Mount Batten, Turnchapel, Oreston and Pomphlett. What we call the Hoe is first recorded as Wynrigg or Wynderigge (Windy ridge); Mount Batten was Hoesterte. Probably 'Hoe' was the word for the whole ridge, which may explain Hooe Lake, caused by a sea break in the ridge. It was much broken by the sea, at Stonehouse Creek, Millbay, Sutton Pool, the Cattewater and Hooe lake entrance.

2. Gilbert Foliot, Bishop of London 1163-88 and a strong opponent of Thomas-à-Becket, is claimed as a member of the family but the evi-dence is slight. Prince, in his *Worthies of Devon*, said he was 'reckoned by Dr Fuller among the natives of this county, and most likely he was

born at Tamerton Foliot.' Just as the lords of the manor of Stoke moved to Keyham early on, so the Foliots moved the Tamerton manor-house to Warleigh on Tamarside, where they were succeeded over the years by the Bonvilles of Shute, Copplestones, Bamfields, and Radcliffes.

CHAPTER THREE   The Town is Born

Principal authorities: For the Valletorts: R. N. Worth's *Plymouth* and his *Stonehouse* (*Trans. Plymouth Inst.*, 1886), *Victoria County History of Devon* (1906), H. R. Watkins *History of Totnes* (1917). Plympton: J. Brooking Rowe's *Plympton Erle* (1906), Hoskins *Devon*. Trade and the sea: J. A. Williamson's *English Channel* (1959).

Notes

1. The Falaise roll in the chapel of William the Conqueror's birthplace commands the greatest authority as a list of the Norman knights at Hastings. Among 'additional names accepted', Robert Furneaux in *Conquest 1066* (1966) includes Renaud de Vautort.

2. Torteval as an early form of Valletort; Cecil Speigalhalter, *Trans. Devon Assn.*, vol. 71 p. 283.

3. Sourpool. The only similar name in Devon is Sewer Mill Cove near Salcombe, of which *Devon Place Names* (1931) says 'Sura 1086, Sure 1242, Shoure 1243, Soure 1275. This may be the Old English plant-name sure, sorrel.'

4. The seine-net suggestion, and much about Plymouth's first market, was dealt with in articles by Robert Pearse in *The Western Morning News* of 29 Sept 1952 and 27 Jan 1954.

5. Plym Bridge. The most extensive records are in *Old Devon Bridges*, Charles Henderson (1938).

6. Many landowners sought market grants for villages on their land as a source of revenue. Some flourished; some remained villages, like Buckland Monachorum, where the Abbot of Buckland was granted a market in 1317, and Tamerton Foliot.

7. The market grant is in the *Calendar of Patent Rolls*, 1247-58; the documents on either side show the King's movements.

8. Around Plymouth, the Priors of Plympton held the advowsons of St Andrew's, Plymstock, Wembury, Brixton, Shaugh, Sampford Spiney, St Budeaux, Tamerton, Egg Buckland, Plympton St Maurice and St Mary, Ugborough, Meavy and Maker. Apart from the rights granted by the Valletorts, they owned Ham and Kinterbury, and land at Cremyll which they made over to the Edgcumbes just before the Dissolution.

9. At the Dissolution, Plympton Priory's annual income was £920 12s 8d. Plymouth's contribution in compensation for loss of the market grant was £20; not a very large proportion.

CHAPTER FOUR   The Royal Port

Principal authorities: Worth's *Plymouth Municipal Records* and his *Plymouth*. For the Earl of Cornwall: *Medieval Cornwall*, by Canon Elliott-Binns (1955), *Buckland Abbey* by Crispin Gill (1951), *Dartmouth*, by Percy

Russell (1950). Trade: Margaret Lattimore, *Study of Plymouth, Vol II.*
Shipping: Dr H. J. Hewitt's paper *Medieval Plymouth (Trans. Plymouth
Inst.* 1960). *The Black Prince's Expedition, of 1355-1357,* Hewitt (1958).
Piracy: *Prejudice and Promise in 15th Century England,* C. L. Kingsford
(Ford Lecture, 1923-4). French raids: *Story of Plymouth,* C. W. Bracken
(1931) and Williamson's *English Channel.* Breton Side: an unpublished
history of Plymouth by Harris (1810), held by Plymouth City Library, and
2,000 Years in Exeter, Hoskins (1961).

Notes

1. The market-cross is mentioned in a dispute of 1310, and is shown
    on the Henry VIII defence map, though the angle of the streets makes
    its location uncertain. But a document of 1342 gives a grant of land
    by the Prior of Plympton to William le Spicer (grocer) and Alice, his
    wife, of land in Bilbury Street, extending to a way leading to the
    market of Sutton, and a way leading from Bilbury Street towards the
    Old Town. Bilbury Street (renamed Exeter Street) forked into Treville
    Street, leading to Old Town Street, and Buckwell Street, leading to
    the site for three centuries of the Guildhall. The site was an open
    triangle made by parting roads, a common enough market site in
    medieval towns which had no central square, and it was equally normal
    for the market site to become the location of the guildhall.

2. I am indebted to Mr Robert Pearse of Tywardreath for these extracts
    from the Pipe Rolls (E/101/158-163) which he found during research
    for his *Ports and Harbours of Cornwall* (1963). Apart from the ships
    named in the text, there was the *Notre Dame* (W. Larcher) 113 tuns,
    Nicholas (Boltwinus Tantone) 161 tuns, *Salvee* (Folford) 120 tuns,
    Nicholas (Robertus de Gantona) 61 tuns, *Sameo* (Joh. Bens?) 96 tuns,
    St Annea (W. Polliforere) 120 tuns, *St Michael* (William de Colifort)
    101 tuns, *St Maria* (W. Argru?) 114 tuns, *St John* (John Torri) 61 tuns,
    Grace Dieu (William Bokerel) 30 tuns. The ship names recur, some-
    times changing captains but always with about the same cargo, sug-
    gesting that they were loaded to capacity. They were 'cogs', the major
    merchantmen and main fighting-units of the day, ranging up to 200
    tuns (none of the Plymouth ships were of this size) with a single mast,
    one large squaresail, and a raised poop and forecastle for fighting.

3. The Friars. Worth and Bracken help: there is more material in Oliver's
    Monasticon Dioecesis Exoniensis (1846).

4. William Adams, an officer of the Sutton Harbour Co Ltd (which was
    created in the last century to take over the former Crown rights in
    the harbour) read a paper to the Plymouth Institution in 1890. The
    harbour was conveyed in 1270 by Roger Valletort to Richard King
    of the Romans, and passed on his death in 1272 to Edmund Earl of
    Cornwall. 1293 records show Sutton profits as part of the Manor of
    Trematon. On Edmund's death in 1310, the harbour reverted to the
    Crown. (Piers Gaveston, Edward II's favourite, held the earldom of
    Cornwall from 1307 until 1312, after which some of his possessions
    were granted to Queen Isabella). On 7 April 1324 the King granted
    to Queen Isabella a weekly market on Tuesdays and Fridays in the
    port and the water of Sutton pertaining to her. All this bears out the

H

view that the harbour was Royal land but the market is a puzzle, unless this served as authority for the wholesale fish-market on the water-side, which paid dues to the Crown.

5. Five Plymouth ships were engaged by the Crown in October 1337, probably carrying supplies to the Army in the Low Countries. There were 213 men in the crews of the *Seynt Saveour, Trynite, Grace Dieu, Kateryne, Margerete,* and *Spiryte*; (Public Record Office, E/101/19/39) The absence of so many men may have facilitated the French raid in Plymouth that autumn. Four of these ships, with the *Seint Spirit* and *Petre* of Plymouth, had been in Royal service in July and August, carrying wool to Dortrecht and Antwerp to help pay for the French wars.

6. Of the fifteen Plymouth ships in Lancaster's expedition, five were called *St Mary*, two *Gracedieu*, two *Godbegot*, and the others *John, James, Thomas, St Saveur, Rode* (Rood), and *Trinity*. Clearly the early Plymouth sailors were God-fearing men, but not imaginative in ship-naming.

7. Population figures: Prof. Hoskins gives tables in his *Local History in England* (1959).

8. Duchy of Cornwall records (sc. 6 817/3) show that, in 1352-3, English ships paying wine-prisage at Plymouth came from Lymington, Hull, Dartmouth, Harwich, Ipswich, Exmouth, Maldon, as well as places indecipherable.

9. It was their ability to sail closer to the wind, by the mid-fifteenth century, that made it possible for our ships to cross the Atlantic by the end of the century.

10. Reference to the panic at Plymouth over Wat Tyler's rebellion appears in the French historian Thierry's *Norman Conquest.* (Everyman edn. Vol. 1, p. 329).

11. Harris remembered Martyn's Gate, with one arch opening to Exeter Street and the other to what was then Green Street but is now called Bilbury Street, and the remnants of the wall running up Green Street.

12. The Causey is a problem. Worth, and Bracken follows him, regards it as the stumpy pier at the Barbican on which was the windlass to wind the harbour defence chain up and down. The chain was certainly at the Causey, and there was a mast which was probably used as a boom, too. The problem is why it was called the Causey, for this can only mean (*Oxford Dictionary*) stepping stones, a way through a marshy place, or a paved way. The first British charts (made by Captain Greenville Collins in 1753) show Sutton Harbour as drying out at low-tide, save for a narrow inlet reaching through the entrance to about the middle of the pool. Perhaps the Causey was a stone-paved way just higher than the mud reaching to the low-water mark, a device common enough in the neighbourhood. It can hardly have reached right across the mouth like the causeway still linking the villages of Newton and Noss, even though the island on the eastern side of the entrance seems to have been called the Causey, too. This may have

been the original form, and the name in time applied to the windlass pier and the harbour entrance, just as 'Barbican', from being the castle's watergate, became the name of a row of houses and today of the whole area.

13. The one remaining piece of the castle, in Lambhay Street, is said by Copeland and Phillips (*Ancient Buildings of Plymouth*) to be ascribed to the late fourteenth century but probably earlier.

CHAPTER FIVE   The Young Borough

Principal authorities: *Plymouth City Charters*, by C. E. Welch (1962), Worth's *History* and *Municipal Records*. Jowett's *History*. For street-names and their meaning: *Devon Place Names*, for which Bracken compiled a list with dates. Wars of the Roses: Kingsford's *Prejudice and Promise, England in the Late Middle Ages* by A. R. Myers (Pelican 1965), *Parliamentary Representation of Devon*, J. J. Alexander (Trans Devon Assn. vol 69). The Tudors: A. L. Rowse's *Tudor Cornwall* (1941), Richard Carew's *Survey of Cornwall* (1602), and Hoskin's *Devon*. Chantries: Oliver's *Monasticon*. Lord Willoughby de Broke: *Devon and Cornwall Notes and Queries*, vols 14, 15 and 18. Leland's *Itinerary* (1535-43).

Notes

1. Elm Road, a cut from the Plympton road at Lipson Bridge to the Tavistock road, formed the boundary for part of its length. It is still steep and twisting; when it was muddy as well, the carters called it Hell Lane; and over the years 'Ell Lane' was made into the respectable Elm Lane and so Elm Road.

2. Plymouth street-names and dates; 1342, Bilbury Street; 1412, Stillman Street; 1459, Notte Street; 1491, Foxhole; 1493, Breton Side, Buckwell Street, Cat Street, Fynewyl Street, Hygh Street, Wympl Street (perhaps where they made whimples, or women's hats); 1500, Looe Street; 1517, Friar's Lane (beside Blackfriars); 1520, Market Street (a name used at various times for both High Street and Whimple Street); 1537, Kinterbury Street; 1577, St Andrew Street; 1584, New Street; 1585, Week Street; 1591, Southside Street; 1616, Mill Lane; 1626, Batter Street; 1637, Woolster Street. From architectural evidence, some of the streets are in fact older but these are the first documentary references.

3. It is not clear whether Plymouth's 1526 clock was inside the Guildhall or, as seems more likely, a public one. Richard Lawrence was paid 24s 6d for the clock and for setting it up; there was another fifteen pence for wire, fifteen pence for ironwork, and fourpence for nails for the frame, a total of 27s 4d. The 1527 records contain the entry 'Itm Rec of master herford for the Clok of the yeld hall that he bought of the Towne, 26s 8d'. One hopes that it was an older clock being sold, not the new one already a failure.

4. Tamerton Foliot's stocks are still preserved in the church porch. The ducking-stool seat, an iron affair, is in the City Museum.

5. The Bonville family held Warleigh and Tamerton at this time, through marriage. The Copplestones acquired the estate by marriage in 1472.

6. This quotation, and the next, is from Jewett's *History*.

7. There were exceptions to the barring of foreigners from the freedom. No 'Alion borne outewards' was to be made free save 'psons of Normandy Gascon Syon Irelond Caleys Berwyke and the bordars of the same Being Englisshe.'

8. There was an aisle dedicated to the Virgin licensed in 1385 (Rowe) and an aisle dedicated to St John the Baptist in 1441 (Worth). One doubts if the first was a very large extension because, at the time, Plymouth was struggling to find money for defence purposes; the second may have been the foundation of the Jabyn chantry. Egg Buckland church had been rebuilt about 1430; the rural districts were prosperous without Plymouth's defence expenses.

9. The Henry VIII defence-map of Stonehouse (opposite page 160) shows a deer park attached to the Durnford manor-house, running down to the edges of Sourpool, and another at Mount Edgcumbe. It would be logical to assume that when Piers Edgcumbe emparked Mount Edgcumbe he took animals from Stonehouse to found his new herd. There are still deer in Mount Edgcumbe Park (a herd of about 150 in 1966) and Lord Mount Edgcumbe tells me they are considered to be one of the oldest strains in the country. Their ancestors may have roamed the Stonehouse park that once covered the western end of Union Street.

10. The year after this, St Andrew's acquired its most famous vicar, Adrian de Castello, but he was never even in England in the seven years of his incumbency. He was principal secretary to Pope Alexander VI, the Borgia who died (some said he was poisoned) after supper in the garden of Adrian's palace. Alexander had made Adrian a cardinal; Henry VII had made him Bishop of Hereford and his Ambassador in Rome; Henry VIII advanced him to the Bishopric of Bath and Wells. Adrian was disgraced for being an accessory to an attempt to poison Pope Leo X in 1517. During his incumbency of St Andrew's (1502-9), his proxy was John Anthony Bonfaunt.

11. In 1523 Exeter had sixty merchants earning more than £40 a year, Totnes thirty, and Plymouth fifteen. The richest merchant in the county was John Giles of Totnes, assessed at £520. In Plymouth, John Pounde (mayor in 1519) had £410, and John Paynter and William Hawkins were over the £150 mark. Colyton was the fourth town, Tavistock the fifth, with another William Hawkins (probably father of the Plymouth man) and Richard Drake named.

CHAPTER SIX   The new World

Principal authorities: *Cabot Voyages* by J. A. Williamson (Hakluyt Society, 2nd series, No CXX), Worth's *History* and *Municipal Records*, Williamson's *Hawkins of Plymouth* (1949) and *English Channel*, A. L. Rowse's *Tudor*

Cornwall and *Sir Richard Grenville*. The Dissolution of the Monasteries: *Devon Monastic Lands*, by Dr Joyce Youings (Devon and Cornwall Record Society, new series, vol 1, 1955); Hakluyt's *Voyages*. For the debacle of San Juan de Ulloa: *The Defeat of John Hawkins* by Raymond Unwin (1960), *Dictionary of National Biography*. *State Papers Domestic*, 1547-80. Rowse's *England of Elizabeth* (1950).

Notes

1. A field beside Efford Lane bore the name of Cockram Park in nineteenth-century tithe-maps. (See page 49).

2. Grisling, defeated in Plymouth, retired to Saltash where he became mayor and tried to reassert the old authority over Sutton Harbour. It became an inter-town battle; Hawkins refused to pay fines imposed in Saltash court and the dispute finally went to the Star Chamber. Plymouth seems to have won, but discreet gifts of hake to Mr Secretary Cromwell may have helped. Hake, always a Plymouth delicacy, was caught by fast trawling off the Eddystone; a certain amount of the catch was taken as 'Castle hake' and sold to help pay for the town defences.

3. The surrender of the Whitefriars was signed by Frater Johes. Myllyn, prior; Frater Symon Apphowell; Friars John Harrys, John Bond, Hev. Hawyn, and Wm Lobbe. The Greyfriars—John Morys, warden of Plymouth; frater John Hunt, vysgardianus; Friars Roger Sparnall, Wm Scherwyll, John Bowgge, Robt Elles, and Thos Tygberd. (*Letters and Papers Domestic and Foreign, Henry VIII*, Vol 13, Pt II, 1538). Was this Scherwyll an ancestor or relation of the Sherwells who became Puritan leaders in seventeenth-century Plymouth?

4. A Sparke daughter married into the Molesworth family of Pencarrow, near Wadebridge, who owned the Whitefriars for a time. Molesworth-St Aubyns are still at Pencarrow. There are still Sparke memorials in St Andrew's Church and Plympton St Maurice; the keystone of Friary Gate bearing the Sparke arms was lost in the wartime destruction of the Plymouth Athenaeum.

5. The well is under a coalhouse in Ladywell; during World War II a precious load of rationed coal went through the rotten floorboards and disappeared into the well.

6. Sparke's account of the second voyage of John Hawkins is reproduced in *The Hawkins Voyages*, edited by Clements Markham (Hakluyt Society, 1878), with a number of Hawkins papers. The other clues to John Sparke come in Plympton records, Hakluyt's *Voyages* and *Early Travels to Russia and Persia* (Hakluyt Society Vols 72 and 73, 1886); one cannot prove that he is the Russian traveller but all the facts hold together and there is no contrary evidence. There were many links between the Atlantic and the Arctic explorers; William and Stephen Burroughs, for example, were natives of Bideford who made their name sailing north-about but later moved into the Atlantic with the familiar Plymouth names.

7. John Hawkins' sister married a son of James Horsewell, their father's great friend.

CHAPTER SEVEN   War with Spain

Authorities: Largely as for the previous chapter. For Drake: Julian Corbett (1890), J. D. Upcott (1927), A. E. W. Mason (1941), Christopher Lloyd (1957) and *The World Encompassed*. General: *Sea Kings of Britain*, G. A. R. Callender (1912), *History of the British Navy*, Michael Lewis (1957). The Armada: *Defeat of the Spanish Armada*, vols 1 and 2 (Naval Record Society); *Enterprise of England*, Thomas Woodroffe (1958).

Notes

1. The five ships with which Drake started his circumnavigation were his flagship *Pelican*, 100 tons, 14 guns; *Elizabeth*, 80 tons, captain John Winter, nephew of Sir William Winter of the Board of Admiralty; *Marigold*, 30 tons, captain John Thomas; *Swan*, 50 tons, storeship, Captain Lydye; pinnace, 15 tons, captain Thomas Moon.

2. Winter fetched up at Ilfracombe, as John Hawkins got back to Padstow in 1565, not of intent but because the crude navigational instruments made it difficult to be sure, after an Atlantic crossing, of making a landfall north or south of Land's End. It emphasises the feats of these early navigators in foreign waters.

3. Drake landed in California in what is still called Drake's Bay and took possession of the land, as New Albion, for England. The Drake Navigators' Guild of California is today a group of amateur historians far more knowledgeable about Drake than any body in Plymouth; both its founder, the late Captain A. S. Oko, its first president, the late Fleet Admiral Chester Nimitz, and other members, have visited Plymouth.

4. Perhaps the last seen of the *Golden Hind* was in 1913 when excavations at Woolwich for a power-station revealed a ship of Elizabethan origin which had been burnt to the waterline, lying in a dock of sloping stone walls. Her ribs of English oak, 16 in by 16 in, had been grown to shape and were set 16 in apart; her outer planking was 6 in thick and the inner 4 in. The keelson was shaped out of pieces of oak 16 in thick 8 ft long and 6 ft wide. Her foremast and bow are probably still under the power-house, but there is much doubt as to whether this ship could be the *Golden Hind*.

5. A brick-built shop on the end of a Victorian row of council houses, behind the 'Breton Arms', is now on the site of Drake's Plymouth house.

6. Fenton was unlucky all through this voyage. When he arrived back in Plymouth in 1583, he first went aground off Drake's Island and then had to chase a pirate who had robbed some Millbrook men out of Cawsand Bay.

7. In the contemporary documents of the Armada I can find no references to the tide times, except that the fireships were sent into Calais on 28 July at midnight, upon the flood. One would expect the fireships to have been launched half an hour or so after slack water, and it is a simple calculation to find that high-water at Plymouth on 19 July was 10.30 or 11 pm. Since that piece of industry, I have found the time of high-water given as 10.31 pm by A. E. Stephens in *Plymouth Haven* (University of London thesis, 1936).

8. Lucas Cocke, the Plymouth captain killed in the Armada fighting, is said to have lived in the now-rebuilt Elizabethan house at 51 Southside Street. His name does not appear in the contemporary list of ships and captains which set out against the Armada, but many unlisted ships joined the fight and Cocke took out his own ship (Prince's *Worthies*).

CHAPTER EIGHT The Second, and Third Armadas

Authorities as in previous two chapters. For the later seamen. A. L. Rowse's *The Expansion of Elizabethan England* (1955) and *Sir Richard Grenville: Elizabethan Privateering*, K. R. Andrews (1964), *Purchas his Pilgrim*. For the Hoe Fort and Gorges: *Acts of the Privy Council, Salisbury Papers*, 1572-1597, *State Papers Domestic* 1591-4, 1595-7. *Dictionary of National Biography*.

Notes

1. The 1589 expedition not only had joint commanders-in-chief but of the six Royal ships three were under soldiers (Sir John Norris in *Nonpareil*, his brother Edward in *Foresight*, Sir Roger Williams in *Swiftsure*), and three under sailors (Drake in *Revenge*, Thomas Fenner in *Dreadnought* and William Fenner in the *Aid*).

2. The Chudley family, said to have originated in Chudleigh, had a house at Strashleigh (now a farm) near Lee Mill. Rowse says they ruined themselves in these maritime enterprises, but they were still a family of note in Devon during the Civil War.

3. The petition to make Drake military governor of Plymouth appears in Whitfeld's *History of Plymouth and Devonport* (p. 50). Presumably, his source was the state papers which he used extensively; he has a direct quotation but gives no reference.

4. The use of the name Drake's Island for St Nicholas's Island, according to Edwin Welch, the former city archivist, was started by his heir, Thomas Drake's great-grandson, another Sir Francis Drake, when he used his forebear's fame to try and turn Plymouth into a Whig pocketborough in the late seventeenth century. (*Devon and Cornwall Notes and Queries*, April 1966).

5. Magellan's ship made the first circumnavigation, Drake the second, and Candish the third. The fourth was made by a Dutchman, Oliver Noort, with an Englishman, Captain Melis who had been with Candish, as his chief pilot. They had six men desert off Plymouth in a small boat.

6. The *Revenge* was Drake's favourite ship but Richard Hawkins thought her unlucky. She went aground under his father at Plymouth in 1586, sprang a leak when bringing Drake back from Lisbon, so that she nearly failed to reach Plymouth, and then grounded on the Winter Shoal in the Sound.

7. The last voyage of Drake and Hawkins is commonly writen off as a bungled job, but the doom-laden account came from a disgruntled army officer, Maynard, who disapproved of everything. Hakluyt's factual report has none of this gloom.

8. The Bagge family is extensively dealt with in *Plympton in the Seventeenth Century* by John Stevens, a typescript in Plymouth Central Library.

9. The John Hele who was deputy town-clerk and arrested by Gorges cannot have been the lawyer of the same name, for he was a Member of Parliament for Exeter, Recorder of Plymouth, and a sergeant-at-law (the top flight of barrister) by this time; too big a man even for Gorges to tamper with. Sergeant Hele was said never to have become Master of the Rolls because he was 'drunk, insolent and over-bearing'; no man to allow himself to be conscripted as a common soldier.

10. Trematon Castle was used as a gaol for Spanish prisoners-of-war. Late in 1596, a dozen escaped, were driven off when they tried to capture a boat, and fled into the countryside, causing some little alarm before they were recaptured. (*Salisbury Papers*, VII, p. 524, 26 Dec 1596).
    There was also a problem with returning English prisoners-of-war. The Mayor questioned Andrew Facey of Stonehouse, who had escaped from the prison in Madrid, been recaptured, tortured, and forced to serve as a pilot in the Spanish Navy before escaping again. He told the Mayor that there were other men still serving Spain, and that they were traitors to Plymouth. John Hill of Stonehouse, forced to serve in the Spanish Navy at Corunna for fifteen months, came back to Plymouth and said he had only served Spain to learn her plans. He was sent to London for questioning by Cecil. (*State Papers Domestic* 1595-7).

11. The town defences which Robert Adams proposed in 1592 were to be a ditch 20 ft wide at the top, 12 ft at the bottom, 12 ft deep, the rubble being used to build the wall. The ditch for the Hoe fort was cut to these dimensions, and the wall there was 13 ft high, 4 ft 8 in wide at the base and 2 ft 8 in at the top. The total amount of wall was estimated at 2,730 yd, the cost £5,005. The 594 yd of fort wall was built, and the last record of accounts shows £2,346 spent. The gates were built, and some of the town wall. One piece ran along the top of the cliff from the old castle to the new fort. Harris records a tower of this wall at the foot of Lambhay Hill still standing in 1810, which explains why Sparke was not allowed to build houses between the forts, and the town's trouble with John Strode of Newnham, who had lime-kilns at Lambhay.

CHAPTER NINE   The Elizabethan Expansion

Principal authorities: Worth's *Municipal Records* and *History*, Bracken and Whitfield; *Old Plymouth*, drawings by Sybil Jerram (1913); *Ancient Buildings of Plymouth*, Copeland and Phillips (1942 and 1955). St Andrew's Parish Register. Contemporary Maps. *Worthies of Devon*, Prince (1810). The Water Act and Leat: papers by Worth and Erskine Risk, *Trans. Devon Assn.* Vol 16 and sequels. Pilchards: *Plymouth Pilchard Fishery 1584-91*, A. L. Rowse (*Economic Journal*, 1932).

Notes

1. Whitfeld's *Plymouth and Devonport* gives extensive extracts from the many versions of the Page of Plymouth murder.

2. Written on this map in a different hand to the rest of the lettering is 'Lypsone Hylle'. It is said to be in the handwriting of Sir Robert Cecil, the first Lord Salisbury (*Trans. Devon Assn.*, vol 30, p. 351). He was Lord High Steward of Plymouth, certainly visited Dartmouth in 1593 and may well, looking at Spry's map, have remembered the steep climb up from Lipson Bridge.

3. E. N. Masson Phillips first produced the roofed market-cross idea in *The Ancient Stone crosses of Devon* (*Trans. Devon Assn.*, vol 69). Mr N. M. Neatby, curator of Saltram, which Bagge was building at about the time he bought the pillars of the market-cross, tells me that there are still some granite pillars in the garden.

4. The Cremyll ferry beach was on the northern side of the tip of Devil's Point, with the road cut down through the cliffs and an inn at the back of the beach. It disappeared with the building of the Victualling Yard. The ferry crossed to Barn Pool.

5. Written across Sourpool on the Adams defence-map of 1592 is 'This was Plimmouth milpoole before the River was brought there by Sir Francis Drake and vi milles builded by him, and this poole made drie for a medow.'

6. An 1856 survey of Crownhill by Captain Cameron R.E., before the military built Crownhill Fort and the Barracks, shows Widey flour mills in the angle between Budshead Road and Tavistock Road, at the top of the first turning on the right in Budshead Road. This was in east Whitleigh manor which was run from Widey; no doubt the Widey name spread across to cover east Whitleigh.

7. A branch from the leat at Roborough took water down to the Bamfyldes, successors of the Copplestones at Warleigh. Worth suggests that, from the Meavy to Roborough, the Plymouth leat was an enlargement of an older leat cut to serve Warleigh, but it seems a vast undertaking for a small community.

8. Preserved in the wall of the Tavistock Road reservoir are fragments of the Old Town conduit. A granite trough is now a drinking-fountain; the inscription cut in granite over it 'Made in the maioraltie of John Trelawnie 1598' dates the first conduit; the arms of Drake and Plymouth on either side come from the 1671 rebuilding. Mayor Trelawny's home was at Ham and he, too, had a branch leat to his house. The Reservoir, built in the last century, is a museum of old stones if one looks; even the granite pillars of the colonade came from the 1603 guildhall.

INDEX

Adams, Robert, 182-3, 197, 202, 232-3
Adrian de Castello, 228
Agaton, 221
Alma Road, 41
Alms houses, 116-17, 210-11
Alva, Duke of, 143, 148
Amadas, family, 124, 130, 195; Philip, 157-8
Amicia, Countess of Devon, 61, 65
Antonio, Don, 158-9, 175
Antony, 132, 166
Armada, Spanish, first, 162-79, 186-7, 205, 230-1; second, 191; third 192
Arms, coat of, 97, 115, 212
Arundell, family, 133, 152, 200
Ashburton, 54, 69, 81, 116, 118, 121, 127, 213
Augustinians, 52, 60

Bagge, James, 188, 203, 214; family, 232-3
Bamfield, family, 202, 224, 233
Barbican, 100, 120, 145-6, 180, 196, 226-7
Barne Barton, 33, 221
Barn Pool, 233
Barrett, Robert, 142
Barton Avenue, 221
Baskerville, Thomas, 185-8
Bastard, family, 42
Batter Street, 227
Battle of Plymouth, 171
Bazas, 59
Beacon Park, 200
Beacons, fire, 119, 200
Bear's Head Rock, 35
Bedford, Dukes of, 130, 134, 138, 177
Bedford Street, 47
Benedictines, 51
Berd, Maurice, 84
Bere Alston, 68
Bere Ferrers, 30, 51, 68, 114, 117
Bickleigh, 107
Bideford, 131, 156, 165, 229
Bigbury Bay, 174
Bilbury, and Street, 17, 21, 24, 26, 33-4, 36, 90, 99, 225-7
Biscay, Bay of, 58, 169, 176, 191
Blackawton, 128-9
Black Book, 96, 133-4, 146, 159, 180, 214
Black Death, 43
Blackfriars, 70-1, 99, 130, 227
Black Prince, 77-80, 84-5

Blythman, John, 179, 206
Bodenham, John, 147; Jonas, 147, 166, 187-8; Roger, 147
Bond, John, 229
Bonville, family, 110, 113, 224, 228
Books, audit, 114; Simon Carsewell's 134; Thomas Tregarthen's, 114, 134
Bordeaux, 20, 58-9, 67-8, 77, 79-81, 83-4, 109, 125
Boringdon, 200
Borough, William, 164
Boswines, Roger, 84, 90, 122
Botus Fleming, 50
Boundary stones, 104
Bovisand, 15
Bowls, game of, 170-1
Breakwater, 219
Breton Arms, 230; Boys, 104; Side, 64, 90, 99, 180, 197, 227
Brittany, 19, 21, 24-6, 39, 46, 51, 58, 69, 77, 82, 89-90, 93, 104-5, 112-13, 119, 121, 132, 153, 180, 184
Brixton, 30, 224
Broke, Sir Robert Willoughby, 117, 119
Brown, Brute, 187
Brutus, 20
Buckfast Abbey, 46, 67, 85
Buckland Abbey, 46, 61, 65-6, 68, 95-7, 121-2, 128, 131-2, 152, 156, 158, 182, 188, 198, 200, 206, 224
Buckland Monachorum, 25, 200, 224
Buckwell Street, 64, 66, 203, 225, 227
Budockside family, 25, 42, 122, 144, 195; Philip, 144, 147; Roger, 144, 147
Budshead, 42, 144, 202, 221; Road, 233
Bull Point, 33
Bull ring, 106
Bulwarks, 119, 124-5, 180, 182, 193
Burghley, Lord, 148, 156, 161, 167-70, 176, 188, 200-1, 213
Burrington, 36, 41-2, 223
Burrough, Sir John, 182-3; William, 229; Stephen, 229

Cadiz, 163-5, 167, 175, 185, 191, 194, 198
Cadover Bridge, 54
Callington, 16, 117
Camel's Head, 26, 73, 100
Candish, Thomas, 161-2, 174, 181, 231